Evolving China: Speed to Quality

转型中国：从速度到质量

吴金铎 著

责任编辑：曹亚豪
责任校对：潘　洁
责任印制：丁淮宾

图书在版编目（CIP）数据

转型中国：从速度到质量／吴金铎著 . —北京：中国金融出版社，2020. 7
ISBN 978 - 7 - 5220 - 0488 - 4

Ⅰ. ①转…　Ⅱ. ①吴…　Ⅲ. ①中国经济—经济发展模式—研究　Ⅳ. ①F120. 3

中国版本图书馆 CIP 数据核字（2020）第 030995 号

转型中国：从速度到质量
ZHUANXING ZHONGGUO：CONG SUDU DAO ZHILIANG

出版
发行　中国金融出版社

社址　北京市丰台区益泽路 2 号
市场开发部　（010）66024766，63805472，63439533（传真）
网 上 书 店　http：//www.chinafph.com
　　　　　　（010）66024766，63372837（传真）
读者服务部　（010）66070833，62568380
邮编　100071
经销　新华书店
印刷　北京市松源印刷有限公司
尺寸　169 毫米 ×239 毫米
印张　20
字数　335 千
版次　2020 年 7 月第 1 版
印次　2020 年 7 月第 1 次印刷
定价　52. 00 元
ISBN 978 - 7 - 5220 - 0488 - 4
如出现印装错误本社负责调换　联系电话(010)63263947

Contents

Chapter 1   Transformation Dilemma

1.1 Internal Contradictions and External Shocks

1.1.1 Past rapid growth and high quality outlook

Since reform and opening up, China has experienced more than 40 consecutive years of sustained economic growth. China has formed a set of development models with Chinese characteristics, which relying on fully supplying demographic advantages and low labor force cost brought by "population bonus", high capital accumulation and investment rate, thereby joining the global industrial chain and sharing the globalization dividend. However, as the world economy enters the new normal, China's development mode is facing more and more challenges. The external environment and internal conditions of China's past development mode, the macro circumstances and the micro foundations have undergone tremendous variations.

The financial crisis that broke out in 2008 brought great impact on the global economic development, which caused serious recession worldwide. The global capital and financial market crisis spread, international trade declined sharply. The developed countries' economy was in a sharp downturn, and the GDP growth rate of emerging markets also slowed down greatly since then. Although China's "Four Trillion" crisis rescue plan has made Chinese economy spared from this crunch, harmness is inevitable. During the financial crisis, the boom of global financial and trade markets has vanished, which has caused severe challenges to China's development mode who dependent on external demand since 2001. The contraction of external demand has led to a sharp decline in global exports. Besides, the collapse of foreign trade enterprises has deteriorated the unemployment in China. "Four Trillion" crisis rescue plan has helped China avoid from recession, but China has suffered serious overcapacity. The shock on China's original economic development mode is not only the consequences of the contraction of external demand from international markets, but also the results of the accumulation of internal contradictions within the original development mode. This reflects in the supply structure: on the one hand, some industries such as steel and coal are overcapacity; some inefficient zombie enterprises who have wasted national credit resources and aggravated bad debts continue to survive. The power and strength of Chinese enterprises' innovation and R&D are inferior to those of developed countries. Industrial division and labor relocation of China are at a low end in the global value chain, and products have low added value and high substitutability. This type of development mode relies heavily on resources consumption, low-cost and cheap labor as well as credit advantages, resulting in a disadvantageous position in international competition. On the other hand, domestic demand is seriously insufficient and excessively external dependently. The development mode under circumstances of overinvestment, energy and resource consumption and zero environmental costs tend to be more and more unsustainable. Resource constraints and environmental restraint are becoming increasingly prominent. The source of China's comparative advantage, sufficient labor supply, has been fade away with the demographic dividend approaching the turning point. There is no longer much room for the surplus labor force of rural areas which unlimited supplied before, while the supply of migrant workers is insufficient with growing wages. The liberalization of the childbearing policy does not significantly improve the birth rate as expected, even since the "second child" policy. Besides, the aging phenomenon is becoming more and more serious in the first tier cities. The demographic dividend tends to disappear, while the new human capital dividend is not yet strong enough. In addition, the advantages of labor force in other developing countries such as Southeast Asian countries and BRICS are more and more obvious than that of China, which brings great threat and challenges to the international competitive advantages of China's original development mode.

Another fact China's development mode faced is that China's economic development is facing middle-income trap. China's per capita GNP in 2018 is $9372[1], ranking in middle-income countries. With the phenomena of slowing down of economic growth, the surplus rural labor force shortage, and rising wages of skilled labor, China might be stuck in the middle-income trap. The reasons about China's slowdown in economic growth, whether it is the result of external shocks of financial crisis or the internal performance of middle-income trap, it is indistinguishable. Instead of transformation problems, what facing China at this stage are cumulative problems and concentrated outbreak of contradictions in the existing economic development modes. The original growth mechanism and development modes can neither effectively deal with the systemic risks and internal contradictions of the industrial structures brought by the crisis, nor can they spontaneously solve the middle-income trap problems and hold back the new external crisis.

Under such circumstances, the transformation of China's economic development mode is imperative. The theme of economic development mode has also been the focus both in academia and government for a long time. The Chinese government formally put forward the topic of changing the mode of economic development in the Seventeenth CPC National Congress and placed it in the long-term strategic plan for

---

① Calculated at the international exchange rate. Data source: China National Bureau of Statistics.

national economic development. The report of the Seventeenth National Congress proposes that the transformation of the economic development mode should start from three aspects: demand structure, factor input structure and industrial structure, so as to carry out strategic adjustment of economic structure. The Nineteenth National Congress report points out that China's economy has shifted from high speed growth stage to high quality development stage. At present, China is at the stage of changing the way of development, optimizing the economic structure and changing the driving force of growth. The adjustment and upgrading of industrial structure play an important part in the transformation of economic development mode. From the perspective of the course of the world's modern economic growth, the change of industrial structure is an important manifestation of the industrialization process, and the substitution of the leading industry indicates the direction of the adjustment and upgrading of industrial structure, so we can make use of the leading industry to comprehensively achieve the transformation of the economic development mode. Therefore, it is of great practical significance to systematically study the role played by leading industries in the process of industrial structure evolution in the middle stage of industrialization. The report of the Nineteenth National Congress pointed out that the transformation of the economic development mode should be carried out mainly from the following aspects: "taking the structural reform on the supply side as the main line, promoting the quality, efficiency and motivation of economic development, and improving the total factor productivity", in which it also propose the specific content and driving force of the transformation of the economic development mode in the new era.

Successful industrialized countries whose industrial evolution practices and upgrading experiences seem to provide ready-made templates for the later comer countries who need structural transformation and evolving of economic development mode. It is true that the experiences of industrial transformation and the successful transformation and upgrading of economic structure in industrialized countries provide helpful and valuable lessons. However, the development mode of industrialized countries is not necessarily universal and suitable for developing countries, even though they could be helpful references. As the different initial conditions and institutional environments, those successful route are not necessarily suitable for the latter developing countries. Full application in emerging countries may not replicate success. The successful realization of industrialization and the smooth transformation of economic structure are the result of the dynamic interaction of various development parameters and initial conditions with internal and external factors over time. For a later comer country like China, taking into account factors such as natural resource constraints, human capital, institutional conditions, international environment, established industrial structure and initial resources constraints, set the industrial priority scientifically and rationally is playing an important role in the process of smoothing transformation of economic development mode and comprehensive sustainable development. The sequence of industrial development is an important driving force for the evolving of industrial structure and development mode. The industrial iteration is not only the process of the continuous rise and development for some industry, but also the procedure of the rising and development of industrial clusters with guiding role and foresight in industrialization. In view of the fact that the theory of industrial evolution originated from the developed countries with mature market economy, this book applies related theory to China's industrial research and economic reform, to combine the comprehensive objectives of China's development into the scope of investigation in light of China's national conditions and the stage of economic development, so as to give objective and rational guidance to harmonious combination of China's industrial iteration and adjustment of industrial structure and the transformation of economic development mode.

This book intends to use the research methods of development economics and evolutionary economics to summarize the historical experiences of the transformation of post industrial countries' priorities in industrial development and the transformation of economic development mode. It reflects the gains and losses of China's leading industries and the adjustment of industrial structure in the past 40 years since reform and opening up, so as to examine the current development and describe the future prospects of China's industries. Scientific and rational advices for China's industrial structure adjustment will help to solve the problems encountered in the process of industrial transformation, in the purpose of accelerating the smooth transformation of China's economic development mode. With this consideration, the book attempts to explain the following questions:

1. What is the transformation dilemma faced with China? What's the relationship between leading industries and the transformation of economic development mode? How could the evolving in leading industries and industrial structures promote the transformation of economic development mode?

2. Why is China's economic development difficult to change? What are the factors affecting the formation and replacement of leading industries? How to make a breakthrough in the transformation process of economic development mode? What's the bottleneck of high quality development mode in evolving China?

3. What is the current situation and potential of China's industrial development? How to make a scientific industrial policy with industry combination under the current new development goal?

4. What's in common for the process of industrial turnover in successful transition countries? Is there a general empirical model for

the transformation of industrial structure to upgrading? What are the references for China?

1.1.2 The central committee's important exposition on the economic development mode since reform and opening-up

Since the reform and opening up, the theme of changing the economic development mode has been highly valued by China. The government report of the fourth session of the Fifth National People's Congress in 1981 put forward ten principles for economic construction centered on improving economic efficiency[①]. The government report adopted at the first meeting of the Sixth National People's Congress in 1983 emphasized that all economic focus should be shifted to the track of improving economic efficiency, and underlined that under the premise of constantly improving economic efficiency, China should strive to maintain a real speed of production and development[②], economic development was required to achieve the unity of efficiency and speed. In the government report of the Thirteenth National Congress of the Communist Party of China in 1987, which pointed out that only by constantly striving to improve economic efficiency, gradually alleviated the contradiction of large population, relatively inadequate resources and serious shortage of material capital in China, and ensure the sustained development of the national economy at a high speed. China must unswervingly implement the strategy of focusing on efficiency, improving quality, stabilizing growth and coordinating development[③], the ultimate objective of economic development

---

① Current Economic Situation and Guidelines for Future Economic Construction[N].People's Daily,1981-12-15(3).

② Government Report[N].People's Daily,1983-06-24(1).

③ Proceeding along the road of socialism with Chinese characteristics—Report on the Thirteenth National Congress of the Communist Party of China[N/OL].[1987-10-25].http://www.people.com.cn/.

should gradually shift from extensive to intensive. In 1992, the report of the Fourteenth National Congress of the Communist Party of China stressed that science and technology were the primary productive forces, and that economic construction must rely on scientific and technological progress as well as the improvement of the quality of workers, improving the role of innovation and technology in economic growth, and promoting the transformation of the entire economic construction from extensive operation to intensive management[①].The fifth plenary session of the fourteenth Central Committee of the Communist Party of China, held in 1995, deliberated and adopted the ninth five-year plan for national economic and social development and the proposals on the long-term objectives for 2010, and put forward two fundamental changes of overall significance: one is the transformation of economic system from planned economy to socialist market economy; the other is the transformation of economic growth mode from extensive to intensive economy. The economic mode should transformed to depend on structural optimization, economies of scale, scientific and technological progress and standardize management[②]. The report of the Eighth National People's Congress in 1996 put forward the implementation of the strategy of rejuvenating the country through science and education and the strategy of sustainable development, insisted on promoting the reform of economic system and the transformation of economic growth mode from extensive to intensive, rationally exploited and economized resources, developed circular economy, coordinating development of economic construction,

---

① Jiang Zemin.Speeding up the pace of reform and opening up and modernization, and winning a greater victory in the cause of socialism with Chinese characteristics: a report at the Fourteenth National Congress of the Communist Party of China[N/OL].[1992-10-12].http://www.people.com.cn/.

② Li Peng.The Central Committee of the Communist Party of China has formulated the "Ninth Five Year plan" for the national economic and social development and the 2010 vision target [N/OL].[1995-09-25]. http://www.people.com.cn/.

resources and environment.[1] At the fifth Congress of the Party held in 1997, the report reiterated that China should actively promote the reform of the economic system and enforce the fundamental transformation of the economic growth mode. At the same time, China should make great progress in optimizing the economic structure, developing science and technology and improving the level of opening-up to the world, so as to achieve a coordination of real economic, social and environmental with faster speed, better efficiency and continuous improvement of the overall quality[2]. At the fifth meeting of the Fifteenth Central Committee of the Communist Party of China, on October 11, 2000, the government passed a resolution: "Recommendations of the Central Committee of the Communist Party of China on the tenth five-year plan for National Economic and Social Development", in which it proposed that in order to achieve the goal of sustained, rapid and healthy development, strategic adjustment of the economic development mode and structural adjustment must be made around the center of economic benefits, relying on institutional innovation and technology[3]. The report of the Sixteenth National Congress of the Communist Party of China in 2002 put forward the goal of building a All-round Construction of Well-off Society, in the way of a new industrialization, adhering to the principle of expanding domestic demand, implementing the strategy of rejuvenating the country through science and education as well as the strategy of sustainable development. It calls for the unification of speed and

---

[1]   Jiang Zemin.The Central Committee of the Communist Party of China has formulated the "Ninth Five-year plan" for the national economic and social development and the 2010 vision target?[N/OL].[1996-03-17]. http://www.people.com.cn/.

[2]   Jiang Zemin.Hold aloft the great banner of the theory of socialism and push the cause of building socialism with Chinese characteristics to the full twenty-first Century.[N/OL].[1997-09-13]. http://www.people.com.cn/.

[3]   Proposal of the CPC Central Committee on formulating the Tenth Five-year Plan for national economic and social development[N/OL].[2000-10-11]. http://www.people.com.cn/.

quality, structure and efficiency of national economic development, and the coordination of economic development with population, resources and environment.[①] On March 14, 2006, the Fourth Session of the Tenth National People's Congress adopted the outline of the eleventh five-year plan for national economic and social development, which proposed accelerating the transformation of economic growth mode, building a resource-saving and environment-friendly society as the basic national policy, accelerating the development of circular economy. It also attach importance to the constraints of resources and environment on economic development, and promote economic development and population, resources and environment coordination. China would continue to promote the strategy of scientific and technological personnel training and technological innovation, accelerate the pace of economic and social informatization, with the principles of clean development, economical development and safe development, and conscientiously follow the new road of industrialization, so as to achieve the coordinated and sustainable development of economy, society and environment.[②] The plan outlined the specific content of the transformation of the economic development mode, which fully reflected the inevitable trend of the transformation of the economic growth mode to the economic development mode. On June 25, 2007, in the speech to the provincial and ministerial cadres' refresher course of the Central Party School, Chairman Hu Jintao first proposed that the key to achieving sound and rapid development of the national economy, was to make significant progress in transforming the mode of economic development and improving the socialist market

---

① Jiang Zemin.To build a well-off society in an all-round way and create a new situation in the cause of socialism with Chinese characteristics[N/OL].[2002-11-08].http://www.people.com.cn/.

② Outline of the eleventh five-year plan for national economic and social development[N/OL].[2006-03-16].Xinhua News Agency.

economy system[①], the proposition of changing the mode of economic development has been formally put forward. On October 15, 2007, the report of the Seventeenth National Congress of the CPC clearly pointed out that the key to achieving sound and rapid development of the national economy lied in speeding up the transformation of the economic development mode and improving the socialist market economy system, accelerating the strategic adjustment of economic structure, paying more attention to energy conservation and environmental protection, to enhance the ability and level of independent innovation, to improve the overall quality of the economy and international competition. The report defined more clearly the specific content of the economic development mode transformation, which could be summarized as "three transformations": economic growth shifted from relying on investment and export to relying mainly on expanding domestic demand and coordinating the development of consumption, investment and exports; Economic development mode shifted from relying on the second industry to relying on the coordination of agriculture, industry and service industries; Economic growth shifted from relying mainly on large numbers of resources and the consumption of unskilled labor force to scientific and technological innovation, technological progress, high-quality workers and scientific management[②]. In February 2010, the chairman of the State Council, suggested that China should accelerate the transformation of the economic development mode, stressed the need to implement and put forward to accelerate the transformation of the economic development mode as a strategy plan, in which it made eight suggestions on

---

① Hu Jintao: Speech at the provincial and ministerial level cadre training class of the Central Party School[N/OL].[2007-06-25].http://www.people.com.cn/.

② Hu Jintao. Holding the great banner of socialism with Chinese characteristics and striving for a new victory in building a moderately prosperous society in all respects[N/OL].[2007-10-15].http://www.people. com.cn/.

accelerating the long-term focus of the transformation of the economic development mode. China should speed up the adjustment and upgrading of the national economic structures, adjusting the economic structure as a channel of economic development mode transformation. The primary task and strategic focus of the transformation of economic development mode were as follows: industrial restructuring, independent innovation, ecological civilization construction, transformation of agricultural development mode, coordination of economic and social development, promoting cultural industry development and transformation of foreign trade development mode[1]. At the third session of the National People's Congress on March 5, 2010, the government report stressed that it was urgent to change the mode of economic development, proposing that China should enter the development track of innovation and technology-driven and endogenous growth, promoting strategic adjustment and revitalization of key industries, and vigorously cultivate strategic emerging industries[2].The report of the Eighteenth National Congress pointed out that accelerating the transformation of the mode of economic development as the main line was a strategic choice related to China's overall development situation. China should speed up the formation of a new mode of economic development and shift the foothold of promoting development to improving quality and efficiency. Deepening reform was the key to speed up the transformation of economic development. Promoting strategic adjustment of economic structure was the main direction to accelerate the transformation of economic development mode. The focus should be on improving the demand structure, optimizing industrial institutions, promoting coordinated

---

① Hu Jintao. Important speech at the provincial and ministerial level leading cadres in implementing the seminar on speeding up the transformation of the mode of economic development[N/OL].[2010-03-05].http://www.people.com.cn/.

② Wen Jiabao. Government work report[N/OL].[2010-03-05].http://www.people.com.cn/.

regional development and urbanization, as well as solving major structural problems that restricted the sustained and healthy development of the economy.[①]

Theme of "changing the mode of economic growth" to "transforming the mode of economic development" is a major improvement of China's economic development strategy and guiding principles, reflecting the deepening understanding of economic growth and economic development by the academia and government. Instead of changing the mode of economic growth by changing the mode of economic development, it does not mean that China has completed the task of changing the mode of economic growth or the mode of economic growth has accomplished. It shows that the understanding of this topic is more comprehensive and scientific. In the process of China's transformation, it is not only the way of growth that needs to be changed, but also the broader and sustainable development of economy, society and environment. The deep-rooted problems and contradictions in the course of China's economic development can not be solved solely by relying on economic growth or transformation of economic growth mode. China needs to achieve sustainable development and push forward the transformation of the economic development pattern with more comprehensive contents.

1.1.3　Difficulties in changing China's traditional economic development mode

As early as 1995, the ninth five-year plan put forward the topic of changing the economic growth mode. In 2005, the eleventh five-year plan raised the transformation of economic growth mode from the

---

① Hu Jintao. Unswerving along the path of socialism with Chinese characteristics and striving for the building of a moderately prosperous society in all respects — a report on the Eighteenth National Congress of the Communist Party of China[N/OL].[2012-11-08].Xinhua News Agency.

perspect of "Scientific Development Concept". In 2007, the Central Committee put forward that the transformation of the mode of economic development was the key point to achieve sound and rapid economic development, thereby highlighted the importance of the economic development mode transformation. The report of the Eighteenth National Congress of the CPC pointed out that "accelerating the transformation of the economic development mode is a strategic choice related to China's overall development situation". The Nineteenth National Congress of the CPC report wrote: "China's economy has shifted from the high-speed growth stage to the high quality development stage, and is now in the key stage of transforming the development mode." After twenty-four years of efforts, China's understanding of the transformation of the mode of economic development was more comprehensive and profound. The economic development mode has also improved significantly, for example, the export mode has transformed from resource intensive primary products to labor and capital intensive products, and industrial products transformed from primary processing to high intensive processing, but this task has not yet been finished. At present, China's economy is in the stage of transformation, it faces many contradictions. These difficulties and obstacles are also the crux of the difficult transformation of China's economic development mode: the contradiction between the speed of economic growth and the quality of development; the contradiction between the upgrading of consumption structure and the lag of structural adjustment[①]; the contradiction between high output and high consumption and high pollution; contradiction between expanding domestic demand and maintaining external demand; contradiction between inclusive growth and widening

---

① Bai Jinfu. Major Contradictions in China's Economic Growth during the Eleventh Five-year Plan[N].Economic Reference Daily,2005-08-27.

gap between rich and poor; contradiction between centralized and unbalanced development and balanced development; contradiction between technology introduction and independent innovation; contradiction between urban integration and dual structure, and the contradiction between maintaining high growth and sustainable development. Regarding the reasons why the traditional economic development mode is difficult to change, many scholars have made useful explorations from different perspectives, which can be summarized as follows:

1. Restrictions on the stage of economic development

The economic development mode is closely related to the stage of economic development, and the characteristics of different historical periods will lead to different modes of economic development. At different stages, development tasks are different, as development condition varies, economic structure has dissimilar characteristics. (1) From the perspective of development tasks, in the initial accumulation stage of economic development or in the early stage of industrialization, material, technological conditions and institutional support are relatively weak. Limited by the development conditions, people can only rely on the high input and consumption of labor and natural resources to expand scale so as to increase production. This extensive development mode, regardless of environmental input, has lower costs and technical requirements. In the stage of economic developing or in the late stage of industrialization, capital accumulation has been relatively abundant, technology and management has also developed considerably, and the system has been improved. However, increasing shortage of natural resources and the increasingly severe environment have gradually emerged. In this stage, the development mode of resource saving, low energy consumption, high efficiency and environmental friendly are often adopted. Therefore, those countries who were in the stage of pursuing quantity expansion and high-speed development, the mode must be high input, high consumption and high output; if countries who were in the stage of efficiency focused, sustainability and circular economy and development quality oriented, which were at the higher stage of development, the improved model will be inclined to be the positive interaction between human capital and technology-intensive, resource-saving and environment friendly. (2) From the perspective of development conditions, the resource endowments, scientific and technological strength as well as material and human capital conditions of a country are not immutable. The factor endowments varies with the different stages of economic development, and the comparative advantage changes accordingly, in this way the source of national competitiveness is different, result in the mode of economic development showing different characteristics. In the initial stage of development, labor force, natural resources are often relatively abundant, while capital, technology and other factors of production are relatively scarce. The formation of competitive advantage mainly depends on the input of labor force, natural resources and other abundant producing factors. With the improvement of the economic development, the relative price of factor endowment will change, the price of labor force and natural resources will rise gradually with the increase of demand, while the relative price of technology and capital will decrease gradually with the increase of supply. The new competitive advantage will make the economic development turn to depend on production factors such as technology and capital, so the mode of economic development will change accordingly. (3) From the perspective of economic structures, the relationship between industries restrict the evolving of economic development mode. Different stages of economic development have different characteristics, which lead to different development modes. In the traditional heavy industry leading structure, resource allocation and industrial policy were biased in favour of the second industry, while the agriculture and third industries are less energy consumption and with less environmental pressure in the society which resources maily serve for the second industry. In the early stage of industrialization, economic development often relies on energy consumption and intensive investment on capital equipments. The limitation of technological conditions make it impossible for capital to completely replace human resources. Therefore, the development model was characterized by high input and low efficiency, capital and labor intensive. The industrial structure dominated by information industry or modern service industry generally showed the characteristics of knowledge, technology and human capital intensive, resource-saving, low consumption and high efficiency.

2. The advantages of traditional factors supporting economic development are gradually weakening, but new growth power such as technological innovation is insufficient. The transformation of the economic development mode is neither unconditional nor permanent. China has made great achievements in economic growth and foreign trade in the past 40 years by virtue of its relatively abundant natural resources as well as cheap and adequately supplied labor force. However, the advantages of economic development conditions in the past are gradually weakening, while the overall domestic innovation is not strong enough to stop foreign technology imports, the new growth momentum in China is green and yellow, thereupon the economic follow-up development is facing transformation problems. (1) Human capital and skilled labor are important conditions for the fundamental transformation of the development mode. China's industrial development has entered the stage of rising labor factor costs. The cost of skilled labor and human capital has become the bottleneck of the further transformation of China's economic development mode. Resources and labor competition in other countries such as Southeast Asian and BRICS have advantages in the labor cost compared with

China. On one hand, labor shortage and the sharp rise in the wages of migrant workers reflect that the labor market in China is no longer comparable with that of the previous adequate supply of rural labor force. Some industrial labor and part of the seasonal labor force are obviously in short supply. The characteristics of unlimited labor supply in China are fading away, as symbol of a turning point for Chinese economy.[①] The competitive advantage formed by the past economic development model has been greatly weakened. On the other hand, the overall level of China's labor quality is still far from that of the developed countries in the world. Since the reform and opening up, great progress has been made for the development of education reform. The level of human capital has been improved to a considerable extent through "Learning by Doing" and introduction of advanced management mode and methods from developed countries. But in general, China's human capital level and talent structure are not well matched the requirements of economic development and industrial upgrading. This is an unfavorable constraint on the transformation of China's economic development mode. (2) New growth powers, such as scientific and technological progress, are weak in promoting economic development transformation, and the contribution of technology to economic growth is still relatively limited, thus delaying the formation of intensive growth mode. Advanced technology is an indispensable condition for the smooth transformation of economic development mode. Those development mode who lack of advanced technology are not sustainable ones. Changing the mode of economic development and improving the quality and efficiency of factors are essentially the process of integrating science and technology into tangible factors and shifting social production boundaries as far as possible. There is still a big gap

---

① Cai Fang. The Turning Point of China's Economy and its Challenges to Development and Reform [J].Chinese Social Sciences,2007(3):4-12.

between China's overall technological level and that of developed countries. Some fields in national economics is lack of advanced core technology, with many key technologies depending on imports. Poor technical conditions made transformation of China's economic development mode impossible. In addition, at present, the main body of scientific and technological innovation in China is still state-owned scientific research institutions instead of private enterprises. There is a disconnection between scientific research and production, resulting in poor market adaptability of scientific and technological achievements, and low conversion rate and low return of scientific and technological achievements. Finally, due to the lack of effective incentive mechanism for scientific and technological innovation as well as patent protection mechanism, the process of transformation from science and technology to real productivity in China has greater externality, weakened the transformation, leading to scientific and technological innovation insufficient and lack of motivation for the transformation of China's economic development mode. (3) Limited capital increment and low utilization efficiency hinder the smooth transformation of the economic development mode. For economic growth, the effective allocation of resources is the most important. Whether relying on factor expansion or technological progress, the final performance is the improvement of investment returns or investment efficiency.[①] The transformation of the economic development mode must be accompanied by capital investment. Adequate capital not only provides convenient conditions for the development of capital-intensive industries, but also offers advanced technology, increasing investment in research and development, which is conducive to better technological independent innovation and new product development. However, there are lots of zombie enterprises in

---

① Zheng Yuxin.Measurement of Total Factor Productivity and Stage Rule of Economic Growth Mode[J]. Economic Research,1999(5):55-60.

China. A large part of assets from state-owned enterprises are in inefficient or even idle state. Consequently there is structural fund shortage in China's real economy: profit driven large amounts of capital flow into the high profit real estate industry. At the same time, the traditional high input, high energy consumption and high pollution industries, such as steel and coal, have a large surplus of capacity, while manufacturing and high-tech industries are constrained by low return on investment, long investment cycle and insufficient capital investment. In addition, foreign central banks maintained easy monetary policy which leading to excessive liquidity in financial markets during the crisis. Liquidity is unevenly distributed in the real economy and capital market, which is also one of the important reasons why China's industrial structure is irrational and its development mode is difficult to change fundamentally.

3. The "institutional friction" between the planned economy and market economy restricts the transformation of the economic development mode. Institution and economic operation mechanism are the key factors for the evolution of economic development mode. Since the reform and opening up, China's economic development pattern has undergone transformation from the traditional planned economy system to the socialist market economy system. However, China's market economy system is not perfect yet, and its operating mechanism does not functioned well. The friction between planned economy and market economy is the deep-seated reason for the unreasonable mode of economic development, which illustrates the difficulty in fundamental transformation.[①] An important sign of successful transformation of economic development mode is the rational allocation and efficient resource usage. The role of market and government in optimizing the

---

① Jian Xinhua.China's Economic Structural Adjustment and Transformation of Development Mode [M].Shandong People's Publishing House, 2010.

allocation of resources is complementary. However, the coexistence of old and new systems makes it difficult for the planned and market forces to play an effective role respectively. On the one hand, the traditional economic development mode endogenous to the planned system who is still active; on the other hand, the new development mode who born under the market economy system is difficult to develop and grow. In the process of system transformation, the inertia of the old system and the path dependence of economic development will make the economic development model incline to go back to the traditional type. In the process of counterbalance between planned economy and market economy, there are still considerable forces to promote economic development to the old way. The institutional frictions between planning and market are manifested in the following aspects: Firstly, the market mechanism is still imperfect and needs to be improved in incomplete market pricing mechanism with resources and elements artificially underestimated, neglecting costs by means of negative externalities such as environment. For a long time, the government still maintains the power to allocate important economic resources. The national planned pricing results in distorted and unreasonable resource prices with low or even zero environmental emission costs, which stimulates the extensive development mode with high investment, high consumption and high emission. It is difficult to change the development path in terms of quantity and scale expansion. Secondly, for a long time, GDP growth has been regarded as an important criterion and references for evaluating the performance of governments at all levels and leading cadres, which have led governments at all levels to blindly pursue GDP growth and chase economic expansion regardless of costs and consequences. In order to increase the performance appraisal chips and behave well in GDP Championship, governments at all levels blindly pursue the growth rate, neglecting the balance of economic structure, and ignoring the quality of development and the sustainability of development. Overconsumption of resources and overlooking for environmental costs have damaged the extension of development and made it more and more difficult to change the mode of economic development. Finally, the existing fiscal and taxation system makes the traditional economic development mode path-dependently. Since our tax revenue mainly comes from value added tax (VAT), and more than half of it comes from production, the goal of local government to increase production and income makes governments at all levels pay close attention to the growth of output value[①]. Government revenue is closely related to the growth of output value. The growth rate of economy increases with the expansion of production, while the local fiscal revenue increases correspondingly. As a result, some local government officials are enthusiastic about the expansion of short-term production scale and the high growth rate of local economy. The practice of paving the stalls, blindly putting projects on and repeating construction, which ignores the sustainability of economic growth as well as the consequences and costs of excessive consumption of resources and environment, blindly pursuing fiscal revenue, further deteriorates the quality of economic development, which makes it harder to achieve higher quality development.

4. Institutional deficiencies are the profound reasons why the mode of economic development is difficult to transform. The imperfect enterprise system, the incomplete mechanism of self-financing, the injury of survival of the fittest mechanism, the large amount of scarce resources occupied by state-owned zombie enterprises, resulting in the inefficiency of resource utilization. Meanwhile the absence of patent system for technology research and development, the imperfect

---

① Wu Jinglian. Economic Growth is Difficult to Change,Three Obstacles[N].Daily Economic News, 2005-11-29.

incentive mechanism for innovation, resulting in the lack of motivation for independent innovation of enterprises, and the serious mismatch between R&D, technological innovation and investment, leading to market mechanism distorts, destroied the balance between supply and demand. For example, in the past, some state-owned enterprises have large domestic demand for their products, so long as the products are produced, they can be sold out[①]. As a result, the development of state-owned enterprises, independent innovation and product quality improvement are lack of incentives. The income distribution system is also unreasonable, the income gap is expanding. So factor rewards is unbalanced in China, the proportion of labor income to gross national income is too small; Besides, the social security system is not perfect, resulting in a large proportion of urban and rural residents' income saved for old-age care and medical treatments, housing and children's education, which makes it difficult to fully release domestic consumption demand. At the same time, the gradually poor domestic supply is increasingly unable to meet the escalating consumer demand. Insufficient internal motive force of economic development is accompanied by ineffective release of internal growth momentum, which accounts for the high capital accumulation rate and low consumption rate and the difficulty of changing the external dependent development mode. There are many drawbacks in the mode of economic development which mainly relying on foreign trade: high dependence on foreign trade, solidification of trade product structure, foreign trade development relying on quantity expansion and low price instead of brand and high added value, the low end of the value chain in the international division of labor system, etc.The macroeconomic regulation system is not yet fully mature in China, so inefficient allocation of government-led resources and decision-making errors are

---

① Li Yining. How Slow the Transformation of Economic Growth Mode Is?[N].Beijing Daily,2005-02-28.

inevitable. In addition, the performance appraisal system that government officials pay attention to are indicators about quantity and speed, ignoring soft indicators such as development quality, resources and environment, result in local governments paying too much attention to GDP growth, neglecting the quality and environment of development, therefore it is difficult to change the traditional development model that depends on quantity and scale expansion.

5. Over-reliance on industrial investment. Catching-up development strategy is an important way for developing countries to achieve economic take-off, but catching-up development will also over-strengthen the role of investment in economic development, and lead to path dependence of investment-driven development, which restricts the transformation of economic development mode. From the early days since the founding of the People's Republic of China to the reform and opening up, China implemented the industrial policy of giving priority to heavy industry, which had played a positive role in a specific historical period. Since the reform and opening up, especially after the introduction of market economy system, China's industrial priority has been constantly adjusted, and its economic structure has also been greatly improved, and is becoming more and more rational. However, in order to create and maintain a higher growth rate to catch up with the developed countries, China has formed an inertial regulation way in economic practice. As long as pressure comes to the economy, investment will increase to ensure growth. It seems that increasing investment is the most effective way to ensure growth, it can bring instant economic results[1], which give rise to path dependence to promote economic growth by overinvestment. At the stage of economic take-off, the economic foundation is relatively weak, goods and

---

[1] Jian Xinhua.China's Economic Restructuring and Transformation of Development Mode[M]. Shandong People's Publishing House, 2010.

production is generally in short supply. It is a wise choice to speed up industrial investment and expand production capacity, and it is also in line with the law of economic development. History has proved that this strategy has played an important role in the development of China's economy. However, in the new period of economic transformation, especially in the case of serious overcapacity in some industries, blindly increased production capacity, or adopted excessive investment to enlarge production capacity or to absorb excess production capacity by investing to maintain economic growth, is becoming more and more unsustainable. These types of growth mode relying on duplication and blind investment, which is undoubtedly inefficient, and it will bring an endless hindrance to economic development. What's more, the extensive development mode of large-scale industrial investment expansion also exposes more and more disadvantage and drawbacks: excessive consumption of resources caused by rapid industrial expansion, as well as increasing environmental pollution. In addition, it can not be neglected that overinvestment in industry also occupies the capital needed for the development of other emerging industries, leading to an increasingly unbalanced internal structure of the industry. This pursuit of speed, neglecting of development quality deviates from the goal of promoting development for the well-being of the people. But it does not necessarily mean that investment is no longer needed for China's economic development. At present, investment still plays an important role in the process of transformation of China's economic development mode, and the transformation of China's economic development mode needs capital and credit as the basic guarantee. However, the focus of the transformation of investment-driven economic development mode lies in the optimization of investment efficiency and investment structure rather than the blind expansion in quantity. Therefore, it is necessary to identify whether the marginal efficiency of investment in specific industries is in the ascending or descending stage, which is of great significance for improving the investment structure and investment efficiency, as well as for changing the investment mode.

1.1.4 Industrial permutations & combinations and economic development mode transformation

Industrial policies and macroeconomic regulation are essential for both developed countries and emerging economies. The successful developed countries, especially Japan and South Korea in economic restructuring and industrial policies during the postwar period, provides references for China in the transformation of economic development mode. As a late comer developing country, the economic development mode must be changed materially if China wants to make a successful transformation. An important content of the transformation of the economic development mode is to upgrade the industrial structure, and to realize the structure adjustment and optimization of the industrial structure. The priority of industrial development and related industrial policies play a decisive role in the process of industrial structure adjustment. The practice in developed countries shows that the economic growth of a country or region and the emergence of new economic growth points are realized through the promotion of leading industries to form strong economic supports and industrial clusters. Therefore, in the current domestic and international environment, whether China could be able to choose the industry priority is not only an important entry point for the transformation of economic development mode, but also an important potential growth engine. In order to realize the optimization and upgrading of the industrial structure and accelerate the transformation of the economic development mode, China should focus on the determination and adjustment of the industrial development sequence along with the different stages of economic development, establishing a production system that takes the leading industry as the core, with mature competitive advantages, and industries coordinated well with each other, so as to straighten out and coordinate the leading and dominant industries in the transformation process of the economic development mode. The choice of industrial development combination and sequence is related to the direction and speed of future growth power, affects the process of industrial restructuring and upgrading. The adjustment and upgrading of industrial structure is realized through the change of industrial development order. Therefore, the choice and determination of industrial development order is key to industrial restructuring, as well as the central issue of the transformation of economic development mode and the overall economic development.

The essence of industrial structure adjustment is the process of the emergence, development and change of leading industries and dependent industries. The main symbol of the transformation and upgrading of industrial structure is the replacement and iteration of pillar industries and collateral industries. The formulation of industrial policy is a process in which the government determines the sequences of industrial structure development according to the overall plan of economic development under certain time and space conditions, advances it step by step, and realizes the rationalization of industrial structure by constantly changing leading industries. In every stage of economic growth, there are corresponding leading industrial sectors, and the leading industries change with different stages of development. Under different stages of economic development and different industrial structures, the development speed of each department is different in a country or region. Some industries can develop faster, others may develop more slowly, meanwhile some industries may even be in a state of recession and contraction. Therefore, the contribution and role of each industry to economic growth are different. At a specific stage of economic development, there will always be one or some relatively advanced industries or departments, which will exceed other industries in the proportion or concentration of output value and greatly affect the development of other industries. With the development of economy, the change of internal and external environment, and the evolving of industrial life cycle, the industries with development advantages will gradually decline in a certain period, and the new leading industries and auxiliary industries will also be differentiated accordingly. Some of the faster-developing industries with great development potential will develop to the forefront, while others will be buried in the market if they can not adapt to the competitive environment. In the bud, some of the larger industries in the national economy gradually declined or even be replaced. The industries that survived and went to the forefront of development gradually replaced the original leading sectors, thereby the industrial order changed, while the industrial structure also evolved. In brief, the development of the whole economy is the direct or indirect effect of the growth and development of the leading industries.

The most important in the industrial priority development order is to select the leading industries. The leading industry must be a source of innovation. Generally, the leading sector has high productivity, effectively introduce technological innovation, absorb a large number of the latest scientific research achievements at a certain stage, and make a series of innovations for the forward-related industries and backward-related sectors of the whole industrial chain through technology diffusion effect and technology spillover. The leading industry also promotes the upgrading of the whole industrial structure by creating new market demand. Economic development always begins with the adoption of advanced technology by a leading sector. The introduction of technology improves production efficiency and reduces the production cost of this sector. As the market share of this sector continues to expand, their market demand for products and services in other relevant sectors is also increasing gradually, thus driving the overall development of the entire industrial chain or industrial clusters and the national economy.

Leading industry plays a dominate and guiding role in the process of economic development. The leading industry of a country or region determines its industrial structure. The resistance and cost of successful industrial restructuring with leading industry as the core are the smallest in the national economics. The evolution of industrial structure is caused by the orderly replacement of the dominant and subsidiary industries of the country or region. The transformation and continuous iteration of the industries drive the adjustment of the industrial structure, which plays an important role in promoting the transformation of the economic development mode. Industrial turnover is the main driving force to promote industrial restructuring, and therefore one of the sources of long-term economic growth. In fact, the process of industrial structure evolution caused by industrial replacement is also the process of economic development mode transformation. It can be seen that the change of leading industries is also an important opportunity for a country or region to adjust its industrial structure and change its economic development mode.

The optimization and upgrading of industrial structure is closely related to the determination of the leading industries in the national economy. The adjustment of industrial structure is essentially to a scientific and rational industrial arrangement, which is also necessary to determine a reasonable industrial development sequences. On this basis, the relationship between leading industry and dominant industry is coordinated. Under the circumstances of the evolving in original development conditions, the weakening of the strength of leading industry and the change of industrial development, new leading industry with potential will emerge and grow. In order to transform the old mode of economic development and ensure the normal operation and metabolism of the whole economic system, all departments should join together to maintain the consistency and continuity of the whole industrial chain, improving the complementarity of industries inside and outside of the region, and strengthen the correlation and interaction between industries. The adjustment of industrial structure is to determine reasonable leading industries and supporting industries, as well as making them coordinated. The industrial development order and industrial arrangement and combination in industrial policy are the process of adjusting the original industrial relationship or reconstructing the organic industrial combination, and realizing the orderly development of industrial combination. In the industrial mix, there are many industries with high degree of correlation and positive externality around the industrial cluster. These industries enjoy a strong driving role from the leading industry with the development of the whole industrial chain. This driving role has both demand and supply influence. With more and more industries joining in, the leading industry promotes the scale of the whole industrial cluster to expand gradually, and the overall competitiveness is also growing. The basic performance of industrial structure optimization and upgrading is that the leading industry with higher growth rate and innovation strength drives other industries to join in so as to extend the whole industrial chain, thus replacing the original leading industry or industrial cluster process. The industry who can undertake to lead the whole economic development is limited by the conditions. If the number of leading industries is too crowd and the coordinating industry are too dispersed, the scarce resources available for development can not be effectively concentrated on most conducive to the transformation of development mode, therefore the leading position and role can not be highlighted, complicating the difficulty of structural transformation.

The significance of studying the transformation of economic

development mode from the perspective of industrial iteration lies in the optimization and upgrading of industrial structure. The key link is to choose the right and reasonable industrial priority for development. Leading industry represents the direction of advanced technology and industry specialization, and guides the process of industrial restructuring and the transformation of economic development mode. Leading industry is the birthplace of advanced technology and management mode, and its development speed is generally higher than the average level of national economy. With the increasing proportion of the output value of the leading industry in the national economy, the infiltration of advanced technology and innovation in the leading industry, the industrial structure is gradually rationalized, and the economic growth or development is brought out with continuous optimization of the industrial structure. However, the choice of industrial priority development order is not an easy task, because it is restricted by resources, economic development, production technology structure and level, as well as policy factors, also the industrial arrangements and combination have to meet the multiple requirements of rationalization and upgrading of industrial structure as well as economic development goals. The order of industrial development should concerntrated on the internal and external factors of the industry, starting with the internal development conditions of the whole industry. Reasonable industrial development sequences can tap the potential of economic development, make the best use of competitive advantages, and make full and effective use of various resources, thus becoming the driving force for development and promoting the substantive transformation of economic development mode. On the contrary, if the choice of the leading industry is unreasonable or the original leading industry is not adjusted timely at the critical moment, the old industrial structures and industrial linkages may depress the development potential of many industries, and even lead to a path dependence on the unreasonable development mode and increase the difficulty of transformation. In this sense, the key to the transformation of economic development mode lies in the adjustment of industrial structure, and the key to the rationalization and upgrading of industrial structure lies in the establishment of industrial priority and the choice of industrial policy arrangement and combination.

1.2 Intension and Extension of Economic Development Mode

1.2.1 Literature reviews of economic growth mode and economic development mode

The discussion of economic growth pattern in socialist countries stems from the view about the expansion of social capital from Karl Marx. He believes that the enlarging of the scale of social production is the expansion of the extension; and the increase of the output efficiency of production means the expansion of intension[①]. On this basis, former Soviet economists further clarified the concept of the mode of economic growth [②], which can be divided into two categories: one could be achieved by investing natural resources, capital and labor, i.e. extension growth, also known as extensive growth; the other can be achieved by improving production efficiency, i.e. connotation growth, also known as intensive growth. The concept was quickly recognized and valued after being introduced into China, which has aroused widespread references and extensive discussion in the theoretical field. Chinese scholars define the concept of economic growth mode from the following aspects:

① Karl Marx. Capital (Volume 3) [M].People's Publishing House,1975.

② Lu Nanquan.A Review of the Economic Growth Modes of the Former Soviet Union[J].Economic Dynamics, 1995 (11):75-78.

emphasizing the mechanism of economic growth, believing that economic growth is the source of growth, growth mechanism and growth path that a country's overall economy depends on to achieve long-term growth, and is the general term of economic operation and dynamic structure of economic growth at the stage of development under certain institutional arrangements.[①] The way of economic growth is understood as the way of economic growth, with the purpose of examining concretely the way in which the total output expands. From the perspective of the driving forces of development, economic development is divided into four stages: resource-driven, capital-driven, labor-driven and productivity-driven. The transformation from one factor-driven development stage to another factor-driven production stage is the transformation of economic development mode[②].

However, the term "mode of economic growth" is rare in western economic literature. According to the research on economic growth abroad and the discussion of domestic scholars, the meaning of the mode of economic growth we mentioned is close to that of the development mode in Western economics. In the study of economic growth, western scholars have different points of view with the development from Chinese national scholars. The former tries to explain the ultimate cause of economic growth and explains why economic growth will differ in different countries or regions. The latter focuses on how to achieve rapid and stable growth in order to shake off from poverty and achieve leapfrog development and economic take-off. Western scholars generally adopt the growth accounting method to investigate the mode of economic growth[③].The economic growth

---

① Zhou Zhenhua.The Structural Effect of Modern Economic Growth[M].Shanghai Sanlian Press, 1995.

② Cai Fang. Turning Point: New Stage of China's Economic Development[M].Social Science Literature Press,2008.

③ Robert Solow. Technical Change and the Aggregate Production Function[J].The Review of Economics and Statistics,1957,39(3):312-320.

factors can be divided into two categories: first, the increase in the input of production factors, including employment and working hours, the age and gender structure of the employed persons, the educational years of the employed, and the size of the capital stock; second, the increase of the output of unit input, including the improvement of resources allocation, scale economy and knowledge progress[①].The growth accounting results not only confirm Solow's conclusion, that is, technological progress is an important source of economic growth, but also deepen our understanding of the components of technological progress: technological progress mainly comes from human capital accumulation. There are three factors that affect economic growth[②]: the increase of knowledge, labor productivity and structural changes. Kuznets associated knowledge strength with production factors and structural factors to emphasize the important influence of structural factors on economic growth, this is the difference between Denison and him, which is an important contribution to the theory of economic development. The conclusion of Kuznet's analysis is almost the same conclusion as Solow and et al, that is, scientific and technological progress is the main source of modern economic growth. Moses Abramovitz extended the growth accounting. He traced the research period back to the early nineteenth Century. By comparing the growth accounting of the five periods, he concluded that the main form of economic growth in the early stage of industrialization was based on capital accumulation rather than technological progress[③].The type of economic growth discussed above implies the meaning of the mode of economic growth, and can also be regarded as the external manifestation

---

① Edward F. Denison. The Sources of Economic Growth in the United Stares & the Alternatives Before us[M].Committee for Economic Development,1962.

② Simon Kuznets. Quantitative Aspects of Economic Growth in Various Countries[M].Commercial Press, 1999.

③ Moses Abramowitz. Thinking about Growth and Other Essays of Economic Growth and Welfare[M]. Cambridge University Press,1989:3-377.

of economic growth mode of development. Many scholars also use TFP (Total Factor Productivity) contribution in economic growth model to measure economic growth or development mode. The growth factors can be summarized into five categories: first, the increase of labor input in quantity and quality; second, the increase of capital and land input in quantity and quality; third, the improvement of resources; the fourth is the scale economy; the fifth is the progress of knowledge and its application in production. Besides labor, land and capital, the rest belongs to the category of TFP, including the role of technological progress, management improvement, organizational innovation and institutional change in economic growth.[①] The mode of economic growth has rich connotations. Growth accounting only the method to identify the mode of growth, but it does not express its essence and rich connotations. At the same time, growth accounting also has many defects. It decomposes output growth machinery into input growth and TFP growth, which is meaningful to some extent and inspires follow-up research on economic growth. However, growth accounting does not constitute a growth theory, because it does not attempt to explain how changes in input and TFP improvements relate to other elements that can reasonably be considered as basic input factors, such as preferences, technology and institutions.

Although the mode of economic development includes the content of the mode of economic growth, replacing the economic growth mode with the economic development mode does not mean that the transformation of the mode of economic growth is past tense, nor does it mean that the task of the transformation of the mode of economic growth has been accomplished.[②] In fact, China is still facing the

---

①   Lin Xianzhai. Theory and Policy Research on Accelerating the Change of Economic Development Mode[J].Seeking Truth, 2010(10).

②   Zhou Shulian. Profound Understanding and Grasping of "Changing the Mode of Economic Development" [J].Learning Theory, 2008(3):12-13.

arduous task of transforming the economic growth mode. Changing the mode of economic development does not exclude the transformation of the mode of economic growth. It is difficult to fundamentally change the economic development mode only by economic growth, the economic process may bring about new problems and contradictions. Therefore, the transformation of the economic growth mode must be accomplished in combination with other tasks. Economic development includes economic growth, optimization of economic structure, enhancement of development quality and upgrading social system and people's life, economic growth refers to the increase of total products and services. It can be seen that economic development includes economic growth, so economic growth mode is included in the content of economic development mode. Apart from the increase in the number of economic indicators, the methods and modes of economic growth, the contents of economic development modes also include more complex contents such as industrial structure transformation, investment transformation, income distribution, urban-rural structure upgrading, resource utilization, sustainable development and so on[①]. The transformation of economic development mode not only includes the task of transforming the growth mode, that is, the task of transforming from extensive mode to intensive mode, but also the quality and sustainability of economic growth, economic structure, resource conservation and environmental friendliness, which emphasizes the importance of inclusive growth and people-oriented, and ultimately achieves inter-regional, economic and social, human and nature, as well as domestic and foreign parties, in the purpose of coordinating development and achieving a win-win development goals.

The economic development mode refers specifically to the

---

① Huang Taiyan. The Connotation and Realization Mechanism of Changing the Mode of Economic Development[J].Qiushi, 2007(18):6-8.

arrangement and combination of various elements to promote economic development and the allocation of resources, as well as the way in which various resources and elements are connected and combined to promote the economy to achieve its expected development goals[①]. Understanding the mode of economic development mainly depends on what factors economic development depends on and how to achieve them. The mode of economic development is the combination of various factors that determine the economic development and how they interact with each other, which is the summation of approaches, means and ways to achieve economic development. The process of economic development is the course of optimizing the allocation of resources and maximization of output. The basic connotation of the economic development mode actually includes the content of the mode of resource allocation[②]: The first is the efficiency of resource utilization, whose core lies on reducing the quantity of resources consumed by unit products and increase the output of unit resources. The second is the efficiency of resource allocation, with the core of allocating resources by alternative uses to different production uses, and maximize the output of resources by optimizing the resources allocation to achieve the Pareto optimal state of production and distribution. Therefore, from the perspective of resource allocation, the connotation of economic development mode is consistent with that of resource allocation mode, and the essence of economic development mode is resource allocation. Generalized economic development mode actually includes institutional factors, such as ownership, enterprise system, distribution mode and other economic systems and their specific forms. The mode of economic development in this book focuses on the determination of

---

① Jian Xinhua. China's Economic Restructuring and Transformation of Its Economic Development Mode[M].Shandong University Press, 2010.

② Shi Jinchuan. On the Mode of Economic Development and Its Transformation: theory, history and reality[J]. Social Sciences, 2010(4):12-18.

development goals and ways to achieve them, the types and modes of usage on production factors, the adjustment and optimization of industrial structure, export-driven and domestic demand-driven, the relationships between accumulation and consumption, speed and structure and efficiency, development and sustainable development factors such as resources and environment, and the relationship between development and employment, as well as the corresponding methods and ways. The economic development mode discussed here is the macro and medium development mode, which does not involve the micro-economy, that is, the development mode of enterprises or individuals. The mode of economic development includes four links: production, distribution, exchange and consumption[①]. Among them, the mode of economic growth involves mainly production, which is a branch of the economic development mode. Economic development mode includes not only production links, but also industrial structures, urban and rural and regional consumption structures, income distribution, resources and environment.

The proposition of economic development mode has gone through a process from single definition to complexity. But so far, there are still many different versions on the understanding and interpretation of the economic development mode. There is no consensus on this topic, and there is no scientific definition of the economic development mode. So this book defines the connotation and extension of the economic development mode, in which includes the mode of resource allocation and the mode of economic growth. It should be pointed out that the concept of the economic development mode actually has the meaning of normative economics. How to choose the appropriate mode of development? Is the existing development mode reasonable? Although

---

① Zhou Shulian. Profound Understanding and Grasping of "Changing the Mode of Economic Development" [J]. Learning Theory, 2008(3):12-13.

the process, content and manifestation of economic development are determined objectively by the level of productivity, who generated and evolved spontaneously, it is also regulated and controlled by the government's goals and plans, so the mode of economic development is a controllable variable. For developing countries, to achieve the goal of economic take-off, it is more meaningful to seek ways of transformation instead of passively letting them take their own course.

1.2.2 Types of economic development modes

1. From the angle of operation mode or economic growth efficiency, the economic development mode is divided into extensive (extension) type and intensive (connotation) type. Extensive development mode refers to the economic development mode who supported by a great quantity of resources and energy consumption, unskilled labor forces and capital input. It has characteristics of highly resources input and consumption, low quality and low efficiency, one-sided pursuit of quantity and speed, ignoring the quality and efficiency of development, lose sight of the contribution of innovation and technology, production efficiency and structural improvement to economic development. The intensive development mode refers to the way to achieve economic development by relying on technological innovation to improve labor productivity and factor use efficiency. It has characteristics of low consumption and investment, good quality and high efficiency[①]. However, this classification can not distinguish the relative contribution of the changes in the input of various factors in the so-called "extensive" development mode. Besides, those types of development mode based on the improvement of total factor productivity is not necessarily superior to the development mode

---

① Li Wuwei and Wang Zhen. Research on Transformation of the Mode of Economic Growth[M]. Shanghai Xuelin Publishing House, 2006.

mainly based on the increase of input of factors[①]. In a sense, "intensive" development mode can be called "total factor productivity" development mode, while "extensive" development mode can be called "factor accumulation" development mode. Although intensive type is inevitably efficient type, extensive type can not be completely equated with inefficient or inefficient type. Because the key to economic efficiency is whether the output is greater than the input, as long as the input is less than the output, it is efficient; the input is more than the output implies this type is inefficient. If the input of production factors increases to a certain scale, it will produce scale benefits, and the utility of production factors can be make full use of, which will lead to the expansion of connotation and intensive development. If the increased production factors are more efficient factors, such as new machinery and equipment as well as the mastery of high-tech labor force, the new projects adopt the latest advanced technology, indicating this kind of economy contain intensive factors, with efficiency improvement[②].

Hungarian economist Janos Kornai compares the concept of "extensive reproduction" and "intensive reproduction" used by economists in socialist countries with the concept of "increase in input of productive factors" and "improvement of comprehensive factor productivity" used by economists in capitalist countries[③④]. He pointed out that the distinction between increased input of factors of production and increased productivity of integrated factors and the related

① Justin Lin, Su Jian. On the Transformation of China's Economic Growth Mode[J].Management World, 2007(11).

② Jian Xinhua. China's Economic Structural Adjustment and Transformation of Development Mode[M]. Shandong People's Press, 2010.

③ Janos.Kornai.The Socialist System—The Political Economy of Communism[M].Princeton University Press, 1992.

④ Janos.Kornai.Translated by Zhang An:Translation of the System of Socialism, Communism Political Economics[M]. Central Compilation and Translation Press, 2007.

terminology were widely used in the West. However, socialist economists prefer to use "extension" and "intensive", which are semantically the same. Increasing factor input equals extensive and extension-type growth, while increasing factor productivity is comparable to intensive or intensive economic growth. From the perspective of extended reproduction [1] , the mode of economic development can be divided into extension and connotation: the expansion of social production places is the expansion of extension, while the improvement of output efficiency means production is the expansion of connotation. Accordingly, the extension growth mode can be understood as the mode that the expansion of reproduction mainly depends on the increase of production factors such as resources, labor and investment, while the connotation growth mode is the way to realize the expansion of reproduction by relying on technological innovation and the improvement of labor productivity. Other scholars focus on the source of power for economic growth, the mode of economic growth or development is divided into input-driven and efficiency-driven. This division is roughly the same as the previous division, that is, input-driven development means economic growth or development mainly depends on the increase of input of production factors; efficiency-driven means that economic growth or development mainly depends on the improvement of labor productivity or factor use efficiency.

2. According to the difference of factor contribution and growth motive force, the economic development mode is divided into labor-intensive, capital-intensive, technology-intensive and knowledge-intensive. Generally speaking, in the early stage of development, a country mainly relies on resources and labor force to achieve economic

---

[1]   Karl Marx. Capital,Volume 3[M].People's Publishing House,1975.

growth, and its development mode tends to be resource and labor intensive; as the development stage enters the middle stage of industrialization, the economic growth is mainly driven by capital, and the development mode tends to be capital-intensive; in the late stage of industrialization, the economic growth is mainly driven by technology and human capital. The development mode tends to be technology-knowledge intensive. However, if the transformation of the mode of economic development from extensive to intensive is an oversimplification understanding as the transformation from resource-intensive to capital-intensive or technology-intensive, and then the extensive growth is equated with resource-intensive and labor-intensive, advocating abandonment of resources and labor-intensive, which is a misunderstanding in the choice of development mode. Some economists' research indicates that, in recent 20 years, China's economic growth pattern belongs to the element accumulation and factor driven type. Capital growth and land investment drive are the main factors, followed by TFP. For China, the resource structure determines the appropriate growth mode, which means that China should be labor based accumulation, so the current capital intensive growth mode and resource endowment do not match well.[1] Some scholars divide the mode of economic development into investment-driven and consumption-driven economic development according to the different driving forces of development. Investment-driven economic development means that economic development mainly depends on investment; consumption-driven economic development means that economic development mainly depends on consumption demand[2]. The

---

[1] Justin Lin,Su Jian.On the Transformation of China's Economic Growth Mode[J].Management World, 2007(11):5-13.

[2] Li Wuwei,Wang Zhen.Research on the Transformation of Economic Growth Mode[M].Shanghai Xuelin Publishing House, 2006.

historical experience of economic development shows that investment is the main driving force in the early stage of industrialization, while consumption-driven economic development is the important way in the higher stage of industrialization. At present, China is in a typical stage of investment promotion. Consumption-driven economic development is the direction of the transformation of China's economic development mode. It should be pointed out here that the economic development mode of a country is closely related to its system, whether it is investment-driven or consumption-driven, or speed-oriented, benefit-oriented or quantity-oriented and quality-oriented[①]. Also, the economic development mode may be government-oriented or market-oriented. Government-led economic development refers to the development that is closely related to the role and changes of the government's administrative forces, and the economic operation is somewhat controled by the government. For example, China's economic development pursues the speed of quantity, and relies heavily on investment with characteristics of government's macro-policy ruling and correlation. Blind pursuit of GDP and large-scale overinvestment in fixed assets are manifestations of government-led economic development. Market-oriented economic development refers to the economic development mainly driven and automatically regulated by market forces, which has little to do with the change of government policies. At present, with the gradual improvement of market economy system, China is trying to change from government-led to market-led, with the purpose of a sound and healthy growth.

3. According to the quality of economic development or the degree

---

① Speed-type or quantity-type growth means one-sided pursuit of quantity, output value and speed, manifested by low quality, poor efficiency and structural imbalance, while the benefit-type or quality-type growth mode focuses on the improvement of the quality and efficiency of economic growth, as well as the coordination of industrial structure, etc.

of economic and social coordination, the mode of economic development is divided into inclusive and exclusive types. The purpose of inclusive development is the coordination and sustainable development of the economy, society, population and environment. Inclusive development requires all the economic and their descendants to share the fruits of economic development in a fair and reasonable way. The most important manifestation is democracy in politics and narrowing the gap in income distribution in the economy. Inclusive development also includes many measurable standards and intangible factors. Among them, the measurable criteria include literacy rate, the popularization and enjoyment of public goods, specifically related to education, health, infrastructure, personal safety, etc. Inclusive growth also includes spiritual and ideological aspects, including the degree of respect and enjoyment of freedom, maximizing and widening the enjoyment of democracy and respect by the population. The ultimate goal of inclusive growth is to enable the fruits of economic cooperation and development to benefit both developed and developing countries, including the most extensive population. Inclusive growth is guided by scientific outlook on development, based on the development of the economy, and based on the transformation of the economic development mode, focusing on improving the quality of economic development, creating a material foundation and guarantee for all mankind to live a prosperous life. Inclusive growth also advocates upholding humanity and social equity, eliminating obstacles to people's participation in economic development opportunities, access to democracy and freedom, and sharing the fruits of economic development, and creating an environment and atmosphere in which everyone has equal access to development opportunities. Inclusive growth requires people-oriented, maximizing the improvement of people's livelihood and effectively improving people's welfare, with all development objectives for the people and development. The results are shared by the people. ①② There is no doubt that inclusive growth is broad-based, friendly growth, inclusively consider the survival and development of the poverty-stricken areas and the poor, as well as the gap between the rich and the poor, rather than laissez faire poverty and inequality in income distribution. Exclusive economic growth is purely the pursuit of economic growth, efficiency and fairness are not balanced. Poor people are discriminated against and excluded from the process of economic growth, unable to enjoy the fruits of social and economic development, excluding growth other than social, economic and political rights, and growing without development③. Inclusive growth also involves the sustainable development of man and nature. Its inclusiveness is embodied in the green growth and low carbon growth mode of environment-friendly and resource-saving④. Exclusive growth, ignoring the non-renewability of resources, making a single claim for resources and environment, does not take into account the sustainability of economic development.

1.2.3 The argument about the way to realize the transformation of economic development mode

On how to realize the transformation of economic development mode, domestic scholars put forward different methods from various

---

① Hu Jintao. Joint Efforts to Meet Challenges and Promote Sustainable Development—an Important Speech on APEC[R/OL].[2009-11-15].Xinhua News Agency.

② Hu Jintao. Deepening Exchange and Cooperation to Achieve Inclusive Growth: Address to the Fifth APEC Ministerial Conference on Human Resources Development[R/OL].[2010-09-16].Xinhua News Agency.

③ Cai Rongxin. Inclusive Growth: Theory Development and Policy System[J].Leadership Science, 2010(12).

④ Li Gang. The Foundation of Learning Sources, Theoretical Framework and Policy Direction of Inclusive Growth[J].Economist, 2011(7).

angles. From adjusting economic structure[1][2]: Wang Yiming (2010) and Zhang Zhuoyuan (2006) believe that the optimization and upgrading of industrial structure should be accelerated, the development of urban and rural areas and regions should be coordinated, the demand of structure should be adjusted, the role of consumption in economic development mode should be emphasized, and the quality of economic development should be improved. Many literatures have analyzed the relationship between technology and investment, technology chain and industry chain. Zheng Yuxin (1999) indicates that the improvement of the status of technological progress in economic growth is the main symbol of the transformation of economic growth mode. Effective allocation of resources is the most important to economic growth, because whether relying on technological innovation or factor expansion, the final external performance is the improvement of investment efficiency or investment quality[3]. Han Jiangbo (2009) believes that if the economic form wants to realize the transition from low level to high level, and fundamentally change the low level development mode based on extensive economic growth mode, the key is to achieve a breakthrough between the core technology chain and the core industry chain in the process of mutual promotion.[4]

There are also many literatures pointing out that the defects of the system hinder the transformation of the economic development mode: Liu Shaowu (2000) suggests that the transformation of the growth mode requires innovation in the organizational system, property right

---

[1]   Wang Yiming. China's Medium and Long Term Economic Growth Trends and Accelerating the Transformation of Economic Growth Mode[J].2010(12):3-14.

[2]   Zhang Zhuoyuan. Changing the Mode of Economic Growth: Government Reform is the Key[J]. Macroeconomic Management, 2006(10):37-38.

[3]   Zheng Yuxin.Measurement of Total Factor Productivity and Stage Rules of Economic Growth Mode[J].Economic Research, 1999(5):55-60.

[4]   Han Jiangbo.Mutual Promotion between the Core Technology Chain and the Core Industrial Chain-based on the Transformation of Economic Development Mode[J].Social Science,2009(3).

system and distribution system of economic activities[①]. Liu Wei (2006) takes advantage of two basic indicators about economic quantity and economic quality, believes that the transformation of growth mode should start with technological innovation, especially from the improvement of social system innovation ability.[②] Jinbei (2006) points out that innovation in theory, technology and management is key to the transformation of economic growth mode. It is believed that the transformation of the mode of economic development should eliminate the two characteristics of large investment in low-cost resources and regional competition dominated by local governments[③]. Cai Fang (2007) believes that in the face of the turning point of China's economic development, China must speed up institutional innovation and policy adjustment so as to maintain the sustainability of economic growth.[④] Yang Shuhua (2009) proposes to use price, tax mechanism and other economic leverage to force the transformation of economic development mode.[⑤] Shi Jinchuan (2010) points out that the key to determine the transformation of economic development mode is to improve the institutional environment for the transformation of economic development mode and gives full play to the basic role of market in resource allocation.[⑥] Moreover, from the perspective of the transformation of government role, Wu Jinglian (2006) points out that

---

① Liu Shaowu.Thoughts on the Role of Institutional Arrangements in Changing the Mode of Economic Growth[J].Management World,2000(6):182-183.

② Liu Wei.The Historical Change of Economic Development and Reform and the Fundamental Transformation of Growth Mode[J].Economic Research,2006(1):4-10.

③ Jin Bei.Scientific Outlook on Development and the Transformation of Economic Growth Mode [J].China Industrial Economy,2006 (5):5-14.

④ Cai Fang.The Turning Point of China's Economy and Its Challenges to Development and Reform [J].Chinese Social Sciences,2007(3):4-1.

⑤ Yang Shuhua.Path Analysis of the Change of China's Economic Development Mode-Based on the Perspective of Economic Driving Force[J].Economic Dynamics,2009(3):30-33.

⑥ Shi Jinchuan.On the Mode of Economic Development and Its Transformation: theory, history and reality[J].Zhejiang Social Sciences,2010(4):12-18.

the transformation of economic growth mode ultimately depends on the transformation of government functions. Whether or not the government is self revolutionary directly related to the success of market-oriented reform and the transformation of economic growth mode.[①] Zhang Zhuoyuan (2006) proposes that only by promoting government reform and reforming the long-standing imperfect cadre performance appraisal and selection system, can we effectively change the mode of economic growth.

Some scholars think from the microcosmic point of view in economic development, Yang Wenjin etc. (2007) suggest that the pressure of rising cost and product price caused by relative shortage of factors, as well as the potential benefits and benefits of technological change, will drive enterprises to change their development modes. He proposes to change the way enterprises obtain profits to realize the transformation of economic growth modes.[②] Wei Jie etc. (2009) believe that improving the ability of independent innovation is beneficial to improving the efficiency of resource allocation, thus promoting the adjustment and upgrading of industrial structure.[③]

From the point of view of factor, Lin and Su Jian (2007) suggests that China should start with the resource endowment structure and adopt the growth mode that can make full use of the comparative advantage of the labor force, rather than relying on the growth mode dominated by capital intensive and independent R&D which does not have the advantage. However, Wang Xiaolu etc. (2009) argue that the contribution of capital to economic growth will continue to increase, but the dependence on human capital is changing from simple

---

① Wu Jinglian.The Choice of China's Growth Mode[M].Shanghai Far East Press,2006.

② Yang Wenjin, Yang Liuqing.On the Conditions and Social Impact of the Transformation of Economic Growth Mode[J].Economist,2007(1):32-37.

③ Wei Jie and Ren Baoping.Theoretical and Empirical Analysis of Factor Productivity and Quality of Economic Growth[J].Journal of China,2009(11):36-44.

expansion to quality improvement. The excessive expansion of government administrative costs and the continuous decline of the final consumption rate of the national economy have hindered the transformation of growth mode. He advocates that economic growth should rely on technological progress, education and expanding domestic demand.[①] Lv Zheng (2009) believes that China's industrial development has entered the stage of rising cost of production factors. Relying on high input, high consumption, low resources and environmental costs, low technology content and low price competition, the extensive growth mode is difficult to sustain. On the basis of adhering to comparative advantage, it will promote transformation of the mode of economic development through restructuring and solving the problem of relative surplus of industrial production capacity. [②] Liu Rongcang and Zhao Jingxing (1999) indicate that the system and open factors have an important impact on the economic growth and development mode of a country, especially developing countries. They believe that changing the mode of economic development should start with improving the quality of production factors and improving the combination and utilization of elements.[③] Huang Taiyan (2007) believes that the transformation of economic development mode should not only refer to the transformation from extensive growth of extension type to intensive growth of connotation type, but also include diversification of development objectives, simultaneous growth of quality and efficiency, people-oriented, comprehensive optimization of economic structure, in

---

①　Wang Xiaolu, Fang Gang, Liu Peng.Transformation of China's Economic Growth Mode and Sustainability of Growth[J].Economic Research,2009(1): 4-16.

②　Lv Zheng.A Fundamental Change in the Way of Development Promoted by Structural Adjustment [J].Qiushi,2009(9):40-42.

③　Liu Rongcang and Zhao Jingxing.On the Factors Affecting the Mode of Economic Growth and its Transformation[J].China Industrial Economy,1999(10):30-35.

order to achieve the goal of resource-saving and environment-friendly under the condition of knowledge-based economy. [1] Liu Shucheng (2007) proposes that in order to achieve sound and rapid economic development, the quality and efficiency of economic growth should be continuously improved, including the stability of the situation, the sustainability of the way, the coordination of the structure and the harmony of the benefits. [2] Zhou Shaoping's (2010) believes that the key to changing the mode of economic development is to realize the strategic transformation of economic development, speed up the adjustment of economic structure, deepen reform and strengthen independent innovation.

Some literatures discuss and put forward countermeasures to change the mode of economic development from the perspective of industry. Liu Wei and Li Shaorong's (2002) empirical analysis indicates that in China's economy, the most effective industries to promote economic growth, except for the construction industry, are almost all sectors of the third industry, but the structural expansion of the service industry will reduce the positive effect of agriculture and industry on the economic scale. The development of the service industry must be based on the development of the first and second industries. [3] Shi Qi, etc. (2009) believe that the upgrading of consumption structure is one of the main forces to promote the upgrading of China's industrial structure. The service industry is the fundamental reason for the change of industrial structure. The driving force of consumption upgrading comes from the industrial expansion of the sector, but also from the unbalanced growth of different industries. Rather, the unbalanced force

---

[1]   Huang Taiyan.The Connotation and Realization Mechanism of Changing Economic Development Mode[J].Qiushi,2007(18):6-8.

[2]   Liu Shucheng.On Good and Fast Development[J].Economic Research,2007(6):4-13.

[3]   Liu Wei and Li Shaorong.Industrial Structure and Economic Growth[J].China's Industrial Economy, 2002(5):14-21.

mainly comes from the promotion of the service industry. Therefore, modern service industry is the main driving force to promote the change of China's industrial structure. They advocate vigorously developing the service industry and promoting the upgrading of consumption structure. [1]

The representative researches on the performance of the transformation of economic development mode are as follows. Ma Qiangwen and Ren Baoping (2010) use the data envelopment analysis method to analyze the performance of the transformation of China's economic development mode. The results show that the proportion of state-owned enterprises and the increase of foreign trade are the main factors that have a negative impact on the performance of economic development mode. The key lies in improving the degree of marketization and adjusting the trade structure and industrial structure. Li Lingling etc. (2011) establish a performance evaluation system based on the transformation of the mode of economic development with economic growth, development momentum, resources and environment support and development results as the basic framework, and concluded that China's economic development mode has changed. It is recommended to speed up economic development by optimizing the structure of income distribution, improving the degree of marketization and the rate of input and output of scientific research, and changing the mode of production as well as exhibition mode. The above studies on the performance of the transformation of China's economic development mode have not fully examined the input structure of the economic development process, nor do they reflect the industrial structure of economic development. Moreover, the index system is too simple to reflect the deep-seated problems of economic

---

[1] Shi Qi, Yin Jingdong and Lv Lin.The Impact of Consumption Upgrading on China's Industrial Structure[J].Industrial Economic Research,2009(11).

development mode. Ma Qiangwen's method of inspecting the performance of economic development mode is more scientific, but the definition of economic development mode is rather one-sided. While Li Lingling and others have a more comprehensive definition of the mode of economic development, the method is too simple to reveal the inherent problems of economic development profoundly, and the credibility of the conclusions needs to be tested.

The above-mentioned literature studies the connotation and conditions of the transformation of economic development mode from the aspects of economic development stage, factors of production, institutional arrangement, factors of economic opening, motive force of economic growth and industry development, or examines and evaluates the effect of the transformation of economic development mode in China from different perspectives. However, most of the existing literature only studies from a certain point of view, and can not comprehensively summarize the scientific meaning of economic development mode, lacking a systematic framework. Although some literatures have expounded the connotation of specific economic development modes, neither they have not deeply analyzed the reasons and mechanisms for the transformation of economic development modes, nor have they explored the ways of transformation of economic development mode from the perspective of industrial development order. Although some literatures consider the ways to change the mode of economic development from the perspective of industrial structure and sustainable development, the research methods can not fully summarize the current situation of the mode of economic development, especially the industrial structure and elements of economic development, nor can they well integrate the new tasks and challenges faced by the current economic, social and resource environment. Therefore, it is necessary to study the present situation of China's industrial structure and the input-output of various sectors of the national economy, the supply factors such as the structure and efficiency of economic development, and the demand factors such as investment, consumption, import and export. It is necessary to explore the path of the transformation of China's economic development mode from the perspective of industrial priority and the choice of leading industries.

1.3 Industrial Priority and Industrial Combination

1.3.1 Criteria for industry priority

Domestic research on leading industries began in the mid 1980s, when some works on successful industrialization experience were introduced to China. Some countries, especially two East Asian countries after World War II, Japan and South Korea, have made great achievements in the transformation and upgrading of industrial structure and industrial policies, which attracted more and more attention from Chinese scholars and governments. Inspired by these experiences, the priority of industrial development and the choice of industries become a hot issue in China's economic development in the late 1980s. Huang Yi you (1988) considers the resource endowment as the basic constraint condition and based on the national conditions of China's abundant labor force, he puts forward that the industrial priorities are labor-intensive export industries, basic industries, raw materials, original components, components and industrial equipment, and potential next generation export industries. [1] Li Boxi and others (1988) start from the realistic obstacles in China's economic development, and think that the bottleneck industry is the most important constraint condition in economic development. Therefore,

---

[1]   Huang Yiyou.On the Selection of Industrial Priorities in China in the 21st Century[J]. Management World,1988(3).

China should focus on resources and give priority to the development of basic industries. [①] Zhu Zhengming etc. (1988) take foreign experience and the theory of interrelationship between industries into account, indicate that the choice of leading industries should be considered from the perspective of demand structure and industrial correlation. According to this standard, automobile and construction industries should be leading industries.[②] The research results of the institute of quantitative and economic research of Chinese Academy of Social Sciences is that China should give priority to the development of transportation, post and telecommunications, the electric power industry and the electronics industry.[③] Xie Fuzhan etc. (1988) consider that priority industries are agriculture, energy, steel, chemical raw materials, transportation and communication, key industries and transportation equipment manufacturing, textile industry and electronic industry.[④] Academic circles have scattered views on the priority of industrial development and leading or pillar industries, covering a wide range of industries. There is no consistent conclusion on which industries should be selected in the industrial arrangement and combination. The reason lies in the great differences in research perspectives and methods, and industrial replacement itself is a process of constant change and development. Scholars have made some meaningful discussions from different perspectives using different methods. They have made useful explorations on the methods of selecting industrial priority development order and the significance of

① Li Poxi,Xie Fuzhan, Li Nurturing.Analysis and Countermeasures for the Development of "Bottleneck" Industries[J].Economic Research,1988(12).

② Zhu Zhengming, Netizens, Shao Chong.A Probe into the Industrial Problems in Australia in China's Industrial Institutions[J].Management World,1988(1).

③ Institute of Quantitative and Economic Research, Chinese Academy of Social Sciences.Research on Technology Progress and Industrial Structure[J]. Quantitative Economics and Technology Research, 1988(1).

④ Xie Fuzhan etc. Nurturing: Strategic Choice of Industrial Structure Adjustment [J]. Management World, 1990 (4).

industrial policy, and have guided the practice of economic development. However, in the face of the new objectives of the current economic development mode and the new requirements of the sustainable development of economy, society, resources and environment, when the market economy is maturing, the selection method of industrial priority development order and the standard of industrial arrangements and combination put forward new requirements and tasks accordingly.

The concept of leading industry was first put forward by American economist Hirshman in 1958.[①] Then Rostow made a systematic study on the leading industry and further defined the definition of the leading industry. The leading industry is derived from the concept of the leading sector proposed by Rostow. Rostow believes that there are wide differences in the growth rates of different sectors of the national economy at any specific stage. In a particular stage of economic development, some sectors have sustained technological innovation capabilities and rich innovation activities, which are far higher than the average growth rate of the national economy. These sectors also have strong and extensive linkages in the entire industrial system. On the basis of the description of the characteristics of the leading departments, Rostow launches the meaning of the leading industry: the leading industry refers to a certain stage of development in a country or region, which is faster than the growth rate of most industries of the national economy, and will soon occupy or occupy a significant position in the national economy. It plays a leading and decisive role in the whole industrial system and economic development.[②] Rostow believes that the leading departments should have the following

---

① Hirshman.Translated by Cao Zhenghai and Pan Zhaodong.Economic Development Strategy[M]. Economic Science Press,1991.

② Walter W. Rostow.Translated by He Liping, etc.Economics from Take-off to Continuous Growth[M]. People's Press,1988.

characteristics: (1) the growth rate of departments with a sustained and higher level of national economy; (2) new production functions are generated by the introduction of new technologies or new systems; (3) greater industrial inducement, technology diffusion and industrial linkage. According to the difference between growth and growth rate, Rostow divides the industrial sectors of the national economy into dominant growth, auxiliary growth and derivative growth sectors. The possible results of innovation or the possibility of new resources development make the leading growth sector having a higher growth rate than other sectors, and can widely promote the development and growth of other industries. For example, during the third industrial revolution, the computer and software development and design and information transmission industries are the leading sectors; the auxiliary sectors are the direct support sectors for the growth results of the leading sectors, such as computer and communication equipment manufacturing and polymer material manufacturing; the derivative growth sectors are related to other growth parameters such as income growth and demand growth, the interconnection of the information economy era. Network technology service industry and cultural entertainment industry are typical derivative growth sectors. Leading and subsidiary sectors are related to supply constraints. If supply constraints are reduced, the two sectors will develop, while the derived growth sectors are generated to meet demand. In all sectors of the national economy, the leading growth sector plays a leading and decisive role. The transformation of economic growth or development mode is the result of the rapid development of the leading sector strength and the development of derivative and auxiliary growth sectors. The replacement of economic growth stage is manifested in the change of the leading sector sequence. According to his own method, Rostow analyzes the important relationship between the economic growth stage and the leading sector turnover, especially the conduction process of the leading sector to drive the economic development, and explores the decisive factor of the industry sector becoming the leading sector. Whether a new department can become the leading department depends on two related factors: one is that in a particular development process, the department not only has a considerable growth momentum, but also has a significant scale effect; the other is that the department has a strong and extensive review and side effects. Rostow's view provides broad hints for future scholars to analyze leading industries. Later, many scholars make more completed and specific definition of leading industries from various perspectives. The representative viewpoints of domestic scholars are as follows: starting from the position and role of the leading industry, the leading industry refers to those industries which play a leading and guiding role in the process of economic development. They have a faster growth rate than other industries and are or have already occupied a dominant position in the whole industrial system. The leading industry, through the industrial linkage, creates its active growth momentum and technology. The achievements of new and institutional innovation and more advantages have penetrated into the whole national economic system extensively and profoundly.[1] From the point of view of market power in the national economy, leading industry means that it influences the overall situation in the process of economic development, who plays a dominant role in the national economy, industrial structure upgrading, guiding and supporting other industries, maintains a high growth rate and can strongly promote the development of other industries, which largely determines the evolution characteristics and trends of potential industrial sectors and structure.[2][3]

---

[1]   Long Maofa and Ma Mingzong.Introduction to Industrial Economics[M].Southwestern University of Finance and Economics Press,1996.

[2]   Lin Shanwei.China Economic Structural Adjustment Strategy[M].China Social Science Press, 2003.

[3]   Jian Xinhua.Industrial Economics[M].Wuhan University Press,2003.

From the perspective of the correlation function, leading industries are the sectors that develop rapidly in the national economy and can drive the development of a series industries. Those industries which have strong forward or backward correlation in the current and future economic development possess the potential to bring other industries into full play, who have close input and output with other sectors of the national economy. Relations, product demand and supply relations between departments will drive the a series of related industrial clusters.[1][2] At a certain stage of economic development, leading industries play a strong leading role in industrial structure and economic development and have a wide range of direct or indirect effects.[3]

From the perspective of technological innovation and technology absorption, leading industries refer to those departments that can actively absorb innovative achievements and advanced technologies, maintain a high growth momentum and have a strong driving role in the development of other related industries.[4] Those departments who first adopt advanced technology, with costs reduction, the expansion of the market and the accumulation of profits, gradually expand their demand for products and services from other sectors, thus driving the growth of a certain regional economy and even the development of the whole national economy, have obvious characteristics of leading industries.[5] Leading industries are those industries or industrial clusters that obtain new production functions through scientific and technological innovation and the growth is rate higher than the average

---

[1]　Yang Gongpu,Xia Da Wei.Modern Industrial Economics[M].Shanghai University of Finance and Economics Press,1999.

[2]　Mao Lingen.Industrial Economics[M].Shanghai People's Publishing House,1996.

[3]　Li Yue, Li Ping.Industrial Economics[M].Dongbei University of Finance and Economics Press, 2002.

[4]　Mao Lingen.Industrial Economics[M].Shanghai People's Press,1996.

[5]　Jiang Shiyin.Research on the Selection of Regional Industrial Structure and Leading Industries[M]. Shanghai People's Publishing House,2004.

growth rate of the national economy by which effectively drive the rapid development of a series of other industries.[1] These industries or industrial clusters can quickly absorb the achievements of innovation and play a regulatory, transformational, commanding and driving role in the national economy.[2]

Most scholars define the leading industry on the basis of Rostow's leading department. The main contents are basically the same. The difference is that the research perspective and the emphasis. To sum up, the definition of leading industries mainly concentrates on the following aspects: the national economy is dominant, absorbing new technologies and innovative achievements, high growth rate, strong market expansion capacity, and has a forward-backward correlation with other industries. This book holds that the leading industry is one or several industrial sectors which play a leading and supporting role in the national economic system and determine the future development path and mode of this sector, the evolution characteristics and trends of industrial structure. Leading industry is the result of innovation, and it can absorb innovation results widely, rapidly and effectively, and promote the development and diffusion of new technologies. The leading industry sector not only has a large proportion in the national economy or may have a high and stable growth rate in the future, but also has a close relationship with other sectors of the national economy through technology diffusion, division of labor and cooperation, as well as strong forward or backward linkages, with supply and demand relations, to promote the development of other relevant industrial clusters, so as to drive the development of the whole national economy. It should be pointed out that the core of the definition of Rostow's

---

① Su Dongshui.Industrial Economics[M].Higher Education Press,2000.

② Zhang Shou and Li Yue.Accelerating the Rationalization of China's Industrial Structure[N]. Guangming Daily,1988-01-09.

leading sector is the industrial linkage effect. Many subsequent scholars also pay great attention to the correlation effect of the industry when determining the leading industries, but this is far from enough, especially under the new requirements of the current sustainable development and multi objective development strategy.

1.3.2 Relations between leading industries and corresponding industries

1. Leading industries and basic industries

(1) Definition of basic industry

Basic industry is a concept derived from the strategic position of national economy, who provides basic development conditions for other industries. It is an industrial sector that plays a strategic basic role in economic development. The basic industry is an important part of heavy industry. It provides labor and production for all sectors of the national economy, and some sectors can directly serve agriculture, light industry and construction industries. Infrastructure creation in basic industries, as well as public service facilities are provided by basic industry to meet the needs of the normal operation of production of the entire national economy. There are several main definitions of its representativeness: He Chengying (1996) puts forward that basic industry refers to the basic industry and infrastructure of economic and social activities, including energy industry and basic raw material industry, as well as public facilities such as transportation, post and telecommunications, ports, airports, bridges, etc. [1] Lin Yin (1998) believes that the basic industry is relative to the processing industry, which mainly refers to the industry that provides input factors for other industries. Basic industries are divided into broad sense and narrow

---

[1]　He Chengying.Research on Industrial Structure Theory and Policy in China[M].China Financial and Economic Publishing House,1997.

sense. The basic industries in narrow sense refer to agriculture, raw material industry, energy (including electricity), transportation, post and telecommunications, and urban public facilities. The broad basic industries also include those third industries, such as education, technology, finance and insurance, business information, which provide invisible products or services to other departments. [1] The basic industries can be classified into the following types: First, the industries with strong consumption tendency. Generally, the products are not suitable for a large number of long-distance dispatching industries, such as food and beverage industry, aquaculture industry. The second is the widespread industry. Its products are in great demand, and the development conditions are not good enough. They are generally widely distributed, such as food processing industry, wood processing industry, furniture manufacturing industry, etc. The third is the basic industries involved in the production of basic means of production such as energy and raw materials, including power, oil, coal, steel and other industries. Fourth, the departments providing infrastructure, such as highway and railway transportation, postal and communications departments. Fifth, industries where products can not be flowed or stored in space, such as environmental governance and environmental protection industries, etc. In summary, the characteristics of the basic industry are as follows:

First of all, the status of basic industries in the national economy shows that they are the opening end of the industrial chain. The forward correlation of industries is limited and the backward correlation is obvious, which often becomes a hard constraint for the development of other industries and restricts the development of other industries. The basic industry is the basis and guarantee for the normal operation of the

---

[1] Lin Yin.China's Industrial Structure towards Twenty-first Century[M].Capital University of Economics and Business Press,1998.

whole national economy. Therefore, the development level and scale of the basic industry restrict the development scale, speed and quality of the whole economy. If the construction speed and development level of infrastructure industry can not keep up with the needs of national economic development, it will restrict and hinder the further development of other industries or even the whole economy, and become the bottleneck of national economic development.

Secondly, basic industries is monopoly in the whole industry. Generally, the basic industries with heavy industry nature belong to capital and technology-intensive industries. They need more mobile capital and fixed capital, long construction cycle, slow investment return, relatively high technology threshold, and some basic industries have strong externalities. Therefore, private decentralized capital is often not strong enough to enter the basic industry. Because of the large investment and high risk in the early stage, and the long period of return on investment, many small and medium-sized enterprises are not motivated enough to participate in the basic industry and launch free competition. Basic industries are generally considered to occupy an important strategic position in the economy of a country or region, which determines the smooth and healthy operation of the national economy. For some natural monopoly industries or non-competitive industries, the state generally presides over them, so the basic industries are monopolistic. Others, such as furniture manufacturing industry, food processing industry, beverage products industry and textile and garment industry, which have low requirements for development, low entry threshold and large market demand, exist in a large number in the market, and the quality of products is largely homogeneous, which belongs to the fully competitive industry.

(2) Similarities between basic industry and leading industry

The connotation and extension of the two concepts of basic industry and leading industry are totally different, but because they both have important strategic position in the national industrial system, they have some similarities in connotation and some overlaps in extension. The similarities between the two are mainly manifested in:

First of all, both of them occupy an important strategic position in the national industrial system. The importance of the basic industry is mainly manifested in the fact that it is the precursor of the industrial system and is in the starting point of the industrial chain. The degree of its development directly determines the development level of the whole national economy. The importance of leading industry is embodied in its guiding role and industrial relevance. If the leading industry is well developed, its industrial linkage will lead to the development and prosperity of a large number of forward-backward and side-related industries. On the contrary, if the leading industry is suppressed, other related industries will not be able to obtain full development opportunities. From this point of view, to a large extent, the leading industry determines the basic characteristics and development direction of industrial structure.

Secondly, basic industries and leading industries are the leading industries in the national economy, and they are in a priority position within the industrial system. The reasons why the basic industry must give priority to the development of other industries are as follows: the inherent law of industrial structure development requires that the basic industry must give priority to development in order to avoid hindering and restricting the development of other industries; and the necessity of the priority development of the leading industry lies in: according to the needs of the level of economic development and the stage of economic development, as well as the sequence requirements of industrial development, the leading industry should be given priority to others. Only through development can other industries be driven to fully develop their potential.

Thirdly, under certain circumstances, basic industries can be regarded as leading industries. The selection of leading industries is generally based on the development degree and stage, industrial structure and resource endowment of different countries or regions. In some specific occasions, some basic industries may conform to all the characteristics of leading industries, have high growth rate, wide industrial linkages and strong technology spillover, and thus may become leading industries.

(3) The difference between basic industry and leading industry

The above analysis shows that there are many similarities between leading industry and basic industry, but they are very different concepts to a large extent. Their connotations and extensions must be strictly distinguished. The main differences between basic industry and leading industry are as follows:

Firstly, there are differences in the operation mechanism and their roles. The fundamental function of basic industry is mainly manifested in the restriction and hindrance to other industries when it can not develop rationally, which becomes the bottleneck of economic development. For the energy industry, almost all production and living sectors need their support. Without the normal operation of the energy sector, the production of industrial manufacturing enterprises can not be carried out, and the service industry can not work normally. The whole industrial chain and even all sectors of the national economy will be in chaos. The leading role of manifested in promoting the development of the entire industrial system through the growth rate which would higher than the average, as well as its related driving role to other related industries. If the real estate industry becomes the leading industry of a region or a country, the development of the real estate industry will not only drive its forward related industries such as iron and steel industry, cement building materials industry, and chemical industry, but also the subsequent development of related industries such as real estate consulting and sales services, finance and insurance industry, wholesale and retail industry. The joint development of these industries have a great driving effect on the rapid start and development of some side industries of the real estate industry, such as transportation and logistics services, catering and entertainment industries. If the development of these industries is not driven by the correlation of the leading industries, they will develop according to their laws as usual. The leading industries act as an accelerator and coordinator, [①] this principle is quite different from that of the basic industry.

Secondly, the mechanism of the emergence and development is different. The principles and criteria of leading industry selection vary greatly with different subjects and stages of development. The method and basis of choosing the leading industry are different, which leads to the variations of the selected leading industry or the leading industry group. Leading industries are often the result of people's subjective selection and conscious cultivation and development according to the development goals and objective reality needs. The basic industry is spontaneously generated by the market and exists objectively. It is not selected by the subjective consciousness, nor can it be changed by the subjective consciousness. It is the result of the spontaneous use of the market. Obviously, the position of the basic industry is not static as the different economic entities are varied from stages. For example, as a basic industry in the agricultural society, the agricultural planting industry has no longer played an important role in the industrialized society.

Thirdly, the stability is different. Compared with the leading industries, it does not exsist wrong direction or improper choice in the basic industries, which is relatively stable. The leading industry depends on a country or region's policy making departments' understanding of the overall development of the economy and their judgment of the future. Its correctness and reasonableness depend on

---

① Yu Rengang.Leading Industry[M].People's Publishing House,2003.

the angle and judgment method. Different angles and methods will lead to different criteria and basis for the selection of the leading industry. Therefore, the leading industries selected at each stage are not entirely consistent. In view of this, the choice of leading industries may be misguided by the misjudgement of policymakers. Once the subjective choice errors occur, or the leading industries do not make timely adjustments in different historical periods, it will lead to the imbalance and inefficiency of industrial structure and hinder the development of economic potential. There is no such problem in basic industries, which basic industries is the result of the spontaneous use of market forces. However, it is an objective fact that the current basic industry has become an important support and guarantee for other industries, and there is no errors due to selection. In addition, as long as the socio-economic environment does not undergo major changes, the categories of basic industries in a country or region will be relatively fixed, and there will be no major changes in a fairly long period of time.

2. Leading industries and pillar industries

（1）The concept of pillar industries

Whether the leading industry and the pillar industry are two different concepts or not, there are different opinions in the theoretical circles. Some think they are the same concept.[1] Some people think that although these two concepts have similarities, they refer to different industries.[2] Hu Zixiang (1996) considers that the pillar industries refer to the industries that play a decisive role in the national economy. The output value of these industries occupies a large proportion of the gross national product, contributes greatly to the upgrading of industrial structure and the improvement of the economic development, as well as

---

① Guo Wanda.Dictionary of Modern Industrial Economics[M].CITIC Press,1991.

② Fang Jia.Research on Industrial Institutions[M].Renmin University Press,1997.

to the added value, tax revenue, profit and employment.[①] Liu Lisheng etc.(1997) indicate that the pillar industry refers to the industry that plays an important role in the development of a particular industrial structure and plays an important role in promoting the development of a large number of industrial movements.[②] Hu Zixiang's definition of pillar industry is reseasonable. It not only accurately describes the characteristics of pillar industry, but also distinguishes pillar industry from other industries.

（2）Linkages between pillar industries and leading industries

Leading industries and pillar industries are all industries that policy-making departments focus on supporting the development goals of the national economy at a specific stage. From the dynamic point of view, there is a substitution phenomenon in their development. The emergence and development of leading industries may strengthen or weaken the existing pillar industries. At the same time, the pillar industries can also develop from the original leading industries. Therefore, leading industries may also be pillar industries, or potential pillar industries in the future.

Firstly, in the process of economic development, pillar industries and leading industries are replaced with different stages of economic development. The leading industries in the industrial system of a country or region represent the direction of the evolution of the industrial structure of the country or region and the future development trend because of their technological advantages. Leading industries represent advanced production technology, so they have higher productivity and lower production costs. With the advantage of low prices, they can obtain a larger market share. These advantages make the resource utilization efficiency of the leading industry higher than

---

① Hu Zixiang.China's Pillar Industry Development Strategy[M]. Economic Management Press, 1996.

② Liu Lisheng,Tan Xiangjun and Ji Wenting.The Road of Revitalization of Chinese and Foreign Pillar Industries[M].China Economic Press,1997.

the average level of the national economy. Therefore, the leading industry, which originally has a small proportion in the national economy, is likely to develop into a pillar industry. In some cases, the leading industries in some countries or regions are also pillar industries. Only those industries with advanced technology, high elasticity of product demand and income, and strong industrial linkages can guide and drive other industries. If the proportion of output value of this industry increases gradually and has the above characteristics, it is not only the leading industry, but also the pillar industry. Some of the existing pillar industries that have matured or declined may be the leading industries in the previous period, while some emerging industries in the pillar industries may be the leading industries now. The leading industries which accounts for the prop proportion become the pillar industries nowadays, while those whose output value proportion is not large enough may develop into the pillar industries in the future.

Secondly, in choosing leading industries, the focus is mainly on the adjustment of industrial structure and the medium-term and long-term goals of national economic development, while the pillar industries focus on the short-term or medium-term goals, the main purpose is to cultivate the main industries supporting national economic development. From the perspective of time, there is a relationship of succession and substitution in their development. The leading industry in the former period often develops into the pillar industry in the latter period. When entering the new stage of development, another new industry will replace the original leading industry. The successful leading industry will become the potential pillar industry in the future. Pillar industries, like leading industries, are often not fixed or constrained by time and space conditions. They are the results of conscious cultivation and development in accordance with specific development goals and conditions in a specific period, and are closely related to the stage of economic development. With the development of economy, people's demand structure changes, leading industries will also change. Once the original development conditions change, the leading industries or industrial clusters will weaken or even disappear, and gradually be replaced or eliminated by the emerging leading industries. With the change of development goals, the original leading industry will be replaced by the new leading industry, but the former leading industry has gradually become a pillar industry in the new era. From the perspective of industrial evolution history, most of the pillar industries have evolved from the original leading industries. If the current leading industry is consistent with the pillar industry, the leading industry will strengthen the role and position of the existing pillar industry. Pillar industry plays an important role in the national economy, which mainly reflects its contribution to the output value and employment of the national economy. Therefore, once the pillar industry is severely attacked, the overall economic development speed, output value scale and even social stability of a country or region will be greatly affected.

（3）Differences between leading industries and pillar industries

First of all, leading industry and pillar industry are two different concepts. Although they are interrelated, only part of the leading industry may grow into pillar industry in the industrial system. Not all the leading industries will eventually become pillar industry. Leading industry has a high growth rate, which only provides the possibility of its rapid growth as a pillar of the national economy, does not mean that leading industry will certainly develop into a pillar industry. With the change of industrial cycle, some leading industries have gradually evolved into pillar industries, but some pillar industries may also become recession industries.[1] Some pillar industries have gradually evolved from leading industries, but not all

---

① Zou Xiaojuan.Research on the Evolution of China's Leading Industries(1949-2000)[M].Hubei People's Publishing House,2011.

pillar industries used to be the leading industries of the national economy. The most prominent feature of pillar industry is its great contribution to value and employment in the national economy, rather than the characteristics of high growth rate and strong correlation effect of leading industry. If some cities have relatively developed coal resources and take the coal mining industry as a pillar industry, it is not because the coal mining industry has the lead or leading role, but because of the abundant supply of resources in the region and the large and continuous market demand at home and abroad, it can create a large amount of national income. Pillar industries do not necessarily have broad prospects for development, for example, cities with resource industries as pillar industries may face industrial transformation and pillar industries transformation due to the serious consequences of resource depletion and environmental pollution. However, the leading industry has broad prospects for development. It determines the speed and scale of economic development and the level of future industrial structure. To a large extent, it determines the trend of the whole industry and the way of future economic development. The focus of the two industries is different. The leading industries mainly focus on the direction of industrial restructuring and the trend of industrial structure evolution in the future, while the pillar industries focus on cultivating the current national economic growth point and shaping the current industrial structure.

Secondly, the pillar industry pays attention to the present, while the leading industry depend on the future trend. Leading industries represent the direction of future industrial development. They mainly focus on the direction of long-term industrial restructuring in the future, the shaping of new industrial structure and the cultivation of national economic growth point. They are the breakthrough and entrance of industrial structure evolution, who are more forward-looking. The important role of pillar industry in the development of national economy is that it can provide most of the national income. Although it occupies a large proportion of the total economic volume in a certain range, it occupies a smaller proportion in a wider range. Other pillar industries account for a large proportion of output value, but the role of industrial linkage is very limited, and can not undertake the task of industrial division of labor. From this point of view, pillar industries do not necessarily have the function of leading industries. Pillar industry is an industry which has a high share in the total economic volume, strong ability to promote employment, great contribution to GDP and high input-output efficiency. However, the proportion of leading industries in the output value of the national economy may not be large enough, but their industrial linkages play a strong driving role, with great development potential, and their proportion in the national economy is rising. Nowadays, the major industries are the pillar industries. The proportion in the national economy is not necessarily large in the future, which means that the future may not still be the pillar of the national economy. But even if the proportion of some industries in the national economy is declining, as long as the proportion of their output value is large enough, the important impact on the national economy output value will still exist, so it can still become the pillar industry of the national economy.

3. Other concepts related to industries

Leading industries refer to those industries that have strong R&D or innovation capabilities, or can absorb advanced technology faster, represent the future direction of industrial development, and need to advance with other industries in order to maintain long-term and stable economic development. It mainly focuses on future research and development, and has been an industry that industrializes innovation and technology. Leading industry is not a large proportion of the current GNP, and its scale and strength are not necessarily very strong, but its development potential is great, or because of its high innovation and technology penetration ability, it represents the trend and direction of future industrial development, which is of great significance for future economic development. Leading industries can often grow and develop into leading or basic industries of the national economy in a relatively short period of time. Leading industry may exist in basic industry, pillar industry, or coordinated auxiliary industry, and its existence is not completely independent on other industries. Some of the leading industries are not well developed in the past. Although they are young and have no obvious advantages in market competition, they represent the direction of economic development. However, with the passage of time, they gradually develop and grow, and the disadvantageous conditions are transformed into advantageous ones. They have great momentum of development and good prospects for development. After selection and cultivation, they may eventually be transformed into leading industry with comparative advantages. Therefore, the leading industry can also be regarded as the industry that can be foreseen the future leading industry.

Another important concept related to leading industries is strategic industries. Strategic industry is a key industry that concerns the development of national economy, as well as the overall and long-term nature of national economy. It refers to the long-term economic development of a country or region, the adjustment and upgrading of industrial structure and the transformation of the mode of economic development play a global and fundamental role in the industry. Conceptually, strategic industries should include basic industries and leading industries, but they can not be confused by definition. For example, a country or region can regard bottleneck industry as a strategic industry in a certain period, but we can not regard bottleneck industry as a leading industry. Therefore, the determination of leading industry should also be understood from the strategic height of national economic development. Strategic industry is the leading industry which is the key development in the long-term development planning stage. It may also be the pillar industry in the current stage, or the leading industry in the current weak. However, it is not exactly the same as the leading industry. No matter the strength is weak or strong, the strategic industry will be the key industry to support the development of national economy for a long time. However, some leading industries may develop into leading industries with key supports, while some leading industries may be eliminated by the industrial system if they do not receive supports over time. The determination and cultivation of strategic industry is the expression and product of the general law of industrial structure evolution and one of the core contents of government industrial policy.

1.3.3 Industrial priority and benchmark of industrial arrangement and combination

The priority of industrial development and the arrangement and combination of industries lay emphasis on the determination of the benchmark of selection. Therefore, the benchmark of leading industry selection has always been the focus of attention of economists at home and abroad since the concept of industrial policy was put forward.

1. Industrial linkage benchmarks

Albert Hirshman put forward an unbalanced development strategy in the book "*Economic Development Strategy*". The book points out that there are two ways to achieve this strategy. The first is to achieve development by means of production shortage, that is to say, to develop into a connected industry after development. The second is to achieve development by overproduction, that is, to develop industries with large forward links. Development policy is to strive for backward and forward linkages. That is to say, the leading sector can promote the effective growth of the economy by expanding the correlation effect. These two criteria become the beginning of the benchmark study on the choice of leading industries. Later generations call these two criteria "industrial correlation benchmark". [①]

Hector believes that the degree of correlation between industries is the correlation degree of input and output correlations of various industrial sectors. The basic idea of this benchmark is that those industries with relatively high degree of relevance first develop, and then affect and drive other industries through forward linkage and backward correlation effects and side correlation effects. Choosing those industries with strong spread and diffusion effect can transfer the dominant radiation of the leading industry to the whole industrial chain, thus driving the development of the whole industry. The idea of this benchmark shows that the products of intermediate products or basic industries are allocated to many other sectors as inputs besides the final demand, so these related industries should be given priority over the final product production industries. He describes the backward correlation as "putting in supply and deriving demand", that is, every non primary activity would lead to the intention to provide its input. Backward linkages are described as "product utilization", i.e. the use of their products as inputs to a new production activity. Later, Rostow uses Hirshman's industrial relevance effect to determine the leading industry based on the correlation degree between industries. He extends the industrial correlation effect to three aspects: backward correlation

---

[①] Hector Seaman believes that backward correlation is more important than forward correlation. The reason why an industry can survive must be the result of some kind of demand that has been formed beforehand, but it can lead to new and less obvious production activities and demands. And forward correlation will never appear in a simple way, it will always accompany the backward correlation caused by "demand pressure".In other words, existing or anticipated needs are a condition of the former interlinkages. When the former connection can not be regarded as an independent inducement mechanism, it is an independent inducement mechanism for the latter, and it is an important and powerful factor for the latter.

effect, side effect and forward linkage effect.[①] Hector and Rostow determine the leading industry sectors based on the correlation effect between industries. They all focus on the radiation and driving role of leading industries, but they only discuss theoretically the correlation effect between industries. The identification of the leading sector needs detailed and operable basis. It is not only a one-sided judgment of the level of industrial development, but also unable to meet more and more diversified economic and social development goals to determine the leading industry only from the perspective of industrial association or the effect of industrial association.

2. Sakahara benchmarks

In order to plan the industrial structure and revitalize the Japanese economy, Japanese economist Sakahara Shirakawa put forward two specific reference benchmarks for the government to formulate industrial policies in the 1920s, later known as "Sakahara benchmarks", namely, the benchmark of elasticity of demand and income as well as the benchmark of rising productivity[②]. These two benchmarks indicate the influence of the leading industry to be selected on the economic development and the goal of industrial policy from aspects of market demand and factor supply, which is a significant development of the theory of leading industry. The demand-income elasticity benchmark requires the government to focus on supporting industries that provide as much national income as possible. The income elasticity of demand is the ratio of product demand to the change of per capita national income under the condition that the price remains unchanged,indicating the amount of change in the final demand for a particular product per unit increase in per capita national income. If the income elasticity is

---

① Walter.W. Rostow,translated by He Liping,etc.Economics from Take-off to Continuous Growth [M].People's Press,1988.

② Guo Wanda.Dictionary of Modern Industrial Economics[M].CITIC Press,1991.

greater than 1, it means that the demand increases faster than the increase of income; when the income elasticity is less than 1, it means that the increase of market demand is less than the increase of income. With the increase of per capita national income, the products with high income elasticity will develop faster. Therefore, the proportion of these sectors in the industrial system will gradually increase, and the market share will continue to expand. Choosing these sectors as the leading industries will conform to the direction of industrial structure evolution.

The benchmark of productivity should be the speed and the level of technological development for the selection of leading industries. Those industries with faster productivity and higher technology should be regarded as the ministry of leading industries. Those industries or departments that can absorb innovations and advanced scientific and technological achievements quickly and effectively developed with productivity, if they are further supported and nurtured, they will not only benefit the technology diffusion and spillover among departments, but also improve the technical level and resource utilization efficiency of the whole economy. In the industrial system, the increase of productivity in various industrial sectors is different. Those sectors with high productivity have high input and output efficiency, which is conducive to the reduction of production costs and the increase of output, and to the improvement of labor productivity of the whole society, thereby increasing economic welfare. According to Sakahara's two benchmarks, income elasticity benchmark is a reference benchmark based on market demand from the perspective of demand, while productivity rise benchmark is a selection benchmark based on production from the perspective of market supply. These two benchmarks are the most important development goals of Japan's economic development at the right time, and have important macro-directive significance for the recovery and take-off of Japan's economy. Although these two benchmarks are important exploration for the industrial structure theory, the industrial policy has a theoretical basis and specific practical guidelines, but his two benchmarks can not fully reflect the characteristics of the leading industries, nor can they achieve diversified economic development goals, so it is not a universally applicable standard.

3. Standards of incentive mechanism of industrial policy

Dani Rodrik summaries up the ten principles of industrial design, aiming at two micro entities of enterprises and government: (1) incentives must be directed against new activities; (2) there must be clear criteria for success and failure; (3) there must be a presupposed suspension clause; (4) government support must be directed against activities rather than industries; (5) the activities of obtaining subsidies must be clearly mentioned, potential for spillover and demonstration effects; (6) authoritative departments that implement industrial policies need to prove their capabilities; (7) there must be a principal person in charge who closely supervises the departments that implement industrial policies and has a clear judgment on the effects of policies, and this person in charge needs the highest level of political authority; (8) government agencies that implement industrial policies must maintain trust with the private sector. The channel of information communication is unblocked; (9) in the best case, the mistake of "selecting losers" should be allowed to occur; (10) the support measures of industrial policy need the ability to update in time, so that self-discovery can become a continuous process[①].

4. Other representative benchmarks

In order to compensate for the shortcomings of these benchmarks, the Japanese government introduced "prevention of over-intensive benchmarks" and "enrichment of labor content benchmarks" to

---

① Dani Rodrik,translated by Hou Yongzhi.The Same Economics, Different Policy Prescriptions[M]. CITIC Press,2016.

supplement them. These two benchmarks were proposed by the Japan Industrial Structure Review Conference in 1971. During this period, the development goals of the Japanese government focused on improving energy efficiency, expanding social capital and preventing and improving public hazards. Over-intensive benchmark required the government choose leading industries, it must take prevention and improvement to public nuisance ability, improvement of energy efficiency, expansion of social capital, unbalance of ecology and environmental pressure that will not cause over-concentration as reference benchmarks. The benchmark of enriching labor content requires that priority be given to industries that can provide safe and comfortable jobs and stable employment environment for leading industries. To sum up, the starting point of over-intensive benchmark is to achieve the goal of sustainable development between economy, society and environment in the long run. The basic requirement of over-intensive environmental benchmark is that economic development does not take the imbalance of society and environment as a price, conforms to the law of scientific development, and is also far-sighted, especially the problem that the current society is facing increasingly hard constraints on resources and environment. As for the benchmark of enriching labor content, when the level of economic development is low, the benchmark of enriching labor content can not become the key criterion for choosing leading industries, but can be used as an important reference index, so it has certain limitations. These two standards further improved the industrial policy basis of Japan at that time. It is far-sighted and scientific to comprehensively investigate the multi-objective development plan, but the operation method has not been discussed in depth.

It is conditional that the leading sector plays the role of industrial linkages. The premise is that is in the industrial system of overall industrial structure coordination. Because of the complex competition and interdependence among industries, some industries may have larger elasticity of demand and higher productivity. However, once the original industrial system is not coordinated well, the reactions between industries are not sensitive. Their development can not lead to the growth and development of other industries, nor will they promote the rationalization of the industrial structure. It is not suitable to play the role of leading industry. However, some industries play a larger role in industrial linkage, productivity rises faster, demand income elasticity is higher, and labor employment can also be greatly promoted, but it is not resource-saving or environment-friendly. Therefore, the choice of leading industries should be considered from various perspectives. There are many literatures about the benchmark of leading industry selection in China. The representative viewpoints are listed as follows:

Table 1–1 The Benchmark of Domestic Leading Industries

Datum	Representative viewpoints
Three benchmark	Zhou Zhenhua (1992): Shortage Substitutes Elastic Benchmark, Growth Stamina Benchmark, Bottleneck Effect Benchmark
Four benchmark	Liu Zaixing (2004), Dang Yaoguo (2004): Industrial Linkage Benchmark and Income Elasticity Benchmark. Growth Benchmark and Labor Employment Benchmark
Five benchmark	Zhang Shengzu (2001): Benchmark of Income Elasticity, Benchmark of Productivity Rise, Benchmark of Industrial Association, Benchmark of Production Coordination and Benchmark of Maximum Growth Potential Wang Li (2004): Sustainable Development Benchmark, Productivity Rise Benchmark, Industrial Linkage Benchmark, Income Elasticity Benchmark, Benefit Benchmark and Comparative Advantage Benchmark Chen Gang (2004): Innovation Benchmark, Productivity Rise Benchmark, Demand Income Elasticity Benchmark, Industrial Relevance Benchmark, Scale Economy Benchmark
Six benchmark	Guan Aiping et al. (2002), Zhao Bin (2011): Sustainable Development Benchmark, Efficiency Benchmark, Industry Linkage Benchmark, Competitive Advantage Benchmark, Demand Benchmark, Technology Progress Benchmark. Technical progress benchmark, economic benefit benchmark, industrial competitive advantage benchmark, sustainable development benchmark, market growth potential benchmark, employment contribution benchmark
Seven benchmark	Wang Maruqiong (1999): Market prospects, Market Competitiveness, Inter-industry Drive, Innovation and Progress, Absorb Labor Capacity, Dynamic Comparative Advantage, World market competitiveness, Sustainable Development Benchmark. Zhang Kuiwei (2004): Dynamic Comparative Advantage Benchmark, Income Elasticity Benchmark, Productivity Rise Benchmark, Industrial Relevance Benchmark, Relative Intensive Benchmark of Factor of Production, Employment Benchmark, Sustainable Development Benchmark

Source: Ye Anning. A Study on the Benchmark of Choice of Leading Industries[D].Xiamen University, 2007.

1.3.4 Summary of selection methods of leading industries

In addition to the benchmark of the choice of leading industries, the standards and their results are also essential parts of the choice of leading industries. At present, there are several methods of choosing leading industries widely used both at home and abroad:

1. Input-output technology

The idea of input-output technology originated from the "economic table" proposed by French economist François Quesnay in 1758. The "economic table" describes quantitatively the flow of goods and services in the economic system. In 1874, general equilibrium mathematical models of multiple commodities in multiple production sectors constructed in Walrus general equilibrium price determinism were the theoretical basis of the input-output technology created by Leontief in 1930s. Leontief published "*The Relationship between Input and Output in the American Economic System*" in 1936. It is the earliest prototype of input-output technology. In 1941, his book "*American economic structure 1919–1929*" put forward the principles and methods of input-output technology. Input-output technology is the quantitative quantification of the interdependence among departments in a complex economic system. It can not only analyze the intensity of the correlation among industries, but also calculate the final use and ultimate demand elasticity of various sectors of the national economy. In 1951, Leontief and Chenery co-published "*The Study of American Economic Structure*", "*Theory and Empirical Study of Input-Output Analysis*", which improve the Input-output Technology in theory and method. Since then, the application of input-output technology has been widely disseminated. Seguy and Ramirez (1975) create a macroeconomic model based on input-output, including agriculture, basic metal manufacturing and transportation.

The results show that the industrial correlation effect of agriculture is the largest. Gerking (1976) estimates the input-output coefficients using the method of parameter estimation. W. G. Tyler (1976) introduces the capitalist market economic system and price system, taking into account the role of the government in the process of economic development, in the framework of input-output analysis, investigated the reasons for the economic development in 1960s. West (1982) put forward an input-output table reflecting the gross economic output. Considering the practice of economic use at that time, we constructed an input-output table of 74 independent sectors and 22 industry groups. The results show that the correlation performance of the industry is very significant. Later, he expanded his research methods, combining input-output technology with measurement coefficient estimation method. Baer (1987) has used the input-output table of Brazil for 1960–1980 years to analyze the changes of the industrial structure in Brazil. The results showed that the industrial structure of Brazil was becoming vertical gradually, and the relationship between income distribution and economic structure was also considered. Geoffrey J.D. (1989) has applied the data from the year of 1959; 1970; and 1975 to the input-output technology to examine the key sectors of the company. Their research examines the input-output coefficient of relevant departments and the institutional barriers to conversion between sectors. Wolff and Nadiri (1993) have used input-output technology to analyze the relationship between R&D input, technological change, and sector correlation; Wolff and Nadiri (1997) have expanded the data to 1987, increasing the number of sectors from 19 to 48. Using input-output technology to analyze the growth of total factor productivity in the United States from 1958 to 1987, the results show the same growth pattern of total factor productivity.

Total R&D investment in the United States is an important determinant of total factor productivity growth, with R&D returns ranging from 10% to 13%. They also have found that intersectoral spillovers play an equally important role in TFP growth, especially in the manufacturing sector. In the framework of input-output analysis, During and Schnabl (1998) have studied the technology spillover effects among sectors using data from Germany, Japan and the United States from 1980 to 1990.

Domestic scholars have also widely applied input-output technology to the study of various hot economic issues. Shen Lisheng (2003) uses input-output technology to study the contribution of China's exports to economic growth. Input-output technology is also applied to China's carbon emissions research. Zhang Youguo (2010) consideres the structural decomposition method based on input and output technology with the constraint relationship between variables, and analyzed the impact of 1987–2007 years of economic development mode change on China's carbon emissions intensity. Guo Zhaoxian (2010) has constructed an extended import competitive economy energy carbon emission input-output model. The two-tier nested structure decomposition method was used to decompose the growth of China's carbon emissions from three dimensions. Guo Zhaoxian (2010) has also constructed a carbon based on the total economic volume, economic structure, energy efficiency, energy consumption structure and carbon emission coefficient. Emission identities were used to decompose the carbon emissions of China for 1995–2007 years from the industrial level and the regional level by using the logarithmic index decomposition method. Input-output technology can be used to study the impact of energy saving and emission reduction. Liao Mingqiu (2011) has tried to incorporate energy saving and emission reduction into the input-output analysis framework, and constructed a theoretical input-output model based on energy saving and emission reduction. Xu Yingzhi etc. (2010) examine the impact of China's foreign trade on energy conservation and emission reduction. Input-output technology is also used in industrial policy research. Zhang Qizi and others (2009) try to find industries that can coordinate the relationship between guaranteeing growth and transforming the mode of economic growth by using input-output technology. The results show that the goal of guaranteeing growth by promoting the transformation of the mode of economic growth is not entirely realistic at the present stage. There is no optimal choice but a sub-optimal one in industrial policy choosing. By using comparable input-output tables, they use DPG to analyze the evolution of China's leading industries in 1992–2005 years and its consequences.

2. Other analytical methods

(1) Analytic Hierarchy Process (AHP)[①]

Analytic Hierarchy Process (AHP) is a multi-criteria decision-making method. By analyzing the related factors and the correlation among them, the complex problems are decomposed into different elements. These elements are merged into orderly hierarchical structure model. The general structure model is divided into target layer, criterion layer and scheme layer. Analytic hierarchy process (AHP) choose the specific method of leading industry as follows: divide the evaluation system of primary leading industry into several layers according to the research purpose, get a series of weights by comparing two matrices, or give weights by comparing the importance of each sub-layer element with that of the upper layer element through expert rating, and then construct a judgment matrix. The relative weights of the comparison elements to the criterion are calculated by the judgment matrix, and the consistency of the judgment matrix is checked. The total ranking

---

① Li Dashan.Theoretical and Empirical Analysis of Regional Industrial Structure[M].People's Press,1998.

weight of each level for the system is calculated, and the total ranking of each sub-target level for the total goal is obtained. The methods employed include Wang Min (2001), Xie Fengjun (2006, 2008), Zhang Xiao (2009), Zhao Fuhou (2010).

（2）Grey relational analysis method[1]

Grey relational analysis is a method to measure the degree of correlation between factors according to the similarity or difference of the status quo or development trend of factors. Xu Jianzhong (2010), Chu Zhaopeng (2009), Huang Guitian, Qi Wei (2010), Zhou Hanqi (2010) as a ways to choose the leading industry. The magnitude of the correlation between the two systems varies with time is called the correlation degree. In the process of the whole system development, if two or more factors change synchronously and the trend of change is consistent, it shows that they have a strong correlation degree; on the contrary, it indicates that the correlation degree is weak. The basic principle of grey relational analysis is to clarify the numerical relationship among subsystems. The specific steps of applying grey relational analysis to the selection of leading industries are:①to determine the reference column, which is the data sequence of a certain industry reflecting the characteristics of the system by comparison sequence and reference sequence. Among them, the comparison sequence is the data sequence composed of those factors that affect the system behavior. The reference sequences and the comparison sequence are dimensionless after determination. ②Generally, a reference sequence has several comparison sequences. The correlation coefficients of each comparison sequence and reference sequence in each period are calculated and sorted. The basic idea of this method is to use the size of correlation degree as the description of sequence

---

① Deng Julong.Grey System Course[M].Huazhong University of Technology Press,1985.

order, and arrange the correlation degree of comparison sequence in order of size to form correlation sequence. These associative sequences can reflect the good or bad relationship between sub-sequences and parent sequences, and good sequences become candidate industries of leading industries.

(3) Deviation-share analysis method

Domestic scholar Dong Jianghua (2007); Gong Xiaojun (2010); Chen Zhongsheng (2010) used the shift share analysis method as the leading industry discriminant method. The method of deviation-share analysis is applied to the choice of leading industries, which is to divide the change of regional economic aggregate into three components: structural deviation component, share deviation component and competitive deviation component, and to evaluate the advantages and disadvantages of regional industrial structure and competitiveness, and to find out the competitive advantages and disadvantages of regional industrial structure. Potential industrial sectors, in order to determine the rational direction of regional future economic development and industrial restructuring.

(4) DEA analysis, data envelopment analysis

DEA method first needs to determine the decision unit (DMU Decision Making Units), which is a non-parametric analysis method used to evaluate the relative efficiency between DMUs with several inputs and outputs. Zhou Hong, Lin Li (2006); Wu Haimin (2006); Zhang Genming (2008) used this method to judge leading industries. The basic idea of choosing the leading industry by DEA method is that in a certain system, based on the actual decision making units, the decision units are divided on the basis of the best principles, namely, each evaluated object is taken as a DMU, and all DMU is combined into the evaluated individuals or groups. Each DMU has the established standard and the same type of input and output indicators. Based on the comprehensive analysis of input-output ratio, the weights of each input-output index of DMU are calculated and evaluated, and the "effective frontier of optimal efficiency" is determined. Then, according to the distance between each DMU and the "effective frontier", the decision-making unit is determined whether DEA is effective or not. The essence of this method is to determine the leading industry according to its relative efficiency.

There are many methods to distinguish the leading industry. The input-output method is widely used. Other methods have more or less limitations in the process of operation. Input-output analysis technology is based on walrus general equilibrium theory and has strict mathematical and economic logic. Input-output analysis technology is the basis of national economic accounting. It can not only reflect the input and output information of various intermediate input factors of national economic development, but also reflect the final demand including national economic investment, consumption (including residents' consumption and government consumption), import and export information, which is exactly the content reflected by the mode of economic development. However, only using input-output technology to analyze the correlation coefficients of various intermediate inputs and final demand as the specific basis of the leading industry may neglect the factors that can not be considered in the input factors, and may not be able to make the best choice to reach consensus on all indicators. Therefore, we need to use the method of measurement to carry out empirical testing and comparison. Analytic Hierarchy Process (AHP) has great subjective randomness in the evaluation of each scale in the judgment matrix. Whether the method of matrix assignment ensures consistency in the whole reciprocal matrix can not make scientific judgment, and the method of positive and negative matrix assignment will magnify the influencing factors in the calculation of standard weight and relative weight, and the results often deviate from the objective reality. It is unscientific to use industrial correlation to determine leading industries only because the classification of reference sequence and comparative sequence is influenced by subjective factors, and the grey correlation analysis lacks a rigorous economic basis. The deviating share method often neglects the small-scale industries in the primary stage of development, and can not effectively analyze the industries in all stages of development at the same time. This method can not well reflect the potential of industrial development in the future, but also does not consider the external constraints of industrial growth space, such as natural, social and economic conditions. Data envelopment analysis (DEA) has a more scientific theoretical foundation, that is, efficiency, which can analyze the relative efficiency of industries more scientifically, but it is a nonparametric estimation method, which has some limitations compared with other parameter estimation methods. At the same time, the principle of input and output operation of data envelopment analysis is a black box operation. It can not relate to the intermediate input and final use of various sectors of the national economy as input-output technology, nor can it describe the mode of economic development in an all-round way. Therefore, this book chooses the standard of leading industry selection in the analysis framework of input-output technology, then estimates and empirically tests the coefficients of intermediate input in various industries, with the purpose to comprehensively and scientifically determine the leading industries in the inspection period, so as to formulate more suitable industrial policies for China's actual industry.

1.4 Research Route, Methods and Innovations

1.4.1 Research guidelines and framework

Firstly, this part introduces the background of the topic, clarifies the reasons for the title selection of this book, propose the dilemma of transformation, then combs the central government's important expositions on the transformation of economic development mode since the reform and opening up, and analyses the reasons why the traditional economic development mode of China is difficult to change, and clarifies the significance of studying the transformation of economic development mode from the perspective of leading industries. Then it defines the concepts of the mode of economic development and the leading industry, discriminate the confusing concepts, and makes a comparative analysis of the concepts difference. Finally, it summarizes the ways of the transformation of the economic development mode at home and abroad and proposes the benchmarks and methods of the leading industry selection.

The second chapter focuses on the related theories of leading industries and economic development. The concept of leading industry is related to many economic thoughts in classical economic growth theory. The second chapter refines the idea of leading industries in the economic development concept of H. Smith and David. Then, the relevant theories of leading industry and economic development are discussed. The representative ones are: the development rule of the first tier industry, the evolution rule of the industrial structure, the industrialization theory of Iwatani principles and the theory of "leading industry evolution", Rostow's "leading industry theory", and Helchman's "unbalanced growth theory".

The third chapter is about the history and current situation of the evolution of China's leading industry and economic development mode. This part first inspects the current economic development stage of China, reviews the process of China's leading industry replacement and the evolution of industrial structure. Then it compares and comments on the three representative schemes of leading industry selection in China. At the same time, it combs and compares the industrial policies of the ninth five-year plan, the tenth five-year plan and the eleventh five-year plan. Finally, taking some typical countries as examples, this book expounds the history of leading industry replacement, industrial restructuring and economic development in relevant countries, and summarizes the successful experience and lessons of failure. These representative countries include the United States, Japan, Germany and Korea.

The fourth chapter is the construction of input-output model of economic development mode and empirical analysis part, which is the core of this book. This part first establishes the input-output row model and column model of economic development mode, then deduces and calculates the correlation coefficients of the input-output model of economic development mode, including consumption induction coefficient, import and export induction, investment multiplier, labor employment coefficient, energy consumption coefficient, environmental emission coefficient and technology spillover effect. The purpose of calculating the correlation coefficient is to investigate the development status and changes of various industries under the goal of changing the mode of economic development. In order to ultimately determine the leading industry under the goal of changing the mode of economic development, this part uses stochastic frontier production function and related models to test the input-output efficiency of economic development, which provides a reference consensus for determining the ultimate leading industry.

The fifth chapter, based on the empirical analysis of the fourth chapter, further analyzes the current situation of China's economic development mode, and investigates the input structure, industrial structure and demand structure of China's economic development. At the same time, taking the current real estate industry as an example, this part analyzes the current situation and future development prospects of the leading industry in China.

The sixth chapter is the policy recommendation. According to the successful experience of the industrialized countries in the last few chapters and the gains and losses of China's leading industries as well as the process of economic development, it first determined the principle of accelerating the transformation of the mode of economic development from the perspective of leading industries, from coordinating the relations of production and industry, enhancing the capability of independent innovation, developing new and high technology industries, transforming traditional industries. This part expounds the realization path of the transformation of economic mode from the aspects of circular economy and industrial service. Finally, it gives some suggestions on the development of some key industries.

1.4.2 Innovations and shortcomings of this book

Firstly, the book uses the basic principles of evolutionary economics and industrial economics to systematically study the general laws of leading industries and economic development modes, and initially constructs a research framework and theoretical system of leading industries selection and economic development mode. This is a preliminary attempt to explore the transformation of economic development mode from the perspective of leading industries.

Secondly, based on the industrial level, this book constructs an input-output model of economic development mode, and uses the relevant data to describe the development status and sustainable development potential of China's industries in a comprehensive and systematic way under the goal of the transformation of economic development mode. Based on this framework, the stochastic frontier production function and model are used to test the input-output efficiency of various industries. A consensus conclusion is reached on the choice of leading industries. It is not only an innovation in the choice of leading industries, but also a new way of thinking for the transformation of the mode of economic development. The input-output analysis framework based on the mode of economic development in this book is a useful supplement and development to the current theory of industrial choice, and also a meaningful attempt to expand the theory of economic development.

Thirdly, this book studies the difficulties and breakthroughs in the transformation of economic development mode from the perspective of leading industry selection and industrial policy orientation, and the research perspective is unique. This book focuses not only on the theoretical relationship between the choice of leading industries and the transformation of economic development mode, but also on the meaningful conclusions drawn from quantitative and empirical analysis to guide the practice of economic development. This book has done some frontier work with this regard.

Finally, the empirical analysis framework is based on input-output technology, so the data used are from input-output tables. The limitation of the input-output table is that it is compiled every five years. In the middle of the year when the final number is 5 and 0, the relevant departments will produce an extended table. Nevertheless, the limitation of data makes the time span of this study is short, and to some extent could possible affects some conclusions.

Chapter 2   Theoretical Origins of Leading Industries and Development Modes

The industrial change and structural evolving are conditional, which may emerge spontaneously under the influence of market mechanism, or comes from external interference and government regulation. Because of the asymmetry information, the existence of public goods and the externality, the market mechanism may fail, which means that the adjustment of industrial structure and the transformation of economic development mode need not only rely on market mechanism, but also government regulation. But is the government's response to market failure necessarily scientific and reasonable all the time? On one hand, the government provides direct subsidies to supporting industries, the market players may swarm into the supporting industries. This may lead to the rapid overcapacity of the supporting industries, such as photovoltaic industry and new energy vehicle industry, and even some enterprises are malicious to deceive. On the other hand, for subsidized enterprises, they may not be the most subsidized enterprises or the most efficient enterprises because of complete information, administrative costs or other reasons. In this case, government regulation may not bring the best results, so government failure may lead to another round of government failure. From the point of the development trajectory of industrial policies around the world, according to the difference between the degree of market participation and the intensity and depth of government intervention, industrial policies can be roughly divided into the following two forms:

The first type emphasizes the industry's self-sustainability, advocates the market's self-regulation, considering that the market competition mechanism can automatically maintain the balance between supply and demand, and competitive industries, which generate excess profits, making investment continuously influx, and these industries have sustainable self-sustainability. Market friction and disharmony among industries can survive the fittest through market competition and price mechanism. There is no need to formulate industrial planning or support some industries. The inclined industrial policy is redundant. The market believes that the government's recognition of the limited sequence of industrial development is less trustworthy and dependable than the market's own strength. Therefore, these countries or regions generally do not actively pursue industrial restructuring or direct support for certain industries under non-special circumstances, but emphasize the self-replacement of industries and the spontaneous regulation of the market. Only when "market failure" occurs in the process of economic development, which can't be adjusted spontaneously or the market lags behind, can we passively take some remedial measures or formulate some industrial policies afterwards.

The second is the market fails and effectiveness loses. It advocates that the government positively lay out industrial planning, actively to make up for the shortcomings of market mechanism, and seek ways and channels for the upgrading of industrial structure by determining the priority of industrial development, formulating industrial policies. Japan is a country that has successfully used its industrial policies to "take off". In a short period of time after the war, Japan has successfully overtaken most of the developed countries in Europe and America. Instead of following the practice of free industrial development of developed countries in Europe and the United States, Japan actively seeks to cultivate and support some key industries, and constantly adjusts and optimizes the industrial structure, thus stepping out of a road of rapid rise supported by industrial policies. In recent years, more and more latecoming countries have recognized and attach importance to second forms. Especially for some developing countries with limited initial economic resources and imperfect market mechanism, they have adopted an unbalanced policy to focus on developing certain industries, sorting out the priority development order, promoting industrial cycle, altering and upgrading the industrial structure. The aim of sustained, rapid and healthy development of the national economy will ultimately achieve the take-off of the "catch-up" national economy. What needs to be explained here is that, because the order of industrial development and alignment and the preferential development order of industrial policies are not static, the route of economic development in some countries is not static. The choice of roads in different countries is altering because of initial conditions and existing bases.

2.1 The Origin of Industrial Policy in Western Classical Economics

2.1.1 Adams's view of economic development and industrial priorities

In the wealth of nations, Adams writes, "the possibility of the growth of national wealth lies in the formation of modern urban society and the consequent industrialization." Smith investigates the impact of agricultural production on national wealth growth and the relationship between industrial growth and wealth growth. He believes that agriculture provided primitive accumulation for the national economy in the early stage of economic development. The rise of cities has brought about trade development and industrial technological progress, improved agricultural productivity, land productivity and indirectly expanded cultivated land. This is the way to increase the wealth of a country by developing agricultural production. At the same time, Smith also believes that due to the differences in factors of production, the marginal income of agricultural production is decreasing, while the marginal income of industry is increasing, so industrial expansion can bring rapid accumulation of national wealth, and industry can make greater contribution to the increase of national wealth. Smith also elaborates on the impact of industrial development on agricultural production. He believes that the process of industrial development is the process of increasing the proportion of industry in the national economy. In this process, the industry continuously absorbs the labor transferred from agriculture. Because of the detailed division of labor, advanced technology, high specialization production efficiency, the relative price of industrial products gradually declines; because of the poor specialization of labor, relatively inferior technology and poor output efficiency, the agricultural sector has led to the increase of the relative price of agricultural products, and the change of the whole national wealth. The improvement was driven by the industrial sector. It can be seen that the core of Smith's view is that the ability of various industries to drive the marginal increase of national wealth is not balanced. It always exists an industry or department that plays a leading role in the increase of national wealth. The leading department will change with time. At the lower stage of economic development, agriculture generally gives priority to development. The original accumulation of agriculture provides the necessary capital for industrial development. Originally, primitive accumulation has created technology and skilled labor force for industrial production, and industry has gradually become the main force in creating national wealth.

Smith's *Principle of National Wealth Creation* has begun to show the rudiment of industrial policy thoughts. His industrial development proposition has the characteristics of unbalanced development, which is the origin of industrial priority and industrial arrangement and combination. The development of the agricultural sector will be restricted by land resources. Under the effect of the law of diminishing returns to land resources, the marginal efficiency of the agricultural sector is difficult to improve. The industrial sector benefiting from division of labor and specialization, as well as technological progress and technology diffusion, its labor productivity will gradually increase, so the source of national wealth will gradually increase by the industrial sector. However, the expansion of industrial production is limited by market scope, specialization, capital accumulation and other conditions, especially capital accumulation. Therefore, just as agricultural production is affected by the law of diminishing returns of land factors, the expansion of industrial production scale will also be affected by the law of diminishing returns on capital investment. According to the same law of diminishing factor returns, the increase of national wealth driven by industry will gradually decrease. However, economic growth itself will not stop. After industry, a new round of national wealth increase will be driven by service industry or even higher-level industries than service industry, which Smith could not realize under the conditions of the level of development at that time. Smith recognizes that the position and role of agriculture and industry in the national economy change with time, the industrial structure evolves constantly, and the leading industries that drive the increase of national wealth are different at different stages of development. But Smith only considers the supply side factors, his research does not analyze the demand at home and abroad, and does not consider the structural factors other than the total supply and demand factors, such as the internal structure of the industry.

2.1.2   David Ricardo's economic development theory and industrial priority

David Ricardo's *Theory of Economic Development*, like Smith's, has attributed economic growth to industrial drive. He believes that economic development is the process where every industry can survive in the competition. Ricardo believes that the law of diminishing returns plays a major role in the input and output of agricultural elements, while industrial development is governed by the increasing rule of capital gains, and economic growth is driven by industrial development. Therefore, additional capital and increasing industrial input will drive the rapid economic growth, which is the pursuit of the idea about unbalanced development of Smith's industry. Further, he believes that if the decline in agricultural returns is greater than the increase in industrial returns, growth will be reduced or even stopped. He implies that the way to prevent this situation is technological revolution and free trade. In terms of free trade, according to Ricardo's theory of comparative cost, the industrialization process and population growth of the United Kingdom make the relative price of agricultural products higher than that of international grain prices. Therefore, the UK should reduce agricultural production and replace the agricultural products of other countries with British comparative advantages.

Ricardo attaches great importance to the impact of capital accumulation on economic growth. He believes that production profit is the source of capital accumulation and indispensable condition for economic development. With the improvement of social progress and development level, the population growing correspondingly, the population growth leads to the expansion of the demand for food, so the use of cultivated land will be increased, and the land will become increasingly barren. Without the improvement of production technology to offset the decline of land remuneration, the price of the means of livelihood will continue to rise and the monetary wage will depreciate accordingly. Under such conditions, both physical and monetary rents will continue to increase, resulting in a decline in profit margins, and when the profit margin falls to a certain extent, the motivation of capitalists to accumulate wealth will disappear and capital accumulation activities will no longer be carried out. Therefore, the expansion of reproduction activities no longer exists, and society will enter a cycle of simple reproduction. The most important way to prevent this situation is to increase agricultural productivity. Because of the law of diminishing marginal remuneration of agriculture, when domestic agriculture reaches the stage of diminishing, the only way is to import relatively cheap foreign agricultural products through free trade.

He also stresses the unbalanced growth. His thoughts about the unbalanced industrial development is a kind of unbalanced mode which relies on additional investments in some sectors of the national economy and focuses on development. He emphasizes the role of industry in the development of national economy, but at the same time, it should not harm the development of the agricultural sector. In addition, he considered the factors of supply and demand from an open perspective. He pays attention to the development of some industries in the international market while giving consideration to the balanced development of other industries. Therefore, to some extent, Ricardo's industrial policy thought originate from the principle of comparative advantage and free trade.

2.2 Relevant Theory of Leading Industry and Economic Development

2.2.1 The development for law of Petty industry

In seventeenth Century, the first research of British economist, William Petty, said that in different historical stages of development, the level of national income of different countries in the world is very different. He believes that the change of income level is closely related to the industrial structure of the national economy. He notes that the majority of the population engaged in handicraft manufacturing and business activities has much higher per capita income than other countries in the continent in the same period. According to the specific situation in Britain, the per capita income of different industries is also quite different. For example, the income level of people engaged in agriculture is four times as much as that of seafarers engaged in transportation[1].

According to this phenomenon, Petty draws the conclusion that the income level of industry is higher than that of agriculture, and that of commerce is higher than that of industry. This discovery points out the direction for exploring the causes of economic development from a new perspective, and expands the analytical framework for finding the causes of economic growth from the perspective of factor compensation. According to Petty, the gap and change of relative income between industries will not only promote the transfer of social labor force from low-income industries to high-income industries, but also promote the improvement of labor productivity in various industries. The exploration of Tier Fitting opens up the study of contribution to economic growth from the perspective of industry

[1]   William Petty. Political Arithmetic[M]. Business Press, 1978.

income difference and industrial structure change, therefore enriches the content of economic development theory.

A similar conclusion has been drawn from the study of the evolution of industrial structure by Colin H., also a British economist. Later generations call this rule "Petty law".

According to the proposition of the three industry classification proposed by British economist Fisher, Colin Clark further examines the evolution of industrial structure and the rule of leading industry replacement. In 1940, Clark publishes his book "conditions for economic progress", which compares the data of labor input and total output of three industries in more than 40 countries in different periods, and obtaines the rule and general trend of labor force in the change of three industries structure with the increase of per capita national income. In his book, he first divides the economic development of countries into three stages:

The first stage is a low-development society dominated by agricultural production. At this stage, most people engages in agricultural production. Because of the low labor productivity, the national income and per capita income of the whole society are at a low level.

The second stage is a society in which manufacturing is the leading the national economy. With the development of economy, the proportion of handicraft manufacturing industry in the national economy has been increasing, and manufacturing industry becomes the main social production. At this stage, the manufacturing industry has greatly improved its output level by virtue of its high labor productivity. With the improvement of the output and income level of manufacturing industry, the labor force gradually shifts from other industries to manufacturing industry, so the overall national income and per capita national income level have been greatly improved.

In the third stage, the developed society is dominated by commerce and related services. With the further development of the economy, business and related services have developed rapidly. As the per capita income level of business and related services is much higher than that of agriculture and manufacturing, the labor force has shifted from agriculture and manufacturing to business and service industries, thus the overall income level and per capita income level of the whole society have increased significantly.

The Petty theorem shows that with the increase of per capita national income, the labor force is transferred from agriculture to industry and then to service industry. The transfer of labor force is accompanied by the transfer of production. This process is also the process of industrial structure evolution and industrial replacement. When the national economy is dominated by agricultural production, the population engaged in agriculture accounts for the majority, agriculture accounts for the vast majority of the labor force, the overall labor productivity of the national economy is low, and the poor output leads to the low level of per capita national income; when the rapid development of industry exceeds and replaces agriculture, and industry gradually occupies the dominant position in the national economy, the overall labor productivity is raised. As a result of the large increase in output and the increase in per capita income, the driving force of income returns has shifted the labor force from agriculture to industry, so the proportion of labor force occupied by industry has increased substantially. Meanwhile, the proportion of agricultural labor force and output value has declined. When the economy develops to the third industry in the largest proportion of the national economy, the overall income level of the national economy goes to a new stage. At this time, the labor force from agriculture and industry flows to the service industry in large quantities. The labor force occupied by the service industry expands rapidly and the output value rises sharply. The output value and the labor force proportion of the first and second industries gradually decrease, and the per capita income of the first and second industries also decreases relatively compared with the service industry.

2.2.2 The evolution of industrial structure

On the basis of the results of the research on petty and Clark, American economist John H. collates the historical data of various countries and makes a thorough investigation on the relationship between the evolution law of industrial structure and economic development by using modern economic statistical methods, and drew a conclusion of general significance. Kuznets's research not only uses the labor sector distribution indicators used by Clark, but also uses the relevant indicators and mathematical statistics methods created by the subdivided industrial sectors to reveal the process of shifting the industrial structure center of gravity with the change in per capita income level. Kuznets mainly analyzes the law of industrial structure change from the following two aspects:

1. Changes in the proportion of three industries in GDP at different levels

Based on the original data of 57 countries, Kuznets comprehensively compiled the relevant data calculated according to the constant price per capita GDP in 1958, and analyzed the overall industrial structure change trend under different benchmarks.

Kuznets concluded that when the per capita GDP is in the low range of $70 to $300, the share of agriculture and agriculture-related sectors shows a significant trend of decline, while the share of industrial and service sectors in the national economy keeps rising. At the same time, the structural changes in the industrial and service sectors are moderate and not obvious. When the per capita GNP is $70, the industrial sector output accounts for 40% of the total industrial and service industry output; when the per capita GNP reaches $300, the proportion rises to 45%. In this wage range, the industrial output is generally rising, but the increase is not significant. When the per capita output value is in the high range of $300 to $1000, the share of industrial sector output value in the total output value of industry and service industry rises from 45% to 55%, up by 10 percentage points, which indicates that the structural change between non-agricultural sectors is significant. Kuznets also points out the situation in less developed countries such as Honduras, the Philippines, and Egypt: even though the per capita output has not increased significantly over a long period of time, within the industrial structure, the share of the agricultural sector still has a significant decline.

2. The proportion of labor force in GDP of three industries at different levels

Kuznets also examined the law of the share of labor in three industries in 59 countries in 1960, and concludes that the share of labor in the agricultural sector decreased significantly with the increase of per capita output value. When the per capita output value was between $70 and $300, the share of labor in the agricultural sector decreased by 34.4%, while when the per capita output value was between $300 and $1000, Agriculture's share of the labor force fell 29.1% again, while in these two regions, the share of the labor force in the industrial and service sectors continued to rise. Generally speaking, the share of labor force in three industries is basically consistent with the change of the proportion of output value in three industries. Kuznets further divides the internal structure of the industry and sorts out the per capita gross domestic product into different intervals according to the gradient. From two aspects of output value and labor force distribution, the law of the internal structural change of the industry was inspected, and the direction of the industrial structure evolution and the leading industry change was revealed. His research conclusions further prove the findings of Petty and Clark, and more accurately analyze the evolution of industrial structure with general significance.

2.2.3 Hoffman and Yuke Iwatani's industrialization theory

1. Rule of thumb in industrialization

A pioneering study of industrialization is Hoffman, a German economist. His theory of industrialization is called "rule of law of industrialization" by later generations. In the article "The Stages and Types of Industrialization" in 1931, Hoffman conducted empirical and empirical analysis of industrialization practices in more than 20 countries during the period from the industrial revolution in the 1880s to the economic crisis in the 1930s. Later, in the article "The Growth of Industrial Economy" published in 1958, his research was intensified with a general model of internal structural changes in which industrial sector was constructed and elaborated. Hoffman believed that a country's economic development is determined by the process of industrialization. He attributed the factors that cause the growth of various industrial sectors in the process of industrialization to the following categories: (1) the relative factors of production factors including resources, labor and capital, quantity; (2) technological progress and innovation; (3) technical proficiency of workers; (4) market resource allocation; (5) consumer preferences, etc.

Hoffman uses a set of criteria to select eight representative products for analysis. He believes that all products in the national economy are ultimately used for consumption or for investment production, so he further divides the eight products into consumer industrial products. And capital industrial products are two major categories, each of which was composed of subdivided four small industrial products. Among them, consumer industrial products included: (1) food, beverage and tobacco; (2) cloth and textiles; (3) fur and leather products; (4) furniture manufacturing. Capital industrial products include: (1) pig iron and non-ferrous metal smelting; (2) machinery manufacturing; (3) vehicle manufacturing; (4) chemical industry manufacturing. In order to facilitate observation and analysis, he uses the ratio of the net output value of the consumer goods industry to the net output value of the capital goods industry to examine the law of industrial development. This ratio was the Hoffman ratio. He implies the Hoffman ratio of the eight categories of products in more than 20 countries, that is, the changed law of the ratio of the consumer goods industry to the capital goods industry. It suggests that although the industrialization time of each country occurred sooner or later and the level of development varied, there is no exception. All of them shows a common trend,that is, the net output value of the capital goods industry increases steadily in the total value of industrial net output, while the consumer goods. The proportion of industrial net output value in the total of industrial net output value gradually declined, and the countries surveyed show roughly the same stage characteristics. According to the above situation, this book further divide the industrialization process into four stages: (1) the dominant stage of the consumer goods industry; (2) the rapid growth stage of the capital goods industry; (3) the stage of capital goods industry catching up with the consumer goods industry, and the capital goods industry gradually achieving a state of balance with the consumer goods industry; (4) the industrialization stage, when capital goods industry dominates the industry. According to Hoffman's industrialization judgment rules and related theories, in the 1920s, the countries in the capital goods industry who catch up with the consumer goods industry are: Switzerland, Britain, the United States, Germany, France, Sweden and Belgium; Representative countries in the stage are: Japan, Denmark, the Netherlands, Australia and Canada; the countries in the consumer goods industry are mainly: India, Chile and other countries.

Hoffman's theory of industrialization has made the research of industrialization process a specific and unified standard. Hoffman's research reveals the main characteristics and general trends of the internal structure evolution of the industrial sector in the process of economic development, such as the proportion of capital goods industry rising gradually, the main transformation point of industrial structure and the final foothold, all of which are relatively scientific. Hoffmann attributes the process of economic development to the process of industrialization. His theory of industrialization stages mainly examines the evolution of heavy industry, and only uses the internal proportional relationship of industry to describe the entire process of economic development, which is one-sided. In addition, he studies industrial goods, and divides industry into capital goods industry and consumer goods industry, but this method is not scientific. According to the numerical standard of 75%, Hoffmann classified capital goods industry or consumer goods industry with 75% or above production as the object of investigation, so his object of investigation could not cover the whole industrial chain of national economy comprehensively, which affectes the generality of his theory.

2. Yuke Iwatani's industrial correlation theory

On the basis of Hoffmann industrialization theory, Japanese economist Yuke Iwatani demonstrates Hoffmann industrialization law again. In contrast to Hoffman's 75% classification of sectors, Iwatani divides the national economy into two categories: consumption and capital, with gross rather than net output as the statistical indicator. The research results of Yuke Iwatani shows that in a long period of history, the output value proportion of industrial goods of consumption materials declined steadily, and the proportion of industrial goods of capital materials in the national economy increased, which is a common phenomenon and a general trend of economic development. According to the ratio calculated by Yuke Iwatani, when the economy is in the middle stage of industrialization, i.e. the stage of heavy industrialization, the ratio of consumption material industrial goods to capital material industrial goods decreases obviously, which is basically consistent with the trend reflected by Hoffman's industrial rule of thumb. However, for those industrialization at higher levels of countries such as Sweden and the United States, during the inspection period according to the division of the final product consumption data of the ratio between industrial products and industrial production data is relatively stable, not consistent with the Hoffman the rule of thumb illustrated the development of industrialization, thus Yuke Iwatani's agrees with Hoffman industrialization of thumb and can't reflect the general law of industrialization.

Based on the above analysis, it can be seen that Iwatani's in-depth study of Hoffmann's industrialization law not only makes the industry classification more accurate, but also conforms to the actual development of industrialization. Iwatani specifies the scope of Hoffmann's industrial rule of thumb: the Hoffmann industrial rule applies to countries in the early and middle stages of industrialization. He further reveales the new trend in the process of industrialization, that is, with the development of the economy, the rate of heavy industrialization will gradually rise under the condition that the production of consumption means and the production of capital means are basically stable. When industrialization reaches a certain stage, the growth of the consumption and capital production sectors remains basically stable.

Under the historical background that heavy industry products are only used to meet the needs of military supplies and economic reconstruction, Iwatani's view was in line with the development reality at that time. When the economic development entered the middle and late stage of industrialization, the industrial sector structure shifted from raw material production to heavy industry manufacturing, especially after the economic development stage entered the developed stage dominated by durable consumer goods. When the relationship between supply and demand of products and the industrial structure changes, especially the production of consumer goods in heavy industry is increasing. The development of heavy industry at this time is mainly the expansion of durable goods production in the machinery industry. Thus, on the whole, the ratio of consumption to capital is not falling as Hoffman describes, but eventually stabilising. The practice of historical development shows that the law of industrial development summarized by Yuke Iwatani is more scientific and closer to the reality of development than Hoffman's.

2.2.4 Chenery's evolution theory of leading industries

Chenery etc. uses the per capita income level as a criterion to divide the whole process from underdeveloped economy to mature industrialized economy into six stages: the first stage, the per capita income is $140~280; the second stage, the per capita income is $280~560; the third stage, the per capita income is $560~1120; the fourth stage, the per capita income is $1120~2100; and the fifth stage, the per capita income is $2100~3360. In the sixth stage, the per capita income is $3360~5040. Then, using Kuznets' multiple regression analysis method, Chenery systematically expressed the economic structure transformation process at different stages of economic development and the general rules of changes in leading industries. He establishes a standard transformation model of industrial structure and tested it by empirical research method. Chenery's research method has important reference value for the study of the general law of industrial structure evolution and industrial replacement, and is a classical method for the study of the trend of economic development and industrial structure evolution. He designes a market share model of

GNP as a standard industrial structure transformation model:

$$X_i = \lg\beta_0 + \beta_1 \lg Y + \beta_2 (\lg Y)^2 + \beta_3 \lg N \qquad (1)$$

In the formula: X_i represents the ratio of the added value of the i industry to the total added value; Y represents the per capita gross national product; and N represents the population.

The results show that when the per capita GNP is between $100 and $1000, the proportion of agricultural added value to total added value decreases from 52.2% to 13.8%, 38 percentage points; the ratio of manufacturing added value to total added value first rises from 12.5% to 13.8%, and then the proportion of manufacturing added value rises again to 34.7%, which is quite obvious. At the same time, the market share of added value of public service industry and general service industry has steadily increased. For manufacturing industry, the inflection point of value-added share is at the level of $300 per capita national income, after which, the share of added value of manufacturing industry will exceed that of agriculture. Later, Chenery etc. make the following improvements to the standard industrial structure model:

1. The market share model of GNP has been improved, that is, three variables have been added to the original model to make the market share model reflect the reality more. The formula is as follows:

$$X_i = \alpha + \beta_1 \lg Y + \beta_2(\lg Y)^2 + \gamma \lg N + \delta_1 \lg(I/GNP) + \delta_2 \lg(E_p/GNP) + \delta_3 \lg(E_m/GNP) \qquad (2)$$

Where I/GNP represents the investment rate of resource allocation; E_p/GNP represents the output rate of primary products; E_m/GNP is the rate of production of industrial goods.

Based on the improved market share model, Chenery uses cross-sectional and time series data of 54 countries from 1950 to 1963 to empirically test the relationship between variables, and analyzes and judged the general trend of the change of added value share of the three industries. He believes that with the increase of per capita GNP, the market share of agricultural added value decreased gradually, and the industrial added value also showes a decreasing trend. Only the market share of service industry added value is rising. With the continuous increase of population, the market share of agricultural and industrial added value shows an upward trend, and compared with industry, the upward trend of agriculture is more obvious, while the market share of service industry added value shows a downward trend. When the investment ratio in the process of resource allocation keeps increasing, the market share of added value of agriculture and industry keeps rising while that of service industry drops gradually. When the output rate of products in the primary industry sector increases, only the market share of added value of the primary industry increases, while the market share of added value of the secondary and tertiary industries shows a decreasing trend. When the rate increases, the secondary and tertiary industries show an upward trend except for the decrease of the market share of the primary industry.

2. Establish three sets of standard industrial structure analysis models. In order to further analyze the characteristics of industrial structure in different countries, Chenery et al. divide the objects into three groups according to the size of population based on the standard industrial structure model, namely: (1) large group (L group), i.e. more developed countries with a population of more than 15 million; (2) medium group (M group), industrial-oriented countries with a population of less than 15 million and relatively scarce natural resources; (3) Group S, a resource-rich country with a population of less than 15 million. From the above improved standard industrial structure analysis model, it can see that the variable coefficients of the econometric model express different meanings. In the standard industry structure determination model of group L, the coefficient δ_1 of I/GNP variable plays an important role. Group S and group M are different.

The output coefficients of δ_2 and δ_3 of variables E_p/GNP and E_m/GNP play a larger role. Compared with group L, coefficients of δ_1 of variable I/GNP is less elastic, while the coefficients of β_1, β_2 of GNP Y and γ of population N are elastic. In group S, the coefficient δ_1 of I/GNP is relatively elastic, which is an important feature of this model. In addition, the output rate of primary products E_p/GNP is an important factor determining the growth of the secondary industry.

According to the research results, from group L, the market share of the secondary industry increases from 10% to 32% when the per capita GNP range from $100 to $400 (according to the constant price of 1958 US dollar), and then gradually extendes. When the per capita GNP increases to about $1200, the market share reaches the highest point of 37%. The market share of primary industry declines with the growth of per capita GDP.

From the point of view of S and M groups, the market share of the first and second industries is similar to that of L groups. In particular, the intersection of the market share curves of the primary industry and the secondary industry is about $270 in GNP. From the point of view of Group S, because it represents the type of primary products, it adopts the development model which is quite different from Group L and Group M. Here, the market share of the primary industry is relatively high, showing a downward trend, but the decline is relatively small. Only when the per capita GNP is greater than $500, the market share of the primary industry will show a downward trend. At the same time, the market share of the second industry increased slowly from the low starting point, and only when the per capita GNP reached $500, it rise rapidly. When the per capita GNP increased to around $750, the market share curve of the primary industry intersectes with the second industry market share curve.

Chenery's standard industrial structure model, especially the improved model, further reveals the complex relationship among industries in the process of industrial structure change, and describes the prominent characteristics and differences among different types of national industrial structure evolution, which further deepens the understanding of the general trends and laws of industrial structure change and industrial replacement.

2.2.5 Rostow's theory on leading industry

Rostow was the first scholar to clearly put forward the theory of leading industry. In his masterpiece "economics from take-off to sustainable growth", he put forward that at any stage of a mature economy, the potential for sustained growth is due to the continuous growth and rapid expansion of leading sectors, and the expansion of these sectors has brought about other related industrial sectors. With dynamic action. Rostow pointes out that the leading industry should have the following characteristics: (1) the Department will rely on innovation and technological progress to generate new production functions; (2) the sustained high rate of growth of the sector; (3) the sector has strong penetration and proliferation effect, which will have an important impact on the development of all other industries. These three characteristics reflect the unique role of leading industries, they are an organic whole, indispensable. Nevertheless, the high growth rate can not fully reflect the unique characteristics of the leading industry, because not only the leading industry but also other industries can maintain a high growth rate. Only those industries with both high technology level and strong diffusion effect can be called the leading industry. In addition to absorbing the general characteristics of technological progress, introducing new production functions and maintaining high growth rate, whether the leading industry has strong diffusion effect has become an important feature that distinguishes it from other industries.

Rostow made a standard and definition of the industrial diffusion effect. He suggests that the diffusion effect was that certain departments played a role of over growth ratio in economic development in various historical stages, and manifested in three aspects: (1) the retrospective effect, which refers to the influence of the leading departments' growth on the departments that provide their own production materials; (2) the side effect, which refers to the leading departments; (3) Forward effect refers to the leading sector's inductive effect on the emergence of new sectors, new technology frontiers, new raw materials and energy, which can help solve the production bottleneck problem. He also believes that the existence and rationality of the concept of the leading sector have been confirmed from practical experience. The role of the leading industry in economic growth is a combination of the three diffusion effects from the rapidly growing sectors. It can be seen that Rostow's "diffusion effect" is not only confined to the effect of technological links among industries, but also has a broader impact on economic development.

With the progress of innovation and technology, the deepening of social division in labor and the increasing of production roundabout, the development of the whole economy will not be limited to one or a few industries. Rather, it is the result of the joint action of certain industrial groups. Rostow calls these groups the "leading sector complex", which we can also call the leading industry group. He believes that the leading sector complex is composed of leading industries and departments with strong links and side links with leading industries. For example, the leading sector representing technological progress. For example, machinery industry and steel, electronics, chemical industry, electric power, petroleum, automobile and other sectors with strong backward links and side links are called the leading sector complex.

The formation of leading sector complex is adapted to the stage of economic development in a country. Economic development manifests itself in the orderly replacement of leading sector complex in each stage of industrialization. Due to the differences in resource endowments, supply and demand structure and industrial policies of various countries, leading sector complexes of different nature will emerge. For example, in the early stage of industrialization, Britain started with textile industry, steam engine railways, steel and other leading sectors to drive the whole economic development, with the United States, Germany, France and Canada roughly similar. In the early stage of industrialization, Sweden and Denmark and other Northwestern European countries depend on rich forest resources and animal husbandry, respectively, with wood processing, pulp production and meat processing, dairy production as the leading industries to drive economic development. However, from the long-term development process of industrialization in various countries, the formation of the leading industry and the leading sector complex is basically similar. They all follow the evolutionary trend of light textile industry-basic industry-processing manufacturing industry to form the corresponding leading sector and leading sector complex. Only in some specific periods, some countries show some differences in the selection of Industrial Development order. However, some developing countries also promote the development of the whole economy by cultivating priority industries, and then forming a leading sector complex with strong forward-backward and lateral linkages. Generally speaking, the leading departments must meet the following three basic requirements:

(1) The industry can reflect the direction of economic development in a particular period of time in the country, and the actual and potential demand for the products of the industry will gradually expand, so that the industry has a higher growth rate than other industries.

(2) The industry can quickly absorb advanced scientific and technological achievements, and has strong technology diffusion effect. On the basis of modern technology and modern management, it can create higher labor productivity and more added value.

(3) The industry has strong forward-backward and side-linkages, which can promote and induce the development of other industries.

The three basic requirements of the leading industry reflect the characteristics of the leading industry synthetically. The leading industry is different from the general industry. The leading industry must be able to indicate the direction of economic development and effectively penetrate technology into other industries to promote their continuous development and growth. As for those industries which only have technology development and higher added value, they may not become the leading industries, because the industries with higher added value may also occur in some subsidiary or derivative growth sectors, which are driven by the development of the leading industries and have achieved rapid growth. Rostow has proposed the difference between the leading growth departments and the leading circular sectors. The former is the introduction of new production functions associated with technological progress, which plays a leading role in economic growth, and has strong forward and backward driving effects on other industrial growth. The latter is mainly affected by profit margins, and its development can bring economic prosperity, but it will also increase the growth of other industries. There is no direct impact, this is a non-leading industries.

Rostow believes that in various stages of economic development, the establishment of leading industries and industrial groups must satisfy the following specific conditions: (1) to have sufficient capital accumulation and require a country's net investment rate (the proportion of investment in gross national product) to reach 10%, it is necessary to encourage savings, to a certain extent, to limit consumption, and to actively introduce foreign capital; (2) adequate market demand, and the effective demand of leading industry products must be constantly expanded, so as to promote the production of leading industry by demand and open up the market for the rapid expansion of leading industry; (3) robust technological innovation and sufficient enough to promote technological innovation in this sector and to induce the production of technological innovation and new potential production capacity in other sectors; (4) ability on system innovation, have a large number of entrepreneurs with management literacy and innovation consciousness, provide management and human support for the development of leading industries, and create good operating conditions from the system. Rostow's definition of leading industry is becoming more and more clear, and it is of great significance both in theory and in practice.

2.2.6 Helchman's "*Unbalanced Growth Theory*"

In 1958, Helchman published the book "the stage of economic development". He pointed out that economic development does not depend on the optimal combination of established factors of production, but rather depends on the full use of potential, scattered, inefficient or ineffective resources under established development goals. In order to explore the inducement factors and operational mechanism of economic growth, he put forward the theory of "unbalanced growth". The main point of this theory is that developing countries before entering the economic take-off should focus on very limited capital and scarce resources to give priority to the development of some industries, but then gradually expand their investment in other industries and drive the development of the whole economy through unbalanced strategies. The contents of Helchman's unbalanced growth theory mainly include the principle of "leading to the maximization of investment" and "connection effect theory".

1. The principle of "maximizing investment "

Under the constraints of limited investment resources, if a country's investment demand is fixed, when the government is faced with a series of investment projects, the existing capital and resources can not bear the total cost of these investment projects, how should a country make project investment choices so as to maximize the efficiency of input and output in order to achieve the purpose of maximizing economic contribution? In order to solve these problems, Helchman classifies two types of investment behavior: substitution and delayed choice. Alternative selection is about which investment projects should be selected, and deferred selection is the decision before which projects should be selected. Helchman believes that compared with the lack of resources, the more serious problem of developing countries is the lack of effective means and ability to use resources. He believes that the selection of investment projects should be based on the principle of maximizing preference for "decision-making", that is, investment projects must satisfy the condition that their own development can lead to the fastest development of other projects. Therefore, the basic guiding idea of Helchman's investment choice is that the priority of investment choice must be based on the conclusion that the progress of a certain industry is more effective on the progress of other industries, and whether it can give priority to development through the development of other industries.

Helchman uses a model of the relationship between "socially-distributed capital" (SC) and "direct productive activity" (DPA) to illustrate "the principle of maximizing decision making", "Socially-distributed capital" refers to the investment in infrastructure, which has indivisible characteristics and high capital-output ratio. SC has a large scale of investment, a long construction cycle, a slow return and a wide range of benefits. The so-called "direct productive activity" refers to the investment behavior of direct investment in industry, which can achieve quick results and directly increase output and income. It is characterized by centralized investment, short cycle and high investment efficiency. Helchman believes that the goal of economic growth is to maximize the DPA output under the conditions of least resources and DPA and SC. If existing resources are insufficient to ensure the minimum balanced growth of DPA and SC, what kind of delayed selection should be made? One possibility is that SC gives priority to growth, known as "super-capacity development". Another possibility is that DPA gives priority to growth, known as "shortage development". Both of these orders can stimulate and stress the national economy. The traditional theory holds that we should choose the SC priority line of expansion, but Helchman believes that the development of "superpower" is only possible in theory, and the path of pursuing balanced development will lead to the disappearance of investment or induced stimulus. He believes that the most effective investment results can be produced through "shortage development" and the "induced decision" can be maximized. Therefore, DPA should be preferred to SC.

DPA priority means that the government should delay investment in infrastructure (SC) such as roads, railways, electricity, telecommunications, hospitals and schools, and should concentrate limited resources on direct production sectors, with the aim of increasing output and gaining investment returns as soon as possible, so as to recycle past investment, as the direct production sector gradually grows and develops. After that, capital will be accumulated, so part of the accumulated capital can be invested in infrastructure sector construction in the reproduction process, in order to expand the growth of SC sector. When giving priority to the development of direct productive activities and obtaining a certain amount of accumulated capital to decide to invest in DPA sector, the country should not develop all DPA sectors in an all-round way, but focus on those DPA sectors that can bring about the greatest investment, concentrate limited resources to obtain the growth of some of the most efficient sectors so as to drive the joint and several growth of other sectors. On the basis of what criteria should be chosen to select the sectors with the largest investment effect, Helchman put forward the theory of "connection effect".

2. Linkage effect theory

When exploring various inducement factors of economic development, Helchman deduces the linkage effect mechanism from the choice of "shortage development" and "super capacity development" under "decision making": input supply, derivative demand or forward linkage effect and backward linkage effect. Helchman believes that the linkage effect refers to the interrelation, mutual influence and interdependence among various industrial sectors in the national economy. "Backward linkages" refers specifically to the linkages between an industrial sector and one or some sectors that provide intermediate inputs, such as the backward linkages of textile industry, agricultural planting industry and machinery manufacturing industry. Forward linkages refer to the linkages between an industry and the departments digesting its output, such as chemical industry, petroleum processing and other industries. In most cases, the backward linkages of an industry are usually raw materials, primary product manufacturing, semi-finished product production or semi-finished product processing, while the forward linkages of an industry are generally the final product manufacturing sector.

Helchman believes that most developing countries have weaker overall industrial links. Generally speaking, agriculture, especially the productive agricultural sector, lacks the linkage effect, and primary product production does not have a large backward link. Because the linkage effect of industrialized countries is most fully exerted, the sectors that should be paid attention to in the development plan can be explored according to the linkage effect of industrialized countries. Helchman believes that as long as an industry has an industry related effect, whether it is pre related or backward related, the sector can drive other industries to generate investment. Induced investment can not only promote the development in front of and back related departments or side related departments, but also promote the development of the whole economy. For economic entities, inducing investment can provide opportunities for enterprises to make profits from investment, promote private investment and the expansion of production scale. On the other hand, it can also exert pressure on the government to make the government take auxiliary actions to achieve the "maximization of inducing decision". For example, when a private investor decides to invest in a place with incomplete infrastructure, the investment project has a greater impact on other industries, it also has a great driving effect on the development of other sectors and even the whole region. In this case, the government will raise funds and resources to build infrastructure and help the whole investment project achieve the expected benefits. Helchman's investment maximization has clearly pointed out the direction and development path of the investment of the latecomer countries. The theory of linkage effect indicates that a country should give priority to the development of a wide range of industries with wide linkage effect when planning the strategy. The core of the theory of unbalanced development is Helchman's theory of inducing maximum investment and linking effect as the selection criteria for the priority development order of the industrial sector.

2.3 Summary of This Chapter

The ideological sprout of leading industry can be traced back to the classical economics era. Rostow and Helchman's economic theory gradually put forward relevant theories of leading industries. Early thoughts on economic development and leading industries, such as those of petty, Clark, Kuznets, Channery and others, are mainly related to the evolution of industrial structure in the process of economic growth. Although industrial structure is closely related to leading industry and economic development, the mechanism of leading industry's action on economic growth is totally different from that of industrial structure adjustment. The research on the relationship between industrial structure and economic growth leads to that the research focus is not on the role of industries which plays a leading role in the national economy in economic growth. Therefore, the purpose and angle of the study do not subjectively prefer the industrial sectors which play a leading role in the national economy. Because the early research on the relationship between industrial structure and economic growth is in the process of continuous exploration and progress, leading to the majority of industrial division is not meticulous enough, data and statistical data are very limited, the research on the leading industries of economic development is too rough, and the focus of the research is mainly on the changing law of industrial structure, ignoring the leading sectors and industrial knots. Research on the mechanism of structure in the process of economic development.

The theory of Rostow and Helchman clarifies the concept of leading industry, focused on the leading sectors in the national economy, and further explained the role of leading industries and industrial structure in the process of economic development. At the same time, it inspires the later scholars to actively seek the development ideas of industrial structure optimization and economic take-off. The core of their research is industrial relevance theory, which is not only an important basis for judging leading industries, but also a major principle for leading industries to play a role. However, it is obviously unreasonable to confine the choice of leading industries to the effect of industrial linkage, especially in the case of more and more complex economic development problems and diversified economic development objectives. In addition, Rostow and Helchman did not propose other criteria for judging the leading industry and operability rules, which made their theories have great limitations in practice.

Chapter 3   Economic Development Model and Empirical Study
—Based on Input–output Framework

3.1   Basic Ideas of Input–output Model Design for Economic Development Mode

The input-output table reflects the comprehensive information of input and output from various sectors of the national economy. Horizontally, the input-output table not only reflects the intermediate input part of economic development, including labor, capital, technology, energy and environmental input (the book regards environmental emissions as negative input of economic development), but also reflects the industrial structure and industrial linkage of the national economy. Longitudinally, the input-output table reflects the final demand situation of various sectors of the national economy. Including consumption (household consumption and government purchases), capital formation and import and export trade, it can be seen that the input-output table reflects the main content of the economic development mode vertically and horizontally. Therefore, the correct compilation of the input-output table containing the contents of the economic development pattern can comprehensively understand the industrial structure, input structure, consumption structure and import and export structure of the national economy, which is particularly important for studying the theme of the transformation of China's economic development mode. In view of this, this chapter will expand the traditional input-output table of the national economy, incorporate the contents of the economic development mode into a unified analytical framework, and take the industry as a carrier to investigate the way of China's economic development. The purpose is to find out the industrial path and the arrangement of industrial choice.

3.1.1 Equilibrium of input–output table of economic development mode in industrial level

1. Input-output lateral model directional equilibrium of economic development mode

From a horizontal point of view, the input-output table mainly reflects the intermediate and the final demand, indicating the distribution and usage of products in various sectors in the national economic system. For each department, there is a following trend balance: total product = intermediate demand product + final demand product. Specifically for the equilibrium of economic development mode: total products = technology intermediate products + energy intermediate products + environment intermediate products + labor intermediate products + capital intermediate products + other intermediate products + all end-use products, including consumption, investment and import and export.

Definition: technology intermediate product input matrix is $x_{ij}^{(1)}$, energy intermediate product input matrix $x_{ij}^{(2)}$, environment intermediate product input matrix is $x_{ij}^{(3)}$, labor intermediate product matrix $x_{ij}^{(4)}$, capital intermediate product matrix is $x_{ij}^{(5)}$; other intermediate product input matrix is $x_{ij}^{(6)}$; technology final product matrix is $Y_i^{(1)}$, energy final product matrix $Y_i^{(2)}$, environment final product matrix is $Y_i^{(3)}$, labor final product matrix $Y_i^{(4)}$. The element of the capital final product matrix is $Y_i^{(5)}$, and the other elements of the final product matrix $Y_i^{(6)}$, element of the total final product Y_i, then $Y_i^{(1)} + Y_i^{(2)} + Y_i^{(3)} + Y_i^{(4)} + Y_i^{(5)} + Y_i^{(6)} = Y_i$, and the total intermediate input matrix is X_i, then $X_i^{(1)} + X_i^{(2)} + X_i^{(3)} + X_i^{(4)} + X_i^{(5)} + X_i^{(6)} = X_i$.

According to the equation of equilibrium, there are：

$$\begin{cases} (x_{11}^{(1)}+\cdots+x_{1n}^{(1)})+(x_{11}^{(2)}+\cdots+x_{1n}^{(2)})+(x_{11}^{(3)}+\cdots+x_{1n}^{(3)})+(x_{11}^{(4)}+\cdots+x_{1n}^{(4)})+ \\ (x_{21}^{(1)}+\cdots+x_{2n}^{(1)})+(x_{21}^{(2)}+\cdots+x_{2n}^{(2)})+(x_{21}^{(3)}+\cdots+x_{2n}^{(3)})+(x_{21}^{(4)}+\cdots+x_{2n}^{(4)})+ \\ \cdots \\ (x_{n1}^{(1)}+\cdots+x_{nn}^{(1)})+(x_{n1}^{(2)}+\cdots+x_{nn}^{(2)})+(x_{n1}^{(3)}+\cdots+x_{nn}^{(3)})+(x_{n1}^{(4)}+\cdots+x_{nn}^{(4)})+ \end{cases}$$

are：

$$(x_{11}^{(5)}+\cdots+x_{1n}^{(5)})+(x_{11}^{(6)}+\cdots+x_{1n}^{(6)})+Y_1=X_1$$
$$(x_{21}^{(5)}+\cdots+x_{2n}^{(5)})+(x_{21}^{(6)}+\cdots+x_{2n}^{(6)})+Y_2=X_2$$
$$\cdots$$
$$(x_{n1}^{(5)}+\cdots+x_{nn}^{(5)})+(x_{n1}^{(6)}+\cdots+x_{nn}^{(6)})+Y_n=X_n \tag{1}$$

In the above formula, $x_{ij}^{(1)}$ indicates the consumption of technology intermediate inputs by j departments corresponds to the first quadrant of part (1) of the input-output table (see Table 3-1 below), $x_{ij}^{(2)}$ indicates the consumption of energy intermediate inputs by j departments, corresponds to the first quadrant of part (2) of the input-output table, $x_{ij}^{(3)}$ indicates the consumption of environmental intermediate inputs by j department, corresponds to the first quadrant of part (3) of the input-output table. $x_{ij}^{(4)}$ representing the consumption of intermediate inputs of labor force by j sector production, corresponding to part (4) of the first quadrant; $x_{ij}^{(5)}$ representing the consumption of capital goods by j sector production, corresponding to part (5) of the first quadrant of the input-output table; $x_{ij}^{(6)}$ indicating the consumption of other intermediate inputs in j sector production, corresponding to part (6) of the first quadrant of the input-output table. $Y_i^{(1)}$ correspond to the second quadrant of part (1); $Y_i^{(2)}$ representing the second quadrant of part(2); $Y_i^{(3)}$ correspond to the second quadrant of part (3); $Y_i^{(4)}$ representing the second quadrant of part (4); $Y_i^{(5)}$ correspond to the second quadrant of part (5); $Y_i^{(6)}$ representing the second quadrant of part (6) in the input-output table, the sum of the six parts represents all end-use products. X_i represents the total input of i department, Y_i represents the total output of i department. From the equilibrium equation, we could get the direct consumption coefficients of various inputs.

Direct consumption coefficients of technology intermediate products:

$$a_{ij}^{(1)} = \frac{x_{ij}^{(1)}}{X_j} \qquad (2)$$

Direct consumption coefficients of energy intermediate products:

$$a_{ij}^{(2)} = \frac{x_{ij}^{(2)}}{X_j} \qquad (3)$$

Direct consumption coefficients of environment intermediate products:

$$a_{ij}^{(3)} = \frac{x_{ij}^{(3)}}{X_j} \qquad (4)$$

Direct consumption coefficients of labor intermediate products:

$$a_{ij}^{(4)} = \frac{x_{ij}^{(4)}}{X_j} \qquad (5)$$

Direct consumption coefficients of capital intermediate products:

$$a_{ij}^{(5)} = \frac{x_{ij}^{(5)}}{X_j} \qquad (6)$$

Direct consumption coefficients of other intermediate products:

$$a_{ij}^{(6)} = \frac{x_{ij}^{(6)}}{X_j} \qquad (7)$$

Formula (2) $a_{ij}^{(1)}$ denotes the number of technical intermediate inputs consumed by the total output of j department. Formula (3) $a_{ij}^{(2)}$ denotes the number of energy intermediate inputs consumed by the total output of j department. Formula (4) $a_{ij}^{(3)}$ denotes the number of environmental intermediate inputs consumed by the total output of j department. Formula (5) $a_{ij}^{(4)}$ denotes the number of labor intermediate inputs consumed by the total output of j department. Formula (6) $a_{ij}^{(5)}$

denotes the amount of capital input consumed by the total output of j department. Formula (7) $a_{ij}^{(6)}$ denotes the amount of other intermediate inputs, substituting (2) (3) (4) (5) (6) (7) for formula (1):

$$
\begin{cases}
(a_{11}^{(1)}X_1 + \cdots + x_{1n}^{(1)}X_n) + (x_{11}^{(2)}X_1 + \cdots + x_{1n}^{(2)}X_n) + (x_{11}^{(3)}X_1 + \cdots + x_{1n}^{(3)}X_n) + (x_{11}^{(4)}X_1 + \cdots + x_{1n}^{(4)}X_n) + \\
(x_{21}^{(1)}X_1 + \cdots + x_{2n}^{(1)}X_n) + (x_{21}^{(2)}X_1 + \cdots + x_{2n}^{(2)}X_n) + (x_{21}^{(3)}X_1 + \cdots + x_{2n}^{(3)}X_n) + (x_{21}^{(4)}X_1 + \cdots + x_{2n}^{(4)}X_n) + \\
\qquad\qquad\qquad\qquad\qquad\qquad \cdots \\
(x_{n1}^{(1)}X_1 + \cdots + x_{nn}^{(1)}X_n) + (x_{n1}^{(2)}X_1 + \cdots + x_{nn}^{(2)}X_n) + (x_{n1}^{(3)}X_1 + \cdots + x_{nn}^{(3)}X_n) + (x_{n1}^{(4)}X_1 + \cdots + x_{nn}^{(4)}X_n) +
\end{cases}
$$

$$(x_{11}^{(5)}X_1 + \cdots + x_{1n}^{(5)}X_n) + (x_{11}^{(6)}X_1 + \cdots + x_{1n}^{(6)}X_n) + Y_1 = X_1$$

$$(x_{21}^{(5)}X_1 + \cdots + x_{2n}^{(5)}X_n) + (x_{21}^{(6)}X_1 + \cdots + x_{2n}^{(6)}X_n) + Y_2 = X_2$$

$$\cdots$$

$$(x_{n1}^{(5)}X_1 + \cdots + x_{nn}^{(5)}X_n) + (x_{n1}^{(6)}X_1 + \cdots + x_{nn}^{(6)}X_n) + Y_n = X_n \tag{8}$$

Formula (8) can be expressed as:

$$\sum_{j=1}^{n} a_{ij}^{(1)}X_j + \sum_{j=1}^{n} a_{ij}^{(2)}X_j + \sum_{j=1}^{n} a_{ij}^{(3)}X_j + \sum_{j=1}^{n} a_{ij}^{(4)}X_j + \sum_{j=1}^{n} a_{ij}^{(5)}X_j + \sum_{j=1}^{n} a_{ij}^{(6)}X_j + Y_i = X_i$$

$$(i = 1, 2, \cdots, n) \tag{9}$$

Formula (9) is expressed in matrix form as follows:

$$A^{(1)}x + A^{(2)}x + A^{(3)}x + A^{(4)}x + A^{(5)}x + Y = x \tag{10}$$

Here we get:

$$(I - A^{(1)} - A^{(2)} - A^{(3)} - A^{(4)} - A^{(5)} - A^{(6)})X = Y \tag{11}$$

$$\text{So } X = (I - A^{(1)} - A^{(2)} - A^{(3)} - A^{(4)} - A^{(5)} - A^{(6)})^{-1}Y \tag{12}$$

Here formula (12) is the input-output lateral model reflecting the mode of economic development.

2. Establishment of input-output alignment model of economic development mode

The alignment equilibrium formula reflecting the development mode can be expressed as: total input = technology intermediate product + energy intermediate product + environment intermediate product + labor intermediate product + capital intermediate product + adjusted added value. The corresponding alignments of the first quadrant (1) (2) (3) (4) (5) (6) and the third quadrant of the input-output table are added together.

According to the equation of equilibrium, there are:

$$\begin{cases} (x_{11}^{(1)} + \cdots + x_{1n}^{(1)}) + (x_{11}^{(2)} + \cdots + x_{1n}^{(2)}) + (x_{11}^{(3)} + \cdots + x_{1n}^{(3)}) + (x_{11}^{(4)} + \cdots + x_{1n}^{(4)}) + \\ (x_{21}^{(1)} + \cdots + x_{2n}^{(1)}) + (x_{21}^{(2)} + \cdots + x_{2n}^{(2)}) + (x_{21}^{(3)} + \cdots + x_{2n}^{(3)}) + (x_{21}^{(4)} + \cdots + x_{2n}^{(4)}) + \\ \cdots \\ (x_{n1}^{(1)} + \cdots + x_{nn}^{(1)}) + (x_{n1}^{(2)} + \cdots + x_{nn}^{(2)}) + (x_{n1}^{(3)} + \cdots + x_{nn}^{(3)}) + (x_{n1}^{(4)} + \cdots + x_{nn}^{(4)}) + \end{cases}$$

$$(x_{11}^{(5)} + \cdots + x_{1n}^{(5)}) + (x_{11}^{(6)} + \cdots + x_{1n}^{(6)}) + H_1 = X$$
$$(x_{21}^{(5)} + \cdots + x_{2n}^{(5)}) + (x_{21}^{(6)} + \cdots + x_{2n}^{(6)}) + H_2 = X_2$$
$$\cdots$$
$$(x_{n1}^{(5)} + \cdots + x_{nn}^{(5)}) + (x_{n1}^{(6)} + \cdots + x_{nn}^{(6)}) + H_n = X_n \tag{13}$$

As in the previous section, we introduce the technology direct consumption factor $a_{ij}^{(1)}$; direct consumption coefficient of energy intermediate input $a_{ij}^{(2)}$, direct consumption coefficient of environmental intermediate input $a_{ij}^{(3)}$, direct consumption coefficient of labor intermediate input $a_{ij}^{(4)}$, direct consumption coefficient of capital intermediate input $a_{ij}^{(5)}$, direct consumption coefficient of other intermediate input $a_{ij}^{(6)}$, substitute them into（13）, we get：

$$\begin{cases} (a_{11}^{(1)}X_1 + \cdots + x_{1n}^{(1)}X_n) + (x_{11}^{(2)}X_1 + \cdots + x_{1n}^{(2)}X_n) + (x_{11}^{(3)}X_1 + \cdots + x_{1n}^{(3)}X_n) + (x_{11}^{(4)}X_1 + \cdots + x_{1n}^{(4)}X_n) + \\ (x_{21}^{(1)}X_1 + \cdots + x_{2n}^{(1)}X_n) + (x_{21}^{(2)}X_1 + \cdots + x_{2n}^{(2)}X_n) + (x_{21}^{(3)}X_1 + \cdots + x_{2n}^{(3)}X_n) + (x_{21}^{(4)}X_1 + \cdots + x_{2n}^{(4)}X_n) + \\ \cdots \\ (x_{n1}^{(1)}X_1 + \cdots + x_{nn}^{(1)}X_n) + (x_{n1}^{(2)}X_1 + \cdots + x_{nn}^{(2)}X_n) + (x_{n1}^{(3)}X_1 + \cdots + x_{nn}^{(3)}X_n) + (x_{n1}^{(4)}X_1 + \cdots + x_{nn}^{(4)}X_n) + \end{cases}$$

$$(x_{11}^{(5)}X_1 + \cdots + x_{1n}^{(5)}X_n) + (x_{11}^{(6)}X_1 + \cdots + x_{1n}^{(6)}X_n) + H_1 = X_1$$
$$(x_{21}^{(5)}X_1 + \cdots + x_{2n}^{(5)}X_n) + (x_{21}^{(6)}X_1 + \cdots + x_{2n}^{(6)}X_n) + H_2 = X_2$$
$$\cdots \tag{14}$$
$$(x_{n1}^{(5)}X_1 + \cdots + x_{nn}^{(5)}X_n) + (x_{n1}^{(6)}X_1 + \cdots + x_{nn}^{(6)}X_n) + H_n = X_n$$

The sum formula is expressed as:

$$\sum_{j=1}^{n} a_{ij}^{(1)} X_j + \sum_{j=1}^{n} a_{ij}^{(2)} X_j + \sum_{j=1}^{n} a_{ij}^{(3)} X_j + \sum_{j=1}^{n} a_{ij}^{(4)} X_j + \sum_{j=1}^{n} a_{ij}^{(5)} X_j + \sum_{j=1}^{n} a_{ij}^{(6)} X_j + H_i = X_i$$

$$(i = 1, 2, \cdots, n) \tag{15}$$

Expressed in matrix as:

$$\hat{A}_c^{(1)} X + \hat{A}_c^{(2)} X + \hat{A}_c^{(3)} X + \hat{A}_c^{(4)} X + \hat{A}_c^{(5)} X + \hat{A}_c^{(6)} X + H = X \tag{16}$$

in (16), there are six diagonal matrices:

$$\hat{A}_c^{(1)} = \begin{bmatrix} \sum_{i=1}^{n} a_{i1}^{(1)} & & & \\ & \sum_{i=1}^{n} a_{i2}^{(1)} & & \\ & & \cdots & \\ & & & \sum_{i=1}^{n} a_{in}^{(1)} \end{bmatrix} ;$$

$$\hat{A}_c^{(2)} = \begin{bmatrix} \sum_{i=1}^{n} a_{i1}^{(2)} & & & \\ & \sum_{i=1}^{n} a_{i2}^{(2)} & & \\ & & \cdots & \\ & & & \sum_{i=1}^{n} a_{in}^{(2)} \end{bmatrix} ;$$

$$\hat{A}_c^{(3)} = \begin{bmatrix} \sum_{i=1}^{n} a_{i1}^{(3)} & & & \\ & \sum_{i=1}^{n} a_{i2}^{(3)} & & \\ & & \cdots & \\ & & & \sum_{i=1}^{n} a_{in}^{(3)} \end{bmatrix} ;$$

129

$$\hat{A}_c^{(4)} = \begin{bmatrix} \sum_{i=1}^{n} a_{i1}^{(4)} & & & \\ & \sum_{i=1}^{n} a_{i2}^{(4)} & & \\ & & \cdots & \\ & & & \sum_{i=1}^{n} a_{in}^{(4)} \end{bmatrix};$$

$$\hat{A}_c^{(5)} = \begin{bmatrix} \sum_{i=1}^{n} a_{i1}^{(5)} & & & \\ & \sum_{i=1}^{n} a_{i2}^{(5)} & & \\ & & \cdots & \\ & & & \sum_{i=1}^{n} a_{in}^{(5)} \end{bmatrix};$$

$$\hat{A}_c^{(6)} = \begin{bmatrix} \sum_{i=1}^{n} a_{i1}^{(6)} & & & \\ & \sum_{i=1}^{n} a_{i2}^{(6)} & & \\ & & \cdots & \\ & & & \sum_{i=1}^{n} a_{in}^{(6)} \end{bmatrix}; \qquad (17)$$

sort (16) out:

$$(I - \hat{A}_c^{(1)} - \hat{A}_c^{(2)} - \hat{A}_c^{(3)} - \hat{A}_c^{(4)} - \hat{A}_c^{(5)} - \hat{A}_c^{(6)}) X = H \qquad (18)$$

$$X = (I - \hat{A}_c^{(1)} - \hat{A}_c^{(2)} - \hat{A}_c^{(3)} - \hat{A}_c^{(4)} - \hat{A}_c^{(5)} - \hat{A}_c^{(6)})^{-1} H \qquad (19)$$

Formula（19）is the input-output alignment model of economic development mode.

Table 3–1 Input–output Model of Economic Development Mode

Output Input		Intermediate products (use)	End product(use)				Total output
		$(1,2,\cdots,n)$	consumption	Investment	Export	Import	
Intermediate input	Technical input	I （1）	II （1）				
	Energy input	I （2）	II （2）				
	Environmental input	I （3）	II （3）				
	Labor input	I （4）	II （4）				
	Capital input	I （5）	II （5）				
	Other inputs	I （6）	II （6）				
Adjustment of added value	Depreciation of fixed assets	III	IV				
	Remuneration of workers						
	Net production tax						
	Net operating surplus						
Total input							

3.1.2 Data sources and industrial classification

The data in this book are from the official website of China economic network, state research network and China Statistics Bureau. When calculating the relevant indicators of various industries, because the available data are inconsistent with the industries studied in this paper, it is necessary to classify the relevant industries first. The industry data in this paper are classified according to the industry standard of the input-output table, after which there are 42 departments. The merging criteria are: the industry data on the input-output table are classified according to the original data and inconsistent according to the following criteria: metal mining and processing industry includes non-ferrous metal mining and processing industry and ferrous metal mining and processing industry; food manufacturing and tobacco processing industry includes beverage manufacturing industry, agricultural and sideline food processing industry, food manufacturing industry and tobacco products industry. Textile clothing, shoes, hats, leather, down and its products industry includes textile clothing, shoes, hats and other fibre products manufacturing industry and leather, fur, feather (down) and its products industry. Wood processing and furniture manufacturing industries include wood processing and wood, bamboo, rattan, brown, grass products and furniture manufacturing industries. Paper printing and cultural and educational sports goods manufacturing industry includes paper and paper products industry, printing industry and recording media reproduction and cultural and educational sports goods manufacturing industry. Chemical industry includes chemical raw materials and chemical products manufacturing, chemical fiber manufacturing, pharmaceutical manufacturing, plastic products and rubber products. Metal smelting and calendering industry includes non-ferrous metal smelting and calendering industry and ferrous metal smelting and calendering industry. General and special equipment manufacturing industry includes general equipment manufacturing industry and special equipment manufacturing industry. The construction industry includes the housing and civil engineering construction industry, the construction installation industry, the construction decoration industry and other construction industries. Transportation, warehousing and postal services include railway transportation, road transport, urban public transport, water transport, air transport, pipeline transportation, loading and unloading, transportation and other transportation services and warehousing. Information transmission, computer services and software industries include telecommunications and other information transmission services, computer services and software industries. The financial industry includes banking, securities, insurance and other financial activities. Real estate industry includes real estate development and operation, property management and real estate intermediary services. Integrated technology service industry includes professional technology service industry, science and technology exchange and promotion service industry and geological exploration industry. Cultural, sports and entertainment industries include press and publishing, radio, film, television and audio-visual industries, cultural and artistic industries, sports and entertainment industries. Public management and social organizations include state organs, the Chinese Communist Party organs, CPPCC and democratic parties, mass organizations, social organizations and religious organizations.

Data of energy and environmental emissions, the national research network only contains industrial subdivision data and data from a non-material production sector, where the immaterial production sector of agriculture and the third industry is estimated. According to the total energy consumption data of China Economic Network, 48 industries were integrated and merged by comparing the input-output table industries. Finally, the food processing industry, food manufacturing industry, beverage manufacturing industry and tobacco processing industry are merged into food manufacturing and tobacco processing industry in the input-output table. The clothing and other fibre products manufacturing industry and the leather, fur, and their products industry are merged into textile clothing, shoes, caps, leather, down and their products industry. Chemical raw materials and chemicals, chemical fiber manufacturing, pharmaceutical manufacturing, plastic products and rubber products are merged into chemical industry. General machinery manufacturing industry and special equipment manufacturing industry are merged into general special equipment manufacturing industry. In addition, the transportation, warehousing and postal industries listed in the input-output table are classified as transportation, storage and postal industries; the wholesale and retail industries, accommodation and catering industries are classified as wholesale and retail and trade retail and catering industries; and other services are classified as non-material production industries. Correspondingly, the sum of energy consumption for living consumption and energy consumption for other industries in energy data is merged into energy consumption for non-material production industries, so that we can get a table of energy input and output for 29 industries. The method of estimating is to get a new non-material production department after classifying the relevant departments, recalculate the direct consumption coefficient matrix and the total consumption coefficient matrix of the input-output table, and then calculate the proportion of the departments to be estimated in all industries. According to this proportion, the indexes of all industries in the non-material production department are estimated. In the process of calculation, as far as possible, according to the investment. Standards for 42 departments in the Input-output Table.

3.2 Correlation Coefficient of Input–output Model of Economic Development Mode

3.2.1 Induced coefficient of domestic demand

Whether from the perspective of coordinating consumption, investment, import and export "troika", or the perspective of economic development from external demand to domestic, as an important component of final demand, the role of consumption in the transformation of economic development mode can not be ignored. According to the contents, the final consumption can be divided into resident consumption and government purchase; from the perspective of industry, the impact of the final demand of various industries on the national economy is different. In order to study the role of the final consumption demand of different industries in the national economy, this book takes advantage of the economic development mode of the preceding section to demonstrate the equilibrium between input and output, and quotes the concept of production induction coefficient. Production inducement refers to the change of the final demand of a certain type, which causes the change of the output of other sectors through the interdepartmental relationship. It is expressed by formula as the sum of the pulling effect of the final product demand of j unit on various sectors of the national economy and the product of j department for the final demand of a certain type. The production inducement coefficient is the ratio of total production inducement and the corresponding final demand. In the input-output alignment model of the previous section, assuming that the final demand column vector is D, according to the formula (19) of the previous section, we can see that the production induction coefficient of a final use can be expressed as [1]:

$$R = (I - \hat{\alpha})^{-1}D \tag{20}$$

When D expressing the final demand of consumption, then R can be expressed as the final demand inducing factor of consumption; similarly, the final production inducing factor of final investment and import and export can be obtained in the same way. The implication of production inducement coefficient is the sum of the pulling effect of a unit on the final demand structure of the i industry on all sectors of the national economy. The larger the production inducement coefficient, the greater the production impact of the final demand of this industry.

Considering that the export of intermediate inputs is not directly

---

[1]   In the input-output theory, the induced production refers to the change of the final demand of a certain type, which causes the increase of the output of other departments through the interdepartmental relationship. The output induced by the final demand of category K to sector I reflects the impact of the final product demand of sector J on the national economy. The production inducement coefficient is the ratio of the total production inducement and the corresponding final demand, which indicates the change of the production of the second sector induced by the change of the final demand of the K type according to the structure of a unit.

related to domestic consumption, in order to analyze the inductive effect of consumption on the national economy, it is necessary to eliminate the influence of export factors. This part adjusts the inducing factor of production. The specific method is: according to the proportion of the export products of each department in the total domestic use, the industry is deducted by share. According to the identity relation in the input-output table, the total domestic use = total output + import-export = intermediate product + domestic final use.

Assume that the proportion of total domestic consumption in China is α, the calculation formula is: α =(Total Output-Export)/Total Use. $\hat{\alpha}$ is a diagonal Matrix for domestic use as a proportion of domestic production, then the formula for calculating the production induction coefficient of final consumption can be expressed as: $R = (I - \hat{\alpha})^{-1}C$, among them, R is the final use of the production induction coefficient column vector. $(I - \hat{\alpha})^{-1}$ is the Leontief inverse matrix that eliminates the effect of exports. C column vector representing final consumption coefficient, R represents the production-induced forehead vector caused by the corresponding final consumption. The production inducement coefficient is the ratio of the production inducement and the corresponding final demand aggregate. The calculation results of the consumption inducement coefficient are present as Table 3-2.

Table 3–2 2002–2007 Domestic Demand Pulling Coefficient

2002		2005		2007	
Education	76.828	Public administration and social organization	37.365	Public administration and social organization	166.52
Health, social security and welfare	31.152	Oil and gas mining	10.987	Scrap waste	65.538
Metal mining industry	12.925	Education	7.508	Oil and gas mining	58.022
Oil and gas mining	9.969	Metal mining industry	5.678	Metal mining industry	55.984
Scrap waste	5.918	Health and social security welfare	5.419	Research and experimental development industry	35.093

continued

2002		2005		2007	
Metal smelting and rolling industry	4.151	Non-metallic mining industry	4.931	Health, social security and welfare	16.620
Integrated technical services	2.589	Petroleum processing and nuclear fuel processing	3.051	Education	10.355
Culture, sports and entertainment	2.566	Management of water conservancy and other public facilities	2.251	Instrumentation and office machinery manufacturing	5.714
Residential services and other services	2.444	The chemical industry	2.242	Water conservancy and other public facilities management industry	2.990
Water conservancy and other public facilities management industry	2.247	Accommodation and catering	2.123	Culture, sports and entertainment	2.234
Research and experimental development industry	2.103	Integrated technical services	2.047	Non-metallic ore and other mineral mining industry	2.098
Petroleum processing and nuclear fuel processing industry	2.073	Culture, sports and entertainment	1.997	Residential services and other services	1.888
The real estate industry	2.053	Metal smelting and rolling industry	1.980	Petroleum processing and nuclear fuel processing industry	1.685
Food manufacturing and tobacco processing industries	1.973	Gas production and supply industry	1.935	Accommodation and catering	1.677
The chemical industry	1.699	Financial insurance	1.913	Food manufacturing and tobacco processing industries	1.661
Gas production and supply industry	1.664	Scientific research	1.671	The real estate industry	1.413
Accommodation and catering	1.662	Residential services and other services	1.640	The chemical industry	1.394
Communication equipment and computer equipment manufacturing	1.552	Leasing and business services	1.518	Gas production and supply industry	1.387
The financial sector	1.539	Communication equipment and computer equipment	1.465	Water production and supply industry	1.376
Agriculture, forestry, animal husbandry and fishery	1.533	The postal service	1.401	Agriculture, forestry, animal husbandry and fishery	1.357

137

continued

2002		2005		2007	
The postal service	1.482	Agriculture, forestry, animal husbandry and fishery	1.378	The financial sector	1.317
Water production and supply industry	1.349	The real estate industry	1.254	Leasing and business services	1.306
Non-metallic ore and other mineral mining industry	1.325	Water production and supply industry	1.235	Communication equipment and computer equipment	1.179
Power and heat production and supply industry	1.128	Food manufacturing and tobacco processing industries	1.210	Information transmission, computers and software	1.093
Electrical machinery and equipment manufacturing industry	1.109	Power and heat production and supply	1.053	The postal service	1.075
Nonmetallic mineral products industry	1.049	Information transmission, computer software industry	1.033	Power and heat production and supply industry	1.060
Leasing and business services	1.020	Transportation and warehousing	0.931	Integrated technical services	0.859
Information transmission, computer software	0.992	Electrical, mechanical and equipment manufacturing	0.925	Coal mining and washing industry	0.852
Textile, clothing, shoes, hats and other products	0.938	Clothing leather down and its products	0.738	Textile, clothing, shoes, hats and other products	0.840
Arts and crafts and other manufacturing industries	0.768	Other manufacturing	0.694	Metal smelting and rolling industry	0.802
Paper printing and cultural and educational products manufacturing industry	0.763	Paper printing and cultural and educational supplies	0.678	Wholesale and retail	0.771
Textile industry	0.748	Nonmetallic mineral products industry	0.581	Transportation and warehousing	0.726
Transportation and warehousing	0.723	Metal products industry	0.570	Arts and crafts and other manufacturing industries	0.606
Metal products industry	0.609	Textile industry	0.479	Paper printing and cultural and educational products manufacturing	0.492
Wood processing and furniture manufacturing	0.588	Wholesale and retail trade	0.445	Electrical machinery and equipment manufacturing industry	0.490

continued

2002		2005		2007	
Wholesale and retail	0.550	General and special equipment manufacturing	0.408	Transportation equipment manufacturing industry	0.409
General and special equipment manufacturing	0.548	Wood processing and furniture manufacturing	0.401	General and special equipment manufacturing	0.394
Coal mining and washing industry	0.485	Transportation equipment manufacturing industry	0.361	Nonmetallic mineral products industry	0.372
Transportation equipment manufacturing industry	0.470	The construction industry	0.003	Metal products industry	0.208
The construction industry	0.003	Scrap waste	0.000	Wood processing and furniture manufacturing	0.203
Public administration and social organization	12.63	Coal mining and washing industry	0.29	Textile industry	0.151
Instrumentation and office machinery manufacturing	−278	Instrument and office machinery manufacturing	2.78	The construction industry	0.020

Data Source: China Input-output Table; China National Bureau of Statistics.

From the calculation results, it can be seen that there are two main types of industries with high consumption-driven coefficient between 2002 and 2007: (1) public services, such as education, health, social security and social welfare, have consumption-driven coefficients greater than 5 in both industries during the inspection period, and the coefficients in the inspection areas of water conservancy, environment and public facilities management are greater than 2, and comprehensive technology services in the year of 2002 and 2007. The five-year coefficients were all greater than 2, and decreased slightly to 0.859 in 2007, approaching 1. The coefficients of residential services and other services were greater than 1 in the period of investigation, 2.444 in 2002 and more than 2 times of consumption induction coefficient. The value of R&D coefficients varies greatly, but they remain above 1. Especially in 2007, the value of R&D coefficients is as high as 35.093. The reason for this change may lie in the fact that a large proportion of fiscal expenditure was invested in R&D in that year, which enlarged domestic demand. The large consumption inducing coefficient of education indicates that the policy of expanding university enrollment, as one of the schemes of expanding domestic demand, is correct and effective. However, the consumption inducing coefficient of education decreases gradually from 2002 to 2007, which also shows that the effect of the policy of expanding domestic demand by education has the law of diminishing marginal utility. It may also be that the population and the population of school-age are decreasing year by year. It also shows that the policy of expanding domestic demand by education in China must be adjusted eventually. Health, social security, social welfare and water conservancy, environment and public facilities management belong to the public expenditure industry of the government. Government expenditure is an important part of domestic consumption, and the public service industry not only has the needs from families, but also government purchases. (2) Resources industry. The coefficients of petroleum and natural gas mining, metal mining and processing, petroleum processing and nuclear fuel processing industries remained above 2 during the inspection period. The mining and dressing coefficients of non-metallic minerals are greater than 1, up to 4.931 in 2005. Resources industry is not only related to production, but also to consumption. It is an indispensable part of the national economy production and life, which belongs to the rigid part of domestic demand and is an important support for production and life. Most of the resource products consumed by residents belong to necessities, such as coal for heating, natural gas for daily use, and demand elasticity is very small. The price of resource products produced is not flexible, and some productive resource products such as industrial electricity are also subject to government control. Unless there are new technologies or new sources for energy use, the domestic demand-driven effects of resource consumption will not be fully released. (3) Industries related to people's living standards, such as culture, sports and entertainment, accommodation and catering, postal industry, water production and supply, power and heat production and supply, gas production and supply, etc. The value of such domestic demand driving factor exceeds 1. These industries are closely related to people's clothing, food and housing. The elasticity of demand for production and supply of water, gas and electricity is relatively stable. However, the demand for accommodation and catering industry and culture, sports and entertainment industry is relatively large, and its development is becoming more active with the improvement of people's quality of life and the increase of income level. There are few imports and exports, so the domestic demand driving effect is very obvious. (4) In the manufacturing industry, the coefficients of chemical industry, communication equipment and computer equipment manufacturing industry, food manufacturing and processing industry exceed 1. However, China's textile industry, clothing, shoes and hats, handicraft and other manufacturing industries with strong competitive advantages, and transportation equipment manufacturing industry have relatively small domestic demand driving factor values, which indicates that domestic demand in these industries has been basically saturated and therefore seldom sold at home, and the products are mainly exported from abroad. But the import and export competitiveness of the chemical industry and computer equipment manufacturing industry domestic demand driving role is also strong, we will analyze it in detail in the next section.

3.2.2 Import and export inducement

In the study of China's import and export induced role, this part uses the concept of production induction in the previous section to examine the driving effect of the final import and export demand of various industries on the national economy. According to formula (20), the formula for calculating the production induced amount of the final import and export demand is expressed as follows: $R = (I - \hat{a})^{-1}E$, in which, α diagonal matrix representing the proportion of total import and export to total demand. $(I - \hat{a})^{-1}$ Is the Leontief inverse matrix of the diagonal matrix constructed, E is the column vector of the structural coefficient of the final import and export demand and the column vector of the proportion of the final import and export demand to the total demand. R represents the column vectors of the production induction coefficients caused by the corresponding final import and export. The calculation results are shown in Table 3-3.

The data show that in the past 2002–2007 years, communications equipment and computer equipment manufacturing, chemical industry, electrical and mechanical and equipment manufacturing, general and special equipment manufacturing, metal mining and mining, metal smelting and calendering processing, transportation equipment manufacturing, textile, clothing, leather, feather and shoe hats and other fiber manufacturing industries are all import and export industries that are highly inducing. Owners are mainly concentrated on the industrial manufacturing industry, which is also a key industry in the period of industrialization in China. The greater import and export inducement also reflects the comparative advantages of these industries to a certain extent: compared with other industries, industries with larger import and export inducement coefficient have stronger competitive advantages in the international market, and may also be related to the historical stage and the demand structure of the international market in this season, during which the demand of these products is relatively strong. On the one hand, the import and export volume of metal mining and dressing industry is relatively large because of the small supply and large demand of some products in the international market; on the other hand, the domestic demand for some products in the industry is relatively large, resulting in the situation that both import and export are vigorous, which shows that the international and domestic markets of China's metal mining and dressing industry products are complementary. It is worth our attention that the instrument and cultural office machinery manufacturing industry and some industries which mainly rely on domestic production and supply and cannot be imported or exported, such as health, social security and social welfare, education, heat, gas and water production and supply, water and environment and other public facilities management industries, have little or even negative import and export inducing effect. In the period of investigation, China mainly imports advanced technology-intensive industries, such as instruments and cultural office machinery manufacturing, and imports are far greater than exports. According to the data, the adjustment item of the final demand item in the input-output table is negative, which offsets the contribution of import and export to total output, and makes the ratio of import and export to total output greater than 1, so the inducing amount of import and export in the industry is negative. This may attribute to the serious loss of tangible and intangible products in the import and export process, and of course, it may also be a statistical error. In addition, the calculation results show that the industries with greater import and export inducement are concentrated in the telecommunication equipment manufacturing industry, electrical, machinery and equipment manufacturing industry and textile industry, have obvious export advantages. They belong to labor-intensive industries. Even the machinery manufacturing industry belongs to the processing trade of assembled parts. The export products are underprocessed and are at the low end among the value chain in the international division of labor. Ming Dynasty, China's foreign trade development mode is still dominated by the traditional extensive form.

Table 3–3 Import and Export Inducement (2002–2007)
(current year price, unit: ten thousand yuan)

2002		2005		2007	
Communication equipment and computer manufacturing	55972.48	The chemical industry	18163.2	Communication and computer equipment manufacturing industry	441630.8
The chemical industry	7866.65	General and special equipment manufacturing	13591.5	The chemical industry	22193.41
Electrical, mechanical and equipment manufacturing	7690.71	Electrical, mechanical and equipment manufacturing	13580.5	General and special equipment manufacturing	18896.06
Textile industry	6949.05	Textile industry	11839.6	Electrical machinery and equipment manufacturing industry	16492.91
General and special equipment manufacturing	6748.99	Clothing leather down and its products	8968.87	Oil and gas mining	15767.85
Clothing leather down and its products	6197.29	Metal mining industry	7584.75	Textile industry	14083.71
Wholesale and retail trade	2972.58	Petroleum processing and nuclear fuel processing	7481.79	Metal mining industry	12861.88
Metal smelting and rolling industry	2550.49	Transportation and warehousing	6394.95	Metal smelting and rolling industry	11215.53
Leasing and business services	2334.44	Metal smelting and rolling industry	6161.84	Leasing and business services	10746.19
Metal products industry	2194.19	Metal products industry	6137.64	Textile and clothing and its products	9627.66
Transportation equipment manufacturing industry	2000.58	Wholesale and retail trade	5992.98	Transportation equipment manufacturing industry	7765.36
Paper printing and cultural and educational supplies	1993.7	Transportation equipment manufacturing industry	4230.25	Transportation and warehousing	6001.50
Oil and gas mining	1939.94	Paper printing and cultural and educational supplies	4042.25	Metal products industry	5408.94
Transportation and warehousing	1918.634	Residential services and other services	3827.35	Wholesale and retail	4654.52
Other social services	1620.66	Food manufacturing and tobacco processing industries	2804.18	Paper printing and cultural and educational products manufacturing	3901.07

continued

2002		2005		2007	
Food manufacturing and tobacco processing industries	1575.11	Wood processing and furniture manufacturing	2677.52	Food manufacturing and tobacco processing industries	3812.35
Agricultural, forestry, animal husbandry and fishery	1204.03	Agricultural, forestry, animal husbandry and fishery	2467.94	Wood processing and furniture manufacturing	3570.09
Wood processing and furniture manufacturing	1095.21	Scrap waste	2044.46	Agriculture, forestry, animal husbandry and fishery	3189.23
Petroleum processing and nuclear fuel processing	899.71	Leasing and business services	1947.53	Petroleum processing and nuclear fuel processing	2478.87
Other manufacturing	698.09	Accommodation and catering	1745.84	Scrap waste	2149.39
Nonmetallic mineral products industry	688.68	Oil and gas mining	1539.01	Arts and crafts and other manufacturing industries	2035.88
Metal mining industry	524.32	Nonmetallic mineral products industry	1292.20	Nonmetallic mineral products industry	2026.36
Non-metallic mining industry	414.90	Other manufacturing	1027.48	Accommodation and catering	1376.96
Accommodation and catering	377.24	Non-metallic mining industry	889.49	Research and experimental development industry	1225.90
Culture, sports and entertainment	367.01	Financial insurance	705.06	Information transmission, computers and software	923.35
Financial insurance	310.51	Information transfer and computer software	520.57	Culture, sports and entertainment	768.83
Information transfer and computer software	253.96	Coal mining and washing industry	395.92	The construction industry	636.53
Coal mining and washing industry	195.49	The construction industry	348.07	Residential services and other services	516.02
The construction industry	185.58	Culture, sports and entertainment	309.80	Non-metallic ore and other ore mining	510.65
The tourism industry	143.71	Public administration and social organization	92.20	Coal mining and washing industry	445.61
Public administration and social organization	68.07	Production and supply of electric heat	77.31	The financial sector	217.83
Power and heat production and supply	62.38	The postal service	43.26	Public administration and social organization	107.87

continued

2002		2005		2007	
Scrap waste	37.12	Gas production and supply industry	0	Production and supply of electricity and heat	83.32
Education career	25.52	Water production and supply industry	0	Education	73.67
Gas production and supply industry	0.002	The real estate industry	0	Health, social security and welfare	62.63
Water production and supply industry	0	Scientific research	0	Gas production and supply industry	0
The real estate industry	0	Integrated technical services	0	Water production and supply industry	0
Scientific research	0	Education	0	The real estate industry	0
Integrated technical services	0	Health, social security and welfare	0	Integrated technical services	0
Health, social security and welfare	0	Instrumentation and office manufacturing	−6507.5	Water conservancy and other public facilities management industry	0
Instruments and cultural office	−3719.49	Communication equipment and computer equipment	−2200688	Instrumentation and office machinery manufacturing	−15288.6

Data Source: China Input-output Table; China National Bureau of Statistics.

3.2.3 Investment multiplier

Investment and consumption, as well as import and export, belong to the final demand part of the input-output table. In this part, we still use the algorithm of production inducement coefficient to calculate the production inducement coefficient of investment, that is, investment multiplier. According to formula (20), the formula for calculating the production induced amount of the final investment demand is expressed as $R = (I - \hat{\alpha})^{-1} I$, in which, $\hat{\alpha}$ is the diagonal matrix of the proportion of fixed asset investment in the total output of the whole society. $(I - \hat{\alpha})^{-1}$ is leontief inverse matrix of diagonal matrix, I is the column vector of the structural coefficient of the final investment demand and the proportion of the final investment demand to the total demand. R represents the corresponding column vectors of the production induction coefficient caused by the investment in fixed assets of the whole society. The calculation results are shown in Table 3-4.

The results show that during the period of 2002–2007, (1) the industries with large investment multiplier and stable investment are mainly concentrated in heavy industry: petroleum processing, coking and nuclear fuel processing, chemical industry and metal products industry. The petroleum processing, coking and nuclear fuel processing industries in 2002, 2005 and 2007 all maintained the top three in the national economy. Secondly, the chemical industry, the investment multiplier coefficient values of the three inspection periods are greater than 5. These two industries are also capital-intensive industries. The large investment multiplier indicates that the marginal output of investment has not yet declined, and investment can still play a greater role in the development of the industry. The investment multiplier of non-metallic mining and processing industry is negative in 2005 and 2007, which indicates that the investment efficiency of this industry is very low. These industries are small and many, widely distributed and scattered, and the waste of investment is serious.

(2) The major industries with greater leverage effect of investment in service industry are information transmission, computer service and software industry, financial insurance industry, leasing and business service industry, wholesale and retail industry, culture, sports and entertainment industry. The service industry itself is not a capital-intensive industry, and the investment efficiency of these highly efficient services is more remarkable in the productive service industry, such as information transmission, computer services and software industry, financial insurance industry, rental and business services.

(3) The investment multiplier of the primary industry or the industry with strong forward linkages with the primary industry is also larger, including agriculture, forestry, animal husbandry and fishery, textile industry, food and tobacco processing industry, wood processing

and furniture manufacturing industry, paper printing and cultural and educational supplies manufacturing industry. It can be seen that the investment in these industries is unsaturated. Investment can bring greater marginal benefits to these industries. It is still profitable to invest in these industries.

(4) The investment multiplier of industries with high operation cost, large investment, long cycle and small marginal output is small. For example, transportation, warehousing, construction, real estate and energy industries such as oil and natural gas exploitation, electricity, heat production and supply, water production and supply industries have negative investment driving effect, which indicates that the marginal return of investment in the above industries has tended to decline marginally and there is overinvestment. In addition, most of these industries with small investment multiplier are state-owned monopoly industries, with large institutions and low investment output efficiency, which shows that investment efficiency is closely related to owner structure and nature of the industry.

Table 3–4   Investment Multiplier

2002		2005		2007	
Scrap waste	158.77	Nonmetallic mineral products industry	68.171	Oil and nuclear fuel processing industry	526.649
Metal mining industry	104.98	The chemical industry	24.065	Metal smelting and rolling processing	32.419
Metal smelting and rolling processing	52.079	Oil and nuclear fuel processing industry	10.279	The chemical industry	15.026
Petroleum processing and nuclear fuel processing	22.972	Gas production and supply industry	9.6648	Paper printing and cultural and educational supplies	10.541
Non-metallic mining industry	10.408	Leasing and business services	8.3479	The postal service	7.7731
Coal mining and washing industry	9.4464	Paper printing and cultural and educational supplies	6.4972	Scientific research	7.7072
Electricity and other production and supply industries	8.3010	Information transfer computer software	5.5274	Metal products industry	5.0853

continued

2002		2005		2007	
Nonmetallic mineral products industry	8.1069	Metal products industry	5.1318	Financial insurance	4.4790
The chemical industry	6.2414	Metal mining industry	4.6108	Culture, sports and entertainment	4.0700
Financial insurance	5.0908	Wood processing and furniture manufacturing	3.9762	Agriculture, forestry, animal husbandry and fishery	3.8362
Paper printing and cultural and educational supplies	4.7786	Culture, sports and entertainment	3.5260	Information transfer and computer software	3.5295
Information transfer and computer software	4.3119	Textile industry	3.2696	Wood processing and furniture manufacturing	3.4808
Leasing and business services	4.0105	Agriculture, forestry, animal husbandry and fishery	3.1894	Textile industry	3.4574
Gas production and supply industry	3.7545	Financial insurance	3.0061	Accommodation and catering	2.8742
Residents and other social services	3.6003	The postal service	2.6487	Leasing and business services	2.8458
Metal products industry	3.5266	Accommodation and catering	2.5784	Food manufacturing and tobacco processing industries	2.5936
Wood processing and furniture manufacturing	3.4631	Transportation equipment manufacturing industry	2.3564	Wholesale and retail	2.5539
Wholesale and retail	2.7364	Scientific research	2.2761	Transportation equipment manufacturing industry	2.4857
Textile industry	2.5750	Wholesale and retail	2.2623	Electrical, mechanical and equipment manufacturing	2.2594
Agriculture, forestry, animal husbandry and fishery	2.4596	Electrical, mechanical and equipment manufacturing	2.2432	General and special equipment manufacturing	2.1971
Transportation equipment manufacturing industry	2.3092	Craft products and other manufacturing	2.0936	Residents and other social services	2.1592
Accommodation and catering	2.0526	Food manufacturing and tobacco processing industries	2.0075	Craft products and other manufacturing	2.0553
Electrical, mechanical and equipment manufacturing	2.0087	General and special equipment manufacturing	1.6053	The tourism industry	1.9428
Other manufacturing	2.0000	Residents and other social services	1.5744	Clothing leather down and its products	1.7460
Integrated technical services	1.8474	The tourism industry	1.5632	Communication equipment and computer equipment	1.6043

continued

2002		2005		2007	
Culture, sports and entertainment	1.8099	Education career	1.5351	Education career	1.3668
Food manufacturing and tobacco processing industries	1.7776	Communication equipment and computer equipment	1.4184	Public administration and social organization	1.2232
General and special equipment manufacturing	1.7003	Clothing leather down and its products	1.3613	Health, social security and welfare	1.1505
Communication equipment and computer equipment	1.4667	Health social security and welfare	1.3285	Instrumentation and office machinery	1.1413
The real estate industry	1.4527	Public administration and social organization	1.2786	The construction industry	1.0596
The tourism industry	1.3914	The construction industry	1.0197	Integrated technical services	0.275
Scientific research	1.3718	Instrumentation and office machinery	0.6796	The real estate industry	0.837
Clothing leather down and its products	1.2991	Scrap waste	0.0000	Water production and supply industry	2.295
Education career	1.2053	Integrated technical services	0.379	Oil and gas mining	4.831
Health social security and welfare	1.1022	The real estate industry	1.212	The production and supply of electricity	5.737
Public administration and social organization	1.0670	Water production and supply industry	2.971	Transportation and warehousing	6.690
The construction industry	1.0377	Coal mining and washing industry	3.231	Coal mining and washing industry	6.935
Instrumentation and office machinery	0.9411	The production and supply of electricity, etc	4.051	Metal mining industry	8.743
The postal service	1.6144	Oil and gas mining	4.276	Nonmetallic mineral products industry	23.08
Oil and gas mining	9.4509	Metal smelting and rolling processing	26.18	Non-metallic mining industry	25.47
Water production and supply industry	31.600	Non-metallic mining industry	46.08	Gas production and supply industry	57.20
Transportation and warehousing	45.618	Transportation and warehousing	293.0	Scrap waste	81.05

Data Source: China Input-output Table; China National Bureau of Statistics.

3.2.4 Employment coefficient

Whatever way economic development takes, it must be conducive to promoting the employment. The way of development which is not conducive to the employment of labor force is not consistent with the core of "people-oriented", and it is also an unsustainable development mode. Therefore, it is necessary to investigate the ability of various industries to promote employment. The partial closed-loop model of economic development mode can be used to calculate the complete pull effect of the final demand of each department on employment. In this part, the input-output model of economic development mode is extended, and the residential sector is regarded as a production sector and considered as one of the intermediate flow matrices. The input-output line vectors of residents' departments represent the sum of the remuneration and income received by residents from various departments. The column vectors of residents' departments reflect the consumption of commodities and services of residents in various departments. Residents' labor remuneration has a chain reaction to the production of various industries. After the increase of labor remuneration, residents' demand for products and services of various departments will inevitably expand, thus stimulating the development of production in various departments. The chain reaction is expressed as a direct consumption coefficient matrix A^* expressed as.

$$A^* = \begin{bmatrix} a_{11} & \cdots & a_{1n} & a_{1,n+1} \\ \cdots & \cdots & \cdots & \cdots \\ a_{n1} & \cdots & a_{nn} & a_{n,n+1} \\ a_{n+1,1} & \cdots & a_{n+1,n} & a_{n+1,n+1} \end{bmatrix} = \begin{bmatrix} A & C \\ W^* & c \end{bmatrix} \tag{21}$$

In the formula, the transverse vector W^* representing the remuneration and income of residents from various industries, C represents the ratio of income and remuneration to consumption of products in various sectors , c represents the payment coefficient of residents. Then the extended total consumption coefficient matrix is obtained by using the extended matrix A^*:

$$B^* = (I-A^*)^{-1} - I \tag{22}$$

And extended complete demand coefficient matrix

$$\tilde{B}^* = (I - A^*)^{-1} \tag{23}$$

$(I-A^*)^{-1}$ reflects the sum of the direct and indirect demand for products from the national economy and other sectors caused by intermediate input. Because of the limitation of data, in order to concentrate the research scope on the employment of labor force, simplify the above model, the occupancy coefficient of labor force in various industries of the national economy is used as the driving role of various sectors in employment. The direct occupancy coefficients of labor force in various industries are expressed by vectors:

$$l_j = \frac{L_j}{X_j}(j = 1,2,\cdots, n) \tag{24}$$

The coefficient of employment-driven effect described as follow:

$$\tilde{l}_j = l_j^T(I - A^{*\prime})^{-1} \tag{25}$$

According to the above methods, the results of the coefficient of employment-driven effect are shown in Table 3-5. The results show that: (1) The industries with higher labor driving coefficient generally enter the industries with lower threshold, such as communication equipment, computer and other electronic equipment manufacturing, textile industry, clothing, footwear and caps, clothing accessories and other fibre products, leather down and its products, construction industry, etc. Textile and apparel leather and down manufacturing industry has simple operation, low requirements for skilled technology, no specific requirements for human capital, and low employment threshold. Although the construction industry has corresponding requirements for technology, it is easy to train the skilled workers, so it has a strong ability to absorb employment. Although the manufacturing industry of communication equipment and computer and other equipment is relatively capital and technology intensive, China is still in the low-end sector in the international industrial chain. Most of our country is engaged in the assembly and processing of simple parts. Although it is capital-intensive, it also invests heavily in labor.

(2) The industry entry threshold is higher in instrumentation and cultural office machinery manufacturing, gas production and supply and non-metallic mineral products industry, as well as in the third industry of education, finance, information transmission, computer services and software industry, and real estate service industry, and the employment coefficient is relatively small. Electrical appliances, machinery manufacturing, instrumentation and cultural office, non-metallic mineral products industry generally has higher technical requirements for practitioners; education, finance and information transmission computer services have higher requirements for human capital and high entry threshold. Others are engaged in industries with certain risks, such as oil and gas extraction industry, and the less popular waste industry employment driving role is not obvious.

(3) In addition, there are also some industries in which the public sector itself does not need much labor, such as public facilities management, public management and social organization, residential services and other services. Certain industries themselves are labor substitutes, which naturally have the function of excluding unskilled labor force, such as information transmission and computer software industry, as well as some capital-intensive industries, such as transportation equipment manufacturing, transportation and warehousing industry and electrical, mechanical and equipment manufacturing industry. The employment coefficient of labor force in these industries is very small.

Table 3–5   Labor Force Driving Coefficient

2002		2005		2007	
Accommodation and catering	0.0850	Gas production and supply industry	0.0836	Water production and supply industry	0.1141
Research and experimental development industry	0.0801	Communication equipment and computer equipment	0.0835	Communication equipment and computer equipment	0.1003
Food manufacturing and tobacco processing	0.0753	Clothing leather and other products	0.0788	Electricity production and supply	0.0999
Gas production and supply industry	0.0752	Transportation equipment manufacturing industry	0.0782	Textile and garment industry	0.0960
Culture, sports and entertainment	0.0627	Electricity production and supply	0.0778	Gas production and supply industry	0.0949
Textile and garment industry	0.0618	Instrumentation and office machinery manufacturing	0.0762	Textile industry	0.0945
Petroleum processing and nuclear fuel processing	0.0606	Textile industry	0.0742	Instrumentation and office machinery manufacturing	0.0945
The postal service	0.0582	Electrical, mechanical and equipment manufacturing	0.0741	Transportation equipment manufacturing industry	0.0927
Communication equipment and computer equipment	0.0580	The chemical industry	0.0737	Petroleum processing and nuclear fuel processing	0.0920
The construction industry	0.0577	General and special equipment manufacturing	0.0718	The chemical industry	0.0919
Electrical machinery and equipment manufacturing	0.0575	Nonmetallic mineral products industry	0.0717	Electrical machinery and equipment manufacturing	0.0907
Wood processing and furniture manufacturing	0.0574	Leasing and business services	0.0716	Leasing and business services	0.0888
Nonmetallic mineral products industry	0.0566	Metal products industry	0.0711	Nonmetallic mineral products industry	0.0876
Metal products industry	0.0558	Integrated technical services	0.0707	The construction industry	0.0875
Instrumentation and office machinery manufacturing	0.0555	Metal smelting and rolling processing	0.0699	General purpose, special equipment manufacturing	0.0854
Metal smelting and rolling processing	0.0555	Paper printing and cultural and educational products manufacturing	0.0696	Paper printing and cultural and educational products manufacturing	0.0844
Arts and crafts and other manufacturing industries	0.0551	Health, social security and welfare	0.0692	Metal smelting and rolling industry	0.0841
The chemical industry	0.0550	Scientific research	0.0683	Metal products industry	0.0837
Textile industry	0.0548	The construction industry	0.0682	Arts and crafts and other manufacturing industries	0.0834

continued

2002		2005		2007	
General purpose, special equipment manufacturing	0.0533	Wood processing and furniture manufacturing	0.0681	Wood processing and furniture manufacturing	0.0827
Integrated technical services	0.0532	Other manufacturing	0.0667	Health and social security benefits	0.0794
Public administration and social organization	0.0528	Non-metallic mining industry	0.0666	Metal mining industry	0.0773
Leasing and business services	0.0525	Metal mining industry	0.0638	Coal mining and washing industry	0.0772
Metal mining industry	0.0518	Petroleum processing and nuclear fuel processing	0.0613	Food manufacturing and tobacco processing	0.0760
Residential services and other services	0.0502	Management of water conservancy and other public facilities	0.0607	Culture, sports and entertainment	0.0758
Water production and supply industry	0.0495	Water production and supply industry	0.0583	The postal service	0.0758
Transportation equipment manufacturing industry	0.0492	Coal mining and washing industry	0.0579	Water conservancy and other public facilities management industry	0.0754
Paper printing and cultural and educational products manufacturing	0.0471	The postal service	0.0566	Research and experimental development industry	0.0750
Transportation and warehousing	0.0471	Culture, sports and entertainment	0.0564	Non-metallic ore and other mineral mining industry	0.0742
Electricity and other production and supply industries	0.0470	Transportation and warehousing	0.0522	Public administration and social organization	0.0716
Non-metallic ore and other mineral mining industry	0.0465	Information transmission, computer software	0.0522	Education	0.0687
Water conservancy and other public facilities management industry	0.0453	Residential services and other services	0.0520	Accommodation and catering	0.0676
Wholesale and retail	0.0449	Food manufacturing and tobacco processing industries	0.0518	Residential services and other services	0.0672
Agriculture, forestry, animal husbandry and fishery	0.0425	Accommodation and catering	0.0504	Transportation and warehousing	0.0647
Education	0.0420	Public administration and social organization	0.0477	Integrated technical services	0.0646
Coal mining and washing industry	0.0414	Education	0.0404	Wholesale and retail	0.0557

continued

2002		2005		2007	
Health, social security and welfare	0.0392	Financial insurance	0.0390	Information transmission, computer software industry	0.0530
Information transmission, computer software	0.0389	Agriculture, forestry, animal husbandry and fishery	0.0329	Oil and gas mining	0.0489
The financial sector	0.0381	Oil and gas mining	0.0305	The financial sector	0.0480
Real estate service	0.0275	Wholesale and retail trade	0.0290	Agriculture, forestry, animal husbandry and fishery	0.0461
Oil and gas mining	0.0266	Real estate service	0.0205	Real estate service	0.0229
Scrap waste	0.0000	Scrap waste	0.0000	Scrap waste	0.0099

Data Source: China Input-output Table; China National Bureau of Statistics.

3.2.5 Energy consumption coefficient

As analysis required, all data units of energy consumption in this part are calculated with 10000 tons of standard coal. Following the standards of industry integration in Section I, the energy consumption departments of the national economy are divided into 29 sectors. Because the measurement units of physical energy products are different, the expression of the nematic equilibrium relationship of the energy input-output model is not of general significance. Therefore, only the energy input-output line model is established here, which can be expressed as follows:

$$\sum_{j=1}^{k}\tilde{z}_{ij}^{EN}+\sum_{j=k+1}^{n}z_{ij}^{EN}+\varepsilon_i^E+\tilde{f}_i^E=\tilde{x}_i^E(i=1,2,\cdots,k) \tag{26}$$

Define the direct consumption coefficient matrix A and the complete consumption coefficient matrix B as follows:

$$A=\begin{bmatrix}A^{EE}&A^{EN}\\A^{NE}&A^{NN}\end{bmatrix}, B=(I-A)^{-1}-I=\begin{bmatrix}B^{EE}&B^{EN}\\B^{NE}&B^{NN}\end{bmatrix}, \tag{27}$$

In which

$$A^{EE}=(a_{ij}^{EE})_{k\times k}=(\tilde{z}_{ij}^{EE}/\tilde{x}_j^E)k\times k \tag{28}$$

A^{EE}, A^{EN} indicate the consumption of energy production industries to energy production industries, and energy consumption of energy production industries to non-energy production industries, a_{ij}^{EE} represent the direct consumption coefficient of energy consumption of j.

1. Direct comprehensive energy consumption

Direct comprehensive energy consumption is the direct consumption of energy in the production process of every unit product. The direct energy consumption coefficient matrix A^E is composed by the first k lines of the direct energy consumption coefficient matrix A:

$$A^E = \begin{bmatrix} A^{EE} & A^{EN} \end{bmatrix} \tag{29}$$

The direct comprehensive energy consumption is the sum of the direct consumption coefficients of all the energy consumption in the unit output production process calculated according to the standard coal. The formula for calculating the direct comprehensive energy consumption of the j product is as follows:

$$d_j^{EE} = \sum_{i=1}^{k} \eta_i a_{ij}^{EE} (j = 1, \cdots, \ k) \tag{30}$$

In which, d_j^{EE} represent direct comprehensive energy consumption of energy products in industry j; η_i represent energy conversion coefficient of i, if we converted various energy sources into standard coal ,the coal consumption coefficient after conversion is expressed as a vector $\eta' = (\eta_i)_{1 \times k}$,

Write it in vector form as follows:

$$D^{E'} = \eta' A^E = \begin{bmatrix} \eta' A^{EE}, \eta' A^{EN} \end{bmatrix} \tag{31}$$

In this section, the results of energy consumption data converted to standard coal are obtained directly, so $\eta' = (\eta_i)_{1 \times k}$ can be omitted.

2. Fully integrated energy consumption

Energy consumption can be divided into primary energy consumption and secondary energy consumption through processing and conversion. The complete energy consumption coefficient matrix B^E is composed of the first k lines of the complete consumption coefficient matrix B, which is expressed as follows:

$$B^E = \left[B^{EE}, B^{EN} \right]$$

Fully integrated energy consumption coefficient is equal to direct integrated energy consumption plus all kinds of energy consumption through consumption of non-energy products, and energy products consumed by non-energy products cause indirect energy consumption in the production process of non-energy products. In order to simplify the model, we do not take the indirect consumption of energy products by energy products into consideration, they expressed by formula as follows:

$$T^{EE'} = A^{EE} + (A^{EE} A^{EN}) + (A^{EE} A^{EN})^2 + \cdots \qquad (32)$$

$$T^{EE} = A^{EE} (I - A^{EE} A^{EN})^{-1} \qquad (33)$$

The energy consumption coefficient is shown in Table 4-6. The results show that between 2002 and 2007:

(1) The industries with smaller energy consumption coefficients are mainly concentrated on non-industrial sectors. Among them, waste, agriculture, forestry, animal husbandry, fisheries, wholesale and retail, catering and other non-material production industries, including waste industry is not the material production sector of the national economy, it exist for the needs of economic development balance. Despite the need to consume a certain amount of energy, it is almost negligible. Agriculture, forestry, animal husbandry, by-fishery, wholesale, retail and service industries and other non-material production sectors compared with the industrial sector, the industry itself is energy-saving in nature. For example, the energy consumption of agriculture, forestry, animal husbandry and fishery per 10000 yuan of GDP in 2002 was 0.5131 tons of standard coal, and it also dropped to 0.366 in 2007, which is very energy-saving.

(2) The energy consumption of light industry and industry with water as production input is small. In the manufacturing industry, light

industries such as food manufacturing and tobacco processing industry, clothing, leather, down and products industry are also energy-saving industries. Water-consuming industries have relatively low energy consumption, such as water production and supply industries, coal mining and washing industries.

(3) Heavy industry is an energy-intensive industry. The major energy-consuming industries are: metal products industry, metal smelting and calendering industry, chemical industry, electrical industry, machinery and equipment manufacturing industry, transportation equipment manufacturing industry, construction industry, general and special equipment manufacturing industry, etc. These are heavy industries. In the production process, they not only have a direct primary energy consumption, but also have an indirect energy consumption of multiple energy use, which is very energy hungry.

Table 3–6 Energy Consumption (Unit: 10000 tons of standard coal)

2002		2005		2007	
Scrap waste	0.0000	Scrap waste	0.0000	Scrap waste	0.1140
Oil and gas mining	0.5131	Wholesale, retail trade and catering industry	0.4875	Agriculture, forestry, animal husbandry and fishery	0.3660
Agriculture, forestry, animal husbandry and fishery	0.5207	Agriculture, forestry, animal husbandry and fishery	0.5367	Wholesale, retail and catering	0.4030
Wholesale, retail and accommodation catering	0.5808	Oil and gas mining	0.5447	Other non-material production industries	0.4485
Other non-material production industries	0.5826	Food manufacturing and tobacco processing industries	0.7071	Food manufacturing and tobacco processing	0.5361
Food manufacturing and tobacco processing industries	0.6929	Other non-material production departments	0.7296	Oil and gas mining	0.5614
Coal mining and washing industry	0.7733	Transportation, warehousing and postal services	0.9481	Transportation, warehousing and postal services	0.6350

continued

2002		2005		2007	
Electricity and other production and supply industries	0.8520	Water production and supply industry	0.9845	Water production and supply industry	0.6769
Water production and supply industry	0.8947	Garment leather down and its products	1.0203	Coal mining and washing industry	0.7276
Non-metallic mining industry	0.9183	Coal mining and washing industry	1.0274	Wood processing and furniture manufacturing	0.7554
Transportation, warehousing and postal services	0.9187	Wood processing and furniture manufacturing	1.1053	Textile and garment industry	0.7878
Garment leather down and its products	0.9630	Textile industry	1.1571	Non - metallic ore and other ore mining	0.7950
Paper printing and cultural and educational products manufacturing	0.9649	Petroleum processing and nuclear fuel processing	1.1896	Gas production and supply industry	0.8398
Wood processing and furniture manufacturing	0.9661	Electricity and other production and supply industries	1.2235	Paper printing and cultural and educational supplies	0.8519
Textile industry	1.0387	Other manufacturing	1.2274	Metal mining industry	0.8654
Metal mining industry	1.0918	Metal mining industry	1.2321	Textile industry	0.8688
Communication and computer equipment manufacturing	1.1354	Paper printing and cultural and educational products manufacturing	1.2370	Petroleum processing and nuclear fuel processing	0.8740
Craft manufactures and other manufacturing industries	1.1690	Non-metallic mining industry	1.2585	Communication equipment and computer equipment	0.9121
Nonmetallic mineral products industry	1.2530	Gas production and supply industry	1.3190	Arts and crafts and other manufacturing industries	0.9488
Instrumentation and office machinery manufacturing	1.2714	Communication equipment and computer equipment manufacturing	1.3838	Instrumentation and office machinery	0.9574
Transportation equipment manufacturing industry	1.3234	The construction industry	1.4339	Electricity and other production and supply industries	1.0069
The chemical industry	1.4230	Nonmetallic mineral products industry	1.4363	Nonmetallic mineral products industry	1.0368

continued

160

2002		2005		2007	
General and special equipment manufacturing	1.4337	Instrumentation and office machinery manufacturing	1.4829	Transportation equipment manufacturing industry	1.0641
Gas production and supply industry	1.4646	Transportation equipment manufacturing industry	1.5420	The chemical industry	1.1311
The construction industry	1.4752	The chemical industry	1.6388	General and special equipment manufacturing	1.1537
Petroleum processing and nuclear fuel processing industry	1.5512	General and special equipment manufacturing	1.6479	The construction industry	1.2376
Electrical, mechanical and equipment manufacturing	1.5813	Electrical, mechanical and equipment manufacturing	1.7471	Metal smelting and rolling industry	1.3056
Metal smelting and rolling industry	1.7308	Metal smelting and rolling industry	1.7977	Electrical machinery and equipment manufacturing industry	1.3225
Metal products industry	1.8254	Metal products industry	1.8899	Metal products industry	1.3671

Data Source: China Input-output Table; China National Bureau of Statistics.

3.2.6 Environmental emission coefficient

In order to investigate the impact of environmental emissions on economic development more clearly, this part extends the original input-output table and introduces the input-output model of economic development mode. In row vectors, a number of pollution departments have been added, in column vectors, pollution elimination departments have been added. For the production sector, the unit of measurement can be value unit or physical unit. As analysis needed, this part converts the units of environmental emissions into tons. Using the balance between production and intermediate use in different sectors, the equation of various pollutants can be obtained.

$$\sum_{j=1}^{n} p_{ij} + r_i = q_i (i = 1, 2, \cdots, n) \tag{34}$$

$\sum\limits_{j=1}^{n} p_{ij}$ represents total amount of pollutants produced in the production sector. r_i indicate the number of pollutants produced in the final demand area, we divides the pollutants into three categories: wastewater, waste gas and waste residue, defines the pollutant generation coefficient, and the formula expressed as follows:

$$a_{ij}^{p} = \frac{p_{ij}}{x_j}(i, j = 1, 2, \cdots, n) \tag{35}$$

By introducing the coefficient of pollution generation into the equation of pollutant formation and transforming it into matrix form, we can get the result: $A^{p}X+R=Q$, in which A^{p} is coefficient matrix of representative pollutants， X,R,Q represent the total output column vectors of the national economy; the pollutant emission column vectors of various final needs and the total pollutant emission column vectors of the national economy are expressed respectively. We use the direct and total consumption coefficients of pollutants to investigate the environmental pollution of various industries under the existing economic development mode.

According to the above ideas and formulas, the calculation results of environmental emission coefficient are shown in Table 3-7. The results show that:

(1) Industries with smaller environmental emission factors are concentrated in non-solid energy production and supply related industries, such as gas production and supply industries, water production and supply industries, which are relatively less polluted than coal, oil and nuclear fuel energy industries, but not pollution-free, or the direct harm of pollution is not obvious.

(2) The environmental emission of industries which are easy to deal with, such as construction industry, handicraft and other manufacturing industries in light industry, garment, shoes, leather and other products industry, wood processing and manufacturing industry,

instrument and cultural office machinery manufacturing industry, has a small environmental emission coefficient. Emissions from these industries can generally be handled easily, and the treatment process is not complicated, and some of them can be recycled, so they are relatively environmentally friendly industries. In addition, the environmental emission factors of non-metallic mines and other mining and processing industries, non-metallic mineral products industry, waste and other industries are relatively small.

(3) The industries with high environmental pollution coefficient are mainly concentrated in the industries with high energy consumption and high cost of pollution treatment, such as chemical industry, electric power, thermal production and supply industry, metal smelting and calendering industry, paper making, printing and cultural and educational products manufacturing industry, petroleum processing, coking and nuclear fuel processing industry, transportation and storage postal industry, agriculture, forestry, animal husbandry and fisheries, and other services. Among them, the main emissions of agriculture, forestry, animal husbandry and by-fishery are that chemical fertilizers and pesticides pollute the environment seriously, and are not easy to deal with, or the cost of processing is high.

Table 3–7   Environmental Emission Coefficient (unit: emission per ten thousand tons)

2002		2005		2007	
Gas production and supply industry	0.966	Gas production and supply industry	0.6081	The construction industry	0.3456
The construction industry	1.751	The construction industry	1.0903	Gas production and supply industry	0.5710
Water production and supply industry	1.789	Water production and supply industry	1.5760	Water production and supply industry	0.9841
Arts and crafts and other manufacturing industries	1.951	Arts and crafts and other manufacturing industries	1.6365	Arts and crafts and other manufacturing industries	1.0571
Non-metallic ore and other ore mining	2.569	Non-metallic ore and other ore mining	2.1072	Non-metallic ore and other ore mining	1.4189
Textiles, clothing, shoes, hats and other products	2.803	Textile, clothing, shoes, hats and other products	2.3966	Instrumentation and office machinery	2.1817

continued

2002		2005		2007	
Instrumentation and office machinery	2.910	Instrumentation and office machinery	2.8547	Textile, clothing, shoes, hats and other products	2.4030
Scrap waste	3.052	Scrap waste	2.9099	Wood processing and furniture manufacturing	2.7730
Wood processing and furniture manufacturing	3.704	Wood processing and furniture manufacturing	2.9667	Nonmetallic mineral products industry	3.1090
Nonmetallic mineral products industry	4.826	Nonmetallic mineral products industry	4.8256	Scrap waste	4.2959
Food manufacturing and tobacco processing industries	6.692	Metal mining industry	5.5518	Metal mining industry	4.7315
Metal mining industry	6.936	Food manufacturing and tobacco processing industries	6.3851	Transportation equipment manufacturing industry	5.0565
Electrical machinery and equipment manufacturing industry	8.224	Transportation equipment manufacturing industry	7.0855	Metal products industry	5.3474
Metal products industry	8.425	Metal products industry	7.1571	Electrical machinery and equipment manufacturing industry	5.5573
Transportation equipment manufacturing industry	10.05	Communication equipment computer manufacturing	8.7763	Communication equipment computer manufacturing	6.5447
Communication equipment computer manufacturing	10.14	Electrical machinery and equipment manufacturing	9.1919	Food manufacturing and tobacco processing	6.6017
Textile industry	13.63	Textile industry	10.769	Coal mining and washing industry	7.3886
Coal mining and washing industry	16.49	General purpose, special equipment manufacturing	11.847	Wholesale, retail and catering accommodation	8.2080
Petroleum processing and nuclear fuel processing	16.80	Oil and gas mining	12.346	Transportation and warehousing	9.0961
General purpose, special equipment manufacturing	17.17	Wholesale, retail and catering accommodation	15.007	General purpose, special equipment manufacturing	10.052
Oil and gas mining	17.29	Coal mining and washing industry	15.094	Textile industry	10.395
Agriculture, forestry, animal husbandry and fishery	20.47	Petroleum processing and nuclear fuel processing	16.977	Petroleum processing and nuclear fuel processing	10.439
Paper printing and cultural and educational supplies	21.06	Paper printing and cultural and educational supplies	17.087	Oil and gas mining	11.359
Transportation and storage postal industry	23.10	Transportation and warehousing	17.688	Agriculture, forestry, animal husbandry and fishery	13.759

continued

2002		2005		2007	
Power and heat production and supply	24.74	Agriculture, forestry, animal husbandry and fishery	18.479	Paper printing and cultural and educational supplies	14.964
Wholesale, retail and catering accommodation	28.07	Metal smelting and rolling processing	25.304	Metal smelting and rolling processing	17.657
Metal smelting and rolling industry	28.95	Other services	27.998	Other services	17.869
Other services	34.07	Electricity and other production and supply industries	29.361	Electricity and other production and supply industries	24.365
The chemical industry	53.52	The chemical industry	47.880	The chemical industry	34.939

Data Source: China Input-output Table; China National Bureau of Statistics.

3.2.7 Technology spillover

The input of science and technology and R&D in a department is not only conducive to improving the innovation and technological progress of the department and the productivity of the industry, but also can promote the development and progress of other industries. Therefore, investigating the technology spillover effect of the industry is of great significance to the transformation of the mode of economic development. This section quantifies technology spillover effects by using R&D traffic matrix:

$$X_{R\&D} = (\hat{F}_{R\&D})(\hat{X}_j)^{-1}(I-A)^{-1}\hat{Y}_t \tag{36}$$

$X_{R\&D}$ represents inter-industry technology spillover flow matrix，$\hat{F}_{R\&D}$ is diagonal matrix representing column vectors of R&D expenditure；$(X_j)^{-1}$ represents the inverse of the diagonal matrix formed by the total input，$\hat{Y}_i$ is diagonal matrix representing the total output of each industry. $X_{R\&D}$ i technologies and innovations that represent R&D investment from i industry and allocated to the final product of other industries, which is technology spillover contribution of industry i to Other Industries; $X_{R\&D}$ represents the R&D gains of industry j from spillovers of technological innovation from other

165

sectors when the industry conducts production activities. The results show that:

(1) The industries with large R&D-driven and spillover effects are concentrated on the service sectors specializing in technology production. There are research and experimental development industry, integrated technology service industry, water conservancy, environmental and other public facilities management industry. There are also industries related to people's livelihood, such as agriculture, forestry, animal husbandry, sideline fisheries, health, social security and social welfare. These industries themselves have a lot of R&D activities, and have a large investment in R&D.

(2) Technology-dependent industries such as technology-intensive industries or capital-technology-intensive industries have greater spillover effects. Chemical industry, information transmission, computer service and software industry, transportation and storage industry are all industries that rely heavily on technology and capital. Depending on technology, it is necessary to invest in R&D. At the same time, the spillover effect of inter-industry R&D is very obvious because the industry itself makes full use of technology.

(3) The industries with less R&D spillover effect are mainly concentrated in the industries with low technology requirements and less R&D activities, mostly in the service sector. The main industries are real estate, accommodation and catering, postal, wholesale and retail, handicraft and other manufacturing industries, waste industries, etc. These service sectors have low demand for R&D, little or no R&D investment, and less frequent use of technology. Most of them belong to labor-intensive type, so the spillover effect of R&D is small. In addition, the development of arts and crafts and other manufacturing industries does not depend on R&D activities, but on the technological improvement and inheritance of artistic workers themselves.

Table 3–8 R&D Spillovers from 2002 to 2007

2002		2005		2007	
Research and experimental development industry	3963754	Scientific research	1821314777	Research and experimental development industry	23538309
Agriculture, forestry, animal husbandry and fishery	375683.5	Integrated technical services	17407128.9	Agriculture, forestry, animal husbandry and fishery	1180816.2
The chemical industry	101032.2	Management of water conservancy and other public facilities	15252238.1	Integrated technical services	844970.2
Health social security and welfare	78163.5	Health, social security and welfare	6434008.0	The chemical industry	307164.3
Integrated technical services	66852.9	Agriculture, forestry, herding and fishing	3765059.7	Health social security and welfare	189805.5
Transportation and warehousing	61892.7	Culture, sports and entertainment	1501798.3	Management of water conservancy and other public facilities	157153.3
Water conservancy and other public facilities management industry	55043.8	Water production and supply industry	948723.2	Transportation and warehousing	100838.9
Information transfer and computer software	43040.7	The chemical industry	741066.9	Information transfer computer software	91266.9
Transportation equipment manufacturing industry	38196.9	Public administration and social organization	684450.1	General purpose equipment manufacturing	77032.6
Communication equipment and computer manufacturing	24230.2	General and special equipment manufacturing	488690.3	Electricity production and supply industry	72684.2
General and special equipment manufacturing	18078.7	Information transfer and computer software	349077.1	Public administration and social organization	34615.2
Food manufacturing and tobacco processing industries	12195.6	Instrumentation and office manufacturing	330422.8	Food manufacturing and tobacco processing	28717.1
Metal smelting and rolling industry	11319.8	The production and supply of electricity, etc.	289543.1	Culture, sports and entertainment	25503.1
Public administration and social organization	10860.0	Transportation and warehousing	254757.2	Communication equipment and computers	18338.3
The financial sector	10826.3	Education	249159.6	Metal smelting and rolling processing	12668.9

continued

2002		2005		2007	
The construction industry	10600.4	Communication equipment and computer manufacturing	171475.8	The construction industry	11803.8
The production and supply of electricity	7010.1	Wood processing and furniture manufacturing	128010.4	Instrumentation and office machinery	9319.9
Culture, sports and entertainment	6021.4	Food manufacturing and tobacco processing industries	113130.7	Education	8862.2
Education	5687.9	The construction industry	104899.9	Metal mining industry	8072.4
Nonmetallic mineral products industry	2907.6	Metal mining industry	91487.8	Wood processing and furniture manufacturing	7802.4
Instrumentation and office manufacturing	2525.4	Metal smelting and rolling industry	79500.8	Petroleum coking and nuclear fuel	2376.5
Wood processing and furniture manufacturing	2435.8	Gas production and supply industry	46527.7	Coal mining and washing industry	2289.5
Non-metallic ore and other ore mining	1766.2	Residential services and other services	32898.9	Gas production and supply industry	1921.6
Textile industry	1248.5	Transportation equipment manufacturing industry	29683.6	Transportation equipment manufacturing industry	1582.4
Oil and gas mining	1120.2	Clothing leather down and its products	18740.9	Nonmetallic mineral products industry	1319.5
Paper printing and stationery	1006.7	Petroleum processing and nuclear fuel processing	17745.5	Electrical machinery and equipment manufacturing	1241.9
Coal mining and washing industry	932.9	Nonmetallic mineral products industry	16370.4	Oil and gas mining	1227.4
Electrical machinery and equipment manufacturing industry	601.9	Electrical, mechanical and equipment manufacturing	14499.2	Leasing and business services	829.6
Residential services and other services	440.4	Paper printing and cultural and educational supplies	11902.6	Textile industry	739.7
Textile and garment industry	344.3	Leasing and business services	11457.5	Paper printing and stationery	734.5
Gas production and supply industry	321.9	Textile industry	10463.5	Water production and supply industry	498.6
Water production and supply industry	264.9	Coal mining and washing industry	7076.1	Resident services and other services	457.7

continued

2002		2005		2007	
Metal products industry	222.4	Oil and gas mining	5692.9	Metal products industry	398.3
Wholesale and retail	154.7	Non-metallic mining industry	4772.5	Textile and garment industry	274.6
The real estate industry	12.65	Metal products industry	3655.8	Non-metallic ore and other mining	212.3
Metal mining industry	0.000	Wholesale and retail trade	701.7	Arts and crafts and other manufacturing industries	70.8
Petroleum processing and nuclear fuel processing	0.000	Arts and crafts and other manufacturing industries	0.000	Wholesale and retail	50.1
Arts and crafts and other manufacturing industries	0.000	Scrap waste	0.000	Scrap waste	0.000
Scrap waste	0.000	The postal service	0.000	The postal service	0.000
The postal service	0.000	Accommodation and catering	0.000	Accommodation and catering	0.000
Accommodation and catering	0.000	Financial insurance	0.000	The financial sector	0.000
Leasing and business services	0.000	The real estate industry	0.000	The real estate industry	0.000

Source: China Input-output Table; China National Bureau of Statistics.

3.3 Empirical Analysis of Input–output Efficiency of Economic Development

In this chapter we will put the demand structure, factor structure and industrial structure into the same analytical framework, and comprehensively investigate the supply factors such as the industrial structure, the input-output of the national economy, the factor structure and efficiency of economic development, as well as the demand factors such as investment, consumption, import and export, and explore the economic development of China with the choice of leading industries. The path of mode transformation has great research value. This paper attempts to construct an input and output model of economic development mode. It integrates demand structure, factor input and industrial structure into a unified analytical framework. Taking industry sector as a carrier, through measuring and estimating the output coefficients of various input factors of China's 42 industries from the year of 2002 to 2007, economic development mode within input output model, the economic development mode of China is investigated. This part will introduce stochastic frontier production function and use Frontier 4.0 software to make an empirical analysis of input-output efficiency based on economic development mode.

3.3.1 Stochastic frontier production function setting

Input-output efficiency is reflected in the production possibility curve, which shows that under the given level of technology and factor input, the actual output keeps close to or away from the production possibility boundary. The frontier production function representing the production possibility boundary is a scientific benchmark to measure the input-output efficiency. The general form of stochastic frontier production function is:

$$y_{it} = f\left(x_{jit}, t\right) \exp\left(v_{it} - u_{it}\right) \tag{37}$$

y_{it} represents output of the department i at t period, $f(\cdot)$ indicates the deterministic frontier output on the production possibility boundary, which is the optimal output under the existing technological conditions. X_{jit} is factor input vector, j represents the input elements of labor, capital, energy, environment, R&D, respectively. Nonnegative u_i is used to express input-output inefficiency index. $\exp(-u_{it})$ represents the distance between actual output and production frontier generated by production efficiency. i, t indicate industry and time respectively.

For technical functions $f(\cdot)$, we assume a logarithmic linear form:

$$\ln f(x_{it}, t) = x_{it}\beta + v_{it} \tag{38}$$

β is coefficient for explaining variables, v_{it} is a random variable. Substitute (38) into (37) we get:

$$\ln y_{it} = \ln f(x_{it}, t) - u_{it} = x_{it}\beta + v_{it} - u_{it} \tag{39}$$

Based on these assumptions, we introduce the time-variant translogarithmic stochastic frontier production function as the econometric test model for empirical analysis.

$$\ln Y_{it} = \alpha_0 + \alpha_1 t + \beta_1 \ln L_{it} + \beta_2 \ln K_{it} + \beta_3 \ln R_{it} + \beta_4 \ln E_{it} + \beta_5 \ln L_{it} + \beta_6 D_1 + \beta_7 D_2 + (v_{it} - u_{it}) \tag{40}$$

$$u_{it} = u_i \eta_{it} = u_i \exp[-\eta(t-T)] \tag{41}$$

α_1 used to measure the speed of technological progress; η indicate characteristic of technical invalidity changes, random variables $\eta < 0, \eta = 0, \eta > 0$ representing technical inefficiency increase, invariable and decrease with time respectively; we set two dummy variables for 42 departments of the national economy:D_1 and D_2, Material production sector (e.g. agriculture, forestry, animal husbandry and sideline fisheries), the value of D_1 is 1; For the non-material production sector (e.g. the financial and insurance industry), the value of D_1 is 0; Non-profit industries (e.g. water production and supply, public health, social security and social welfare), the value of D_2 is 0;other cases, D_2 values 1. $(v_{it} - u_{it})$ represents random perturbations, which consists of two parts: v_{it} obeys the standard normal distribution, indicates the random error variable and represents the noise error caused by the impact of uncontrollable factors in the system. u_{it} represent the technical inefficiency term changing over time,who obeys the non-negative tail-breaking normal distribution $u_{it} \sim N^+(\mu, \sigma^2), v_{it}$ independent of u_{it}. The model parameters determined by formula (40) (41) can be estimated by OLS or maximum likelihood estimation. For the sake of estimation, here we define: $\gamma = \sigma_u^2 / \sigma_v^2 + \sigma_u^2, \gamma \in (0,1), \gamma$ is used to determine whether the model is reasonable or not. It represents the proportion of technical inefficiency in the random perturbation term of regression equation. When γ infinitely close to zero, which means that the gap between the actual output and the maximum possible output frontier of the system mainly comes from the noise error caused by uncontrollable random factors, so it is meaningless to adopt the stochastic frontier model; when γ infinitely close to 1, which shows that the error of the production function mainly comes from random variables U_{it}, indicating that the stochastic frontier model is used appropriately, especially the stochastic frontier model. When $\gamma = 1$, shows that the stochastic frontier model is the deterministic frontier model, and there is no stochastic impact effect.

3.3.2 Data and variable selection and model estimation

Samples selected from this econometric model are cross-sectional data of total output, labor input, capital investment, R&D investment, energy consumption and environmental input in China's 42 industries in 2002, 2005 and 2007. The relevant data are from the China Statistical Yearbook, the national research network and the China economic network. Estimates of standards and missing data for industry integration are consistent with those above.

In this chapter, the total output of each industry is used to measure the output of the explained variables. The data are derived from the vertical total output data of each industry in the input-output table. Labor input is expressed by the number of employees in various industries; capital input is expressed by fixed assets investment data; scientific research input is expressed by research and development investment of various industries; environmental input includes energy input and environmental emissions; energy consumption is expressed by energy consumption output per 10000 yuan of each industry; environmental emissions are expressed by tons of emission data of "three wastes" per 10000 yuan. The difference relates to other variables that have not been considered to affect productivity.

1. Model estimation results

According to the previous regression model, we use the cross-sectional data of 42 industries in 2002, 2005 and 2007 to estimate the transcendental logarithmic production function. In order to make the influence coefficients of various inputs on total output more intuitive, we first use the logarithmic terms of five inputs plus two dummy variables and time terms for regression estimation. The comparison results of OLS and MLE are shown in Table 3-9. In both OLS and MLE estimates, except for the time term, the impact of other intermediate inputs on total output is positive. MLE estimates are better than OLS estimates (the sigma-squared value of MLE is larger than OLS).

Table 3–9   OLS and MLE Estimated Results

OLS estimates				MLE estimates			
Variable	Coefficient	Standard-Error	T-ratio	Variable	Coefficient	Standard-error	T-ratio
Intercept term	0.107935E+2	0.804028E+0	0.134243E+2	Intercept term	0.137504E+2	0.522822E+0	0.263004E+2
lnL	0.239118E+0	0.630526E-1	0.379235E+1	lnL	0.125128E+0	0.406262E-1	0.307998E+1
lnK	0.148269E+0	0.516225E-1	0.287219E+1	lnK	0.137318E+0	0.295297E-1	0.465016E+1
lnR	0.638342E-2	0.194012E-1	0.329023E+0	lnR	0.737889E-2	0.196116E-1	0.376252E+0
lnE	0.229666E+0	0.618106E-1	0.371565E+1	lnE	0.234491E+0	0.621120E-1	0.377529E+1
lnI	0.297556E-1	0.298369E-1	0.997273E+0	lnI	0.112929E-1	0.164553E-1	0.686278E+0
Dummy1	0.454700E+0	0.160723E+0	0.282909E+1	Dummy1	0.473129E+0	0.172899E+0	0.273643E+1
Dummy2	0.537077E+0	0.171036E+0	0.314015E+1	Dummy2	0.381315E+0	0.206949E+0	0.184256E+1
Time	−0.89955E-2	0.204049E-1	−0.44085E+0	Time	−0.192877E-1	0.217019E-1	−0.888757E+0
sigma-squared 0.525788E+0				sigma-squared 0.24319E+1 0.26126E+1 0.93086E+0			
				gamma 0.95941E+0 0.45580E-1 0.21049E+2			
log likelihood function = -0.13361740E+03				mu −0.16585E+1 0.32382E+1−0.51217E+0			
				log likelihood function =−0.83055878E+02			
				LR test of the one-sided error = 0.10112304E+03			

Table 3-10 and Table 3-11 are the results of OLS and MLE estimates of the econometric models which incorporate logarithmic primary and quadratic terms into the transcendental logarithmic production function, respectively. Obviously, MLE estimation results are better than OLS results. At 5% significant level, the goodness of fit of MLE is 0.8093 than that of OLS is 0.647. The logarithmic likelihood function of MLE regression is -73.811, and the LR test is 73.328, which is significant at 1% significant level. The result of MLE estimation is 0.9079, approaching 1, which indicates that the error of stochastic frontier production function mainly comes from the stochastic variables in the system. It is appropriate to use the stochastic frontier model.

According to MLE's estimation results, the efficiency of labor input and capital input to total output was positive in 2002–2007, which indicated that labor and capital contributed a lot to economic growth, and economic development depended on labor and capital input was effective. Environmental emissions have a negative effect on output, which is also in line with the assumption in this book.

The production efficiency of R&D input and energy input is negative, which indicates that China's R&D input and energy input are negative in general. This can be explained from two aspects: First, the overall impact of R&D and energy on economic growth is positive. The coefficient estimation results of the above single regression test and the square terms of various inputs are positive, but because of R&D, the overall impact of R&D and energy on economic growth is positive. Energy and energy may be excessive or inadequate for a single industry, so overall it is negative efficiency. Second, China's energy input efficiency is negative, indicating that China's energy input is greater than output, and energy use is inefficient. The negative effect of R&D efficiency reveals that the overall level of R&D in China has no scale effect during the period of investigation, or that R&D investment is insufficient or uneven in industry, or that R&D investment is in the stage of diminishing marginal returns. As for the specific reasons, further research is needed.

According to the estimation results, the two dummy variables set up according to the monopoly nature of the national economy and whether or not they have the profit characteristics are significant, indicating that the establishment of our dummy variables is reasonable. The coefficients of the two dummy variables are larger than those of the input factors, which shows that monopoly or competitiveness and profitability are the important factors affecting efficiency. Competitiveness is also closely related to the profitability and self-sustainability of the industry. Therefore, competitiveness and profitability are also the important basis for the transformation of the mode of economic development and the choice of industrial arrangement and combination.

Table 3–10 OLS Estimatied Results

Variable	Coefficient	Standard-error	T-ratio
Intercept term	0.27689777E+02	0.36228773E+01	0.74896059E+01
lnL	−0.19476808E+01	0.55707759E+00	−0.34962469E+01
lnK	0.21477624E+00	0.16076202E+00	0.13359887E+01
lnR	0.21429975E-03	0.58246955E-01	0.36791579E-02
lnE	−0.18318200E+00	0.23040789E+00	−0.79503354E+00
lnI	−0.10552326E+00	0.77001403E-01	−0.13704069E+01
（lnL）2	0.78941589E-01	0.19623599E-01	0.40227885E+01
（lnK）2	−0.38141675E-02	0.13387605E-01	−0.28490290E+00
（lnR）2	0.63283072E-03	0.44117276E-02	0.14344284E+00
（lnE）2	0.20706445E-01	0.15795703E-01	0.13108910E+01
（lnI）2	0.79298716E-02	0.31257743E-02	0.25369303E+01
Dummy1	0.11621997E+00	0.17010507E+00	0.68322462E+00
Dummy2	0.82799280E+00	0.15938190E+00	0.51950242E+01
Time	−0.10015991E-01	0.17758741E-01	−0.56400342E+00
sigma-squared 0.64711239E+0			
gamma 0.75000000E+0		log likelihood function =−0.11047546E+03	

Table 3-11 rank the values of the input-output comprehensive efficiency coefficients of 42 industries. From 2002 to 2007, the construction industry, wholesale and retail industry, communication equipment, computer and other electronic equipment manufacturing industry, financial insurance industry, wood processing and furniture manufacturing industry, electrical, machinery and equipment manufacturing industry are the first industries with higher production efficiency in the national economy. We have also made a corresponding analysis of the specific input-output coefficients [1]. Among 42 industries, the top 15 are mainly concentrated in: (1) Construction and real estate related industries. (2) Consumer services, such as wholesale and retail trade, residential services and other social services, financial insurance, accommodation and catering, and education. (3) Productive services, such as financial insurance and real estate services, are closely related to other productive industries such as construction. (4) Manufacturing industry, in which light industry is dominated by communication equipment, computer and other electronic equipment manufacturing, wood processing and furniture manufacturing, garment and leather down and its products; heavy industry is dominated by electrical, machinery and equipment manufacturing, transportation equipment manufacturing, general and special equipment manufacturing.

Table 3–11 Estimates of Efficiency Coefficient

Ranking	Category	Coefficient Value
1	Construction business	8.84E–01
2	Scrap and Waste	8.70E–01
3	Wholesale and retail business	8.62E–01
4	Manufacturing of Communication Equipment, Computer and Other Electronic Equipment	8.42E–01
5	Financial and Insurance Industry	8.04E–01

---

[1] The waste industry and public management and social organizations are not candidates for leading industries. The reason is that they are the maintainers of economic and social operations, not the creative sectors of the main economic output. Waste industry is the organizer of the normal operation of the environment, while public management and social organizations are the organizers of the normal operation of social order.

continued

Ranking	Category	Coefficient Value
6	Wood Processing and Furniture Manufacturing	7.63E–01
7	Electrical, Machinery and Equipment Manufacturing Industry	7.54E–01
8	Resident Services and Other Social Services	7.50E–01
9	Garment, Leather, Down and Its Products Industry	6.63E–01
10	Transportation Equipment Manufacturing Industry	6.42E–01
11	Accommodation and catering	6.16E–01
12	Estate	6.15E–01
13	Public administration and social organizations	6.03E–01
14	Education	5.95E–01
15	Manufacturing of General and Special Equipment	5.88E–01
16	Leasing and Business Services	5.54E–01
17	Agriculture	5.34E–01
18	Food Manufacturing and Tobacco Processing Industry	4.78E–01
19	Health, Social Security and Social Welfare	4.78E–01
20	Metal Products Industry	4.74E–01
21	Information transmission, Computer services and Software industry	4.01E–01
22	Textile Industry	4.00E–01
23	Instruments and Instruments and Cultural Office Machinery Manufacturing Industry	3.86E–01
24	Paper Printing and Cultural and Educational Supplies Manufacturing Industry	3.45E–01
25	Craft products and other manufacturing industries	2.99E–01
26	Petroleum Processing, Coking and Nuclear Fuel Processing Industry	2.73E–01
27	Production and Supply of Electricity and Thermal Power	2.56E–01
28	Transportation and warehousing	2.54E–01
29	Integrated Technology Services	2.46E–01
30	Chemical Industry	2.45E–01
31	Culture, Sports and Entertainment	2.40E–01
32	Metal Smelting and Calendering Industry	2.30E–01

continued

Ranking	Category	Coefficient Value
33	Scientific research	2.18E−01
34	Non-metallic Mine Mining and Processing Industry	2.13E−01
35	Non-metallic Mineral Products Industry	2.05E−01
36	Oil and Gas Exploitation Industry	1.84E−01
37	Metal mining and dressing industry	1.75E−01
38	Coal mining and washing industry	1.58E−01
39	Tourism	1.34E−01
40	Gas production and supply industry	1.12E−01
41	Postal industry	1.10E−01
42	Water production and supply industry	1.06E−01

3.4　Summary of This Chapter

Based on the input output model of the economic development mode, this chapter calculates the relevant input and output coefficients of the 42 industries in China for 2002–2007 years, and investigates the domestic demand inducing effect, import and export inducing effect, investment multiplier, labor employment driving function, energy consumption coefficient, environmental emission coefficient and technology spillover effect. This part synthesizes the goal of the transformation of the mode of economic development and balance the importance of various factors, so as to reach a consensus on the choice of industries that are conducive to the transformation of the mode of economic development, this chapter then uses the generalized stochastic frontier production function model to make an empirical analysis, and comprehensively inspects the above. The results of the analysis are as follows:

(1) During the period of investigation, the mode of economic development of our country tends to be labor-intensive and capital-

intensive. Labor and capital investment are still the main contributors to the development of our national economy. China's energy input is generally negative efficiency, energy input and output efficiency is low, energy utilization is more common, transportation process loss is serious, coupled with the low level of technology in some industries, energy use is generally at a negative efficiency, and China's energy input and output are inefficient. The effect of R&D input on total economic output is not obvious. The reason may lie in insufficient total R&D input, which does not reach the minimum threshold of the scale effect of R&D input. It may also be due to the uneven distribution of R&D input among industries, excessive R&D input in some industries, and insufficient R&D input in some industries, which leads to the inefficiency of R&D input and output in general. Of course, it is also possible that R&D investment in China is in the stage of declining factor rewards, or that the scale effect of R&D has not yet been brought into play. It can be seen that at this stage, China's economic development mode still belongs to the traditional labor and capital-intensive.

(2) The estimation results of stochastic frontier production function show that the comprehensive input-output efficiency of construction industry and real estate related industries is high. Combining with the calculation of the correlation coefficient of input-output model based on the mode of economic development, it can be seen that the consumption-pull coefficient of real estate industry is higher in 2002–2007, the employment-pull coefficient of construction industry is larger, and the environmental emission coefficient of construction industry is also higher. The survey also shows that the construction industry is environmentally friendly, while the construction industry also has a large R&D spillover effect. Therefore, the construction industry and real estate related industries are the leading industries in

China at this stage. During the period of investigation, the stochastic frontier production efficiency of China's manufacturing industry was relatively high, among which light industry was dominated by communication equipment, computer and other electronic equipment manufacturing, wood processing and furniture manufacturing, garment and leather down and its products, and heavy industry was dominated by electrical, machinery and equipment manufacturing, transportation equipment manufacturing, general and special equipment manufacturing. By investigating the input-output correlation coefficient, we can see that the consumption pull coefficient, import-export inducement effect and labor employment driving coefficient of telecommunication equipment, computer and other electronic equipment manufacturing industries are larger. While telecommunication equipment and computer and other electronic equipment manufacturing industries are energy-saving and environmentally friendly. The stochastic frontier production efficiency of wood processing and furniture manufacturing industry, garment, leather, down and its products industry is higher, the import and export inducement effect is greater, and the investment multiplier and labor employment driving factor are higher.

(3) The comprehensive input-output efficiency of wholesale and retail industry, residential service industry and education industry is relatively high, and this kind of consumer service industry is the second best choice of leading industry, because consumer service industry can not be neglected in the process of economic development mode transformation, no matter from the domestic demand pulling role, labor employment driving role or from the point of view of energy conservation and environmental protection. In addition, the comprehensive input-output efficiency of the financial insurance industry with the nature of producer services is relatively high. At the same time, the development of the industry has a strong industrial

correlation with the development of construction, real estate and manufacturing industries, and it is an auxiliary industry of the national economy.

The above empirical results show that the construction and real estate related industries should be the leading industries in the national economy at this stage, considering the intermediate input-output efficiency, domestic demand induction, labor force driving, import-export pulling effect, investment multiplier driving effect, energy saving and environmental protection effect, R&D spillover effect and input-output efficiency. Communication equipment and computer and other electronic equipment manufacturing industry in manufacturing industry, wood processing and furniture manufacturing industry, garment, leather, down and its products industry is also the second best choice of industrial arrangement and combination in this period. In addition, financial services and consumer services are the auxiliary industries of the national economy.

Chapter 4　Evolution of China's Leading Industries and Economic Development Modes

4.1 An Investigation of the Current Stage of Economic Development in China

Economic development is a process of coordination with consumption, investment, import and export trade, technology and system. Estimation on economic development stages and their characteristics is an important basis to formulate a scientific development strategy. In different stages of economic development, the industrial development sequence is different and the economic development mode is varying. The economic development stage of a country or region restricts the choice of leading industries and the mode of economic development. The choice of leading industries and the mode of economic development depend largely on the stage of economic development. Therefore, it is necessary to have a correct understanding about China's current development stage.

Many economists have done a lot of in-depth research on the criteria for dividing the stages of economic development from different perspectives. Liszt (1841) divided economic development into five stages: the primitive and uncivilized stage, the animal husbandry period, the agricultural period, the agro-industrial period and the agro-industrial and commercial period. In the critique of political Economy,

Karl Marx (1859) divided human society into Asian times, primitive society, feudal society, modern capitalist society and socialist society according to the mode of economic development. After the second world war,with the vigorous development of the second industrial revolution, a variety of emerging industries have emerged, and the economic circle has more comprehensive classification of the stages of economic development. Rostow (1960) in his book "The Stage of Economic Growth-Declaration of the Non-Communist Party", absorbed the German historical school economic development stage, Schumpeter's innovation theory, the way of dividing the Keynesian macroeconomic analysis methods such as theory, from the history perspective of the world economy, the human society is divided into five stages: traditional society, creates the premise for the take-off stage, to mature and the phase of mass consumption. In 1971, he proposed "thoery of sixth stage", the "pursuit of quality of life", in "politics and growing stages". The third and sixth stages are the two "abrupt changes" in social development, which are also the most significant. From the perspective of industrial structure, Hoffman divided the industrial development stage with the proportion of capital goods industry and consumer goods industry. Hoffman divided the industrialization process into four stages: the stage dominated by the consumer goods industry; the stage when the growth of capital goods industry exceeds the growth of consumer goods industry; growth of capital goods industry and balanced development of consumer goods industry; capital goods industry is dominant; the stage that realizes industrialization. Lewis's dualistic economic development war stage theory divides the economic development of developing countries into two stages: the stage dominated by traditional agricultural sector and the stage dominated by modern industrial sector. In the first stage, the infinite supply of labor and capital is scarce, when capital accumulation to catch up with the labor supply, labor infinite supply features disappear, economy entered the second phase of development, namely all factors of production are scarce, economic development into the industrialized society, Lewis believes in developing countries today are still in the first stage. The above studies have drawn meaningful conclusions on the classification of economic development stages from different perspectives. However, combined with the research purpose of this paper, the above classification standards are too rough and fail to formulate a specific and unified standard for economic development stages from the industrial level.

Many scholars take industrialization stage as an important basis to judge the stage of a country's economic development. In the process of industrialization,due to the limitation of technology and capital, most of the changes in industrial structure started from the light industry, and then gradually transferred to the basic industry sector dominated by raw material processing and energy industry, and entered the development stage centered on heavy industry. As basic industry sector development mature,provide the perfect conditions for the development of other sectors, and lay a good foundation, transfer to the processing and manufacturing industry concentration, when increasing value-added products, industrial processing degree deepening, industrialization has entered the phase of high degree of finish, after the innovation and technological progress, driven by the industrialization gradually into the technology intensive phase. Generally, industrialization is in the primary stage when the industrial structure tends to be dominated by the production of raw materials and the construction of basic industries. When the industrial structure is in the stage of high processing or the rapid development of heavy industry, that is, the process of industrialization is in the middle stage. When the internal structure of industry changes from the processing stage to the technology-intensive stage, the technology-intensive processing industry becomes the leading industry. The later stage of industrialization is characterized by technological innovation and technological progress as the main driving force of industrial growth. And the industrialization process corresponding to the leading industry of the evolution of the trajectory is: pretreating manufacturing industry as the leading-basic industries as the leading industry as the leading-technology intensive processing industry as the leading-modern service industry as the leading factor, the blunt low level to high level of industry evolution process is also the pattern of economic development to realize the process of transformation. Since industrialization is the period with the fastest speed and scale expansion in the process of economic development, the evolution process of industrial structure and the change process of economic development mode can also be partly reflected.

The output value of the three industries can partly reflect the characteristics of the stage of economic development. Before industrialization or in the early stages of industrialization, agricultural output value accounted for a larger proportion in the national economy, and the proportion of industry in the national economy was relatively low. However, the tertiary industry based on business and service industry also accounted for a larger proportion in the national economy in some preindustrial countries. At that stage, the pillar of the national economy in general is not industry, but agriculture or services in the tertiary industry, represents the direction of economic development industry. To satisfy basic life need, the first and third industry largely exist for development of industrial development, the present productive agriculture and the characteristics of the service or agriculture. With the advancement of industrialization, the proportion of agricultural output value continues to decline, while the proportion of industry gradually rises, and the proportion of service industry also increases. However,the speed is relatively slow compared with that of industry. The process of industry becoming the leading of national economy is also the process of industrialization. After the reform and opening up, the adjustment of

China's industrial structure and the change of leading industries began to correct the imbalance of industrial structure caused by the preferential development of heavy industry. However, the trend of industrial structure change in China basically follows and conforms to the general rule of industrial structure adjustment in industrialized countries. Since the middle and late 1990s, the leading industry of China's economic development has been industry, because the proportion of the secondary industry is higher than that of the secondary industry in the general industrialization mode.

In terms of which stage China is in industrialization, many domestic scholars have analyzed from different perspectives, and their opinions are basically the same: China is in the middle stage of industrialization. More authoritative view has the following kinds: Jiang Xiaojuan integrates the index analysis of per capita income, GDP structure, employment structure and urbanization level, and concludes that China is in the period of overlapping the two stages of completing traditional industrialization and promoting industrial modernization because of the significant deviation between the process of industrialization and various "standard models" [1]. Wang Yueping synthesizes Chenery's theory about measuring the stage of development, from the accumulation process, the industrial structure, openness and trade structure, employment structure and urbanization, social development and income distribution using 25 indicators, selection of data in 1998, the analysis results show that the industrialization level of China in $480~640 per capita gross domestic product price (1964, in US dollars) stage, economic development has entered the industrialization intermediate stage. [2]

---

[1] Jiang Xiaojuan.Upgrading of Industrial Structure at the Turn of the Century[M]. Shanghai Far East Press,1996.

[2] Wang Yueping.Adjustment and Upgrading of Industrial Structure in China: theory, demonstration and policy[M]. China Planning Press,2001.

4.2 Replacement of China's Leading Industry, Evolution of Industrial Structure and Transformation of Economic Development Mode

With the development of the economy, the industrial structure is constantly changing, leading industries are varying with time, industrial focus and direction are different, and the economic development model is also changing over time. Since the founding of the People's Republic of China, China's leading industries have experienced the following stages of evolution:

The first stage: 1952–1978, initial stage of industrialization led by heavy industry

After the founding of the People's Republic of China, under the guidance of the national economic reconstruction and catch-up strategy, China chose the strategy whose development priority is heavy industry. This development mode is the concrete practice of the marxist-leninist thought of development priority by means of production in China. Through the preferential development of heavy industry, especially national defense and basic industries represented by steel, the national economy, especially heavy industry, has developed rapidly since then. The strategy of giving priority to the development of heavy industry has not only accumulated the material capital and technological foundation needed for the construction of the national economy, but also transformed China from an agricultural country into an industrial power with a relatively complete industrial system. Giving priority to the development of heavy industry has also successfully transferred a large number of rural surplus labor and natural resources, promoting the rapid economic development. Development of heavy industry is endowed with super economic goal and task, industries especially heavy industry as the center of the whole economic development, under foreign trade condition has not yet started. So the severe suppression of domestic demand, relying on investment, pooling resources development model of the development of heavy industry in China started played an important role in the process of industrialization. However, long-term economic development is inclined to heavy industry, which not only causes the overinflated industrial structure and neglects the light industry and the tertiary industry, but also crowding out the resources needed by the development of other industries, resulting in the serious imbalance of the proportion of light and heavy industries, the stagnant development of the tertiary industry, the deformed industrial structure and the backward economic development mode. The policy of concentrating resources to develop heavy industry has resulted in a serious shortage of domestic consumption and a difficult improvement of people's livelihood. The abnormal industrial structure not only hinders the rational utilization and optimal allocation of resources, but also causes the national economic development to rely heavily on the input of resources, capital and unskilled labor, with high input, high consumption and low output, and low input-output efficiency. This mode of development is produced in a particular historical period and under a special international environment, and bears the heavy responsibility of super-economic objectives. It is of great significance to China in economic reconstruction and post-development, but the focus on growth and ignores the extensive development mode of growth quality does not make the people get the benefits of economic development, greatly violated the principle of people-oriented and sustainable development, so it can be said that the development mode of this period is not beneficial to our citizen.

Second stage: 1978–1990s, Consumer durables and textile industry dominant

From the early stage of reform and opening up to the mid-1980s,

China's economy recovered from the hindrance and destruction caused by political and cultural struggles. Since the Third Plenary Session of the Eleventh Central Committee, China has begun to explore a development path suitable for itself, shifting its development strategy from heavy industry to coordinated development of various industries. During this period consumer durables and textile industry became the leading industries of the national economy. The representative policy of industrial structure adjustment in this stage is as follows: based on agriculture, simultaneously develop agriculture, forestry, animal husbandry and fishery; In 1981, the State Council implemented the principle of "preferential development of raw materials, fuel and electric power supply, priority of renovation measures, priority of bank loans, construction, foreign exchange and imported technologies, and transportation support". China focus on adjusting the internal structure of industry, slowing down the development of heavy industry in a planned way, and placing the development of the consumer durables industry in an important position. During this period, in addition to the production of basic heavy industrial products for national defense and military industry and the development of the national economy, heavy industry also produced durable consumer goods such as television sets and washing machines. In addition, the relationship between heavy industry and other industries began to change: heavy industry serves agriculture and tertiary industry. For example, the development of the chemical industry focuses on supporting agriculture, producing fertilizers, pesticides, plastic films and other products. The leading industry policy favored light industry and consumer goods industry, so the light textile industry and food manufacturing industry developed rapidly. During this period, the adjustment of industrial structure achieved obvious results, and the proportion of industry and agriculture was gradually coordinated. At the same time, the consumer goods industry has made great progress and people's living standards have been improved. In 1989 our country issued "the decision of the state council on the current industrial policy points", shown in the table below, which focus on support and priority to the development of industry, as the relationship between the infrastructure and basic industries of national economy is essential. Generally they are all about light or heavy indusry which are energy saving, suggests that our country has specific measures to change the extensive pattern of economic development. In addition, driving power of the national economy is no longer limited to investment, consumption and import and export as new economic growth points.

Table 4–1 Prioritized and Restricted Industries

Give priority to developing and supporting industries	An industry that strictly controls and restricts its development
1.Agriculture and agro-industry	1.Cars and motorcycles
2.Light industry and textiles	2.High energy consumption products
3.Infrastructure and basic industries (transportation and energy)	3.High consumption products (such as aluminum,copper and chemical fiber products) produced with domestic scarce raw materials
4.Mechanical and electronic industry	4.Backward production methods,serious waste of resources and pollution of the environment (such as gasoline and diesel power generation)
5.High-tech industry	5.Low-quality liquor,common artificial leather,etc
6.Export industry to earn foreign exchange	—

Source: Ministry of Industry and Information Technology of China.

Third stage: Late 1990s-the present, heavy chemical industry dominant

Since the middle and late 1990s, after the sustained and rapid development of consumer goods industry, the shortage of industrial goods in China has been basically solved. Since 1992, the state has successively formulated a series of documents to determine the key industries for economic development, and the change of leading industries makes the economic development enter a new round of rapid development. In October 1992, the 14th National Congress of the

Communist Party of China (CPC) proposed the revitalization of mechatronics, petrochemicals, automobile manufacturing and construction, making them the pillar industries of the national economy.[①] The government promotes the adjustment of industrial structure with the key support of some industries, and at the same time,it also gives corresponding support in foreign trade policy. For example,we will encourage the export of processing agricultural and sideline products, textiles and home appliances with competitive advantages. We will encourage the import of new technologies and key equipment. At this stage, electronic and communication equipment, electrical and mechanical equipment and equipment, transportation and other industries rapidly grew into the leading industries of the national economy with the advantages of added value, industrial association and employment promotion. At the same time, transportation equipment, general and special machinery and equipment also became the backbone of the national economy. In the 21st century, due to the upgrading of consumption structure and the acceleration of urbanization, heavy industry has driven a new round of growth. Real estates, automobile and electronic communication have become the new leading industries of economic development. The development of these industries has driven the development of iron and steel, non-ferrous metals, chemical industries and other industries, but also pulled the development of electricity, coal, oil and other energy industries.

4.3 Comparison and Review of Existing Leading Industry Selection Schemes

At present, there are plans for leading industries in China and many provinces, including plans from Chinese Academy of Social Sciences,

---

① Accelerating the pace of reform, opening up and modernization, and winning a greater victory for the cause of socialism with Chinese characteristics.[N/OL].[1992-10-12].People's Daily online.

the former state planning commission and the development research center of the State Council. These schemes belong to the bottom-up selection schemes,which are characterized by the selection of leading industries by representative provinces and regions,the expansion of the scope to all provinces and regions of the country, and the rise to a more national macro level, forming a hierarchy of leading industries from the bottom up.

4.3.1 Program of Chinese academy of social sciences

Zhou shulian, professor of Chinese Academy of Social Sciences, put forward a set of choices for key industries and regional leading industries in China's industrial policy research and regional industrial policy research. The scheme systematically has studied and put forward the focus on the development of industry in China, on analysis of the current situation of the macro regional industrial structure (including three regions and countries respectively), puts forward some detailed developed region, the medium developed regions and underdeveloped region representative province industrial structure adjustment and the leading industry selection scheme.

1. National key industries selection scheme

One of the main contents of industrial policy is to determine the key industries in a certain period. The industrial system of a country can be divided into: Firstly, the main part of the industrial system can be called the pillar industries of the national economy. These industries not only provide most of the national income of a country, but also their internal composition and technical level determine the stage of the industrial structure in the process of evolution. Secondly, the leading industry in the development of national economy,which has a leading technological position, represents the direction or trend of the change of industrial structure. Leading industry has broad development prospects, and may grow into the future leading industry, driving the entire industrial structure to a higher level. Thirdly, it has been highly mature and has gone through the development limit. Therefore, in the whole industrial system, the relative position of industries tends to decline gradually. Such industries may have been pillar industries in the past, or even developed into leading industries. But these industries have begun to grow old and can be called recession industries over time.

The above three industries can be called "sunrise industry" and "sunset industry" respectively, which roughly outline the basic scope of the evolution process of a country's industrial structure, and are the basis for the selection of leading industries in this plan. This classification of industrial structure is based on the theory of industrial life cycle. In the choice of regional leading industry, not every industry in the flourishing period of life can become the leading industry. Only those emerging industries which are in the flourishing period of life and have high correlation degree and can drive the development of other industries can become the leading industries. Therefore, in addition to considering the life cycle of the leading industry, the position and influence of the industry in the regional industrial structure should also be considered.

The plan holds that the selection of leading industries should not only consider the general rules and theories of the evolution of industrial structure, but also relate to the specific realities of the country, such as the current situation of industrial development, technical and financial support, and resource endowment conditions. The plan holds that the industrial structure of China in the 1990s was characterized by the transformation from an agricultural country to an industrial country. The industrial structure was in the stage of rapid industrial expansion, and heavy industry was the leading industry of the national economy. At the same time, it also pointed out the problems existing in China's industrial structure at that time. Then, the technical level of the whole industry is generally low and the mode of production is backward. In addition, from the perspective of regional industrial structure, there is still the problem of inter-regional industrial convergence. The industrial structure of different provinces or regions imitates each other, ignoring the regional reality and blindly copying the model of other provinces.

The plan puts forward the order arrangement of the key development of China's industry in the 1990s and even a longer period of time. On the whole, it is advocates that basic industries such as agriculture, energy, transportation and important raw materials should be the key industries supported by the state. The internal goal of the processing industry is to improve the technical structure and improve the technology. We will give priority to the development of industries and actively develop industries that earn foreign exchange through exports. In terms of specific strategies, we should focus on strengthening the virtuous circle among the three industries: basic industry, processing industry and export foreign exchange earning industry. Firstly, the positive interaction between the basic industry and the processing industry should be formed, the development status of the basic industry should be improved so that the bottleneck of the processing industry would not be formed, the existing production capacity of the processing industry should be strengthened, and focus on the improvement of the profit rate and structure level of the processing industry. The development of processing industry should also provide advanced technical equipment and capital accumulation for the development of basic industry, and reduce the pressure on basic industry by saving energy use and improving energy consumption efficiency. Secondly, it forms a virtuous circle between the export industry and the industry that meets the domestic market demand. We will vigorously develop the export of labor-intensive products, import raw materials and advanced technology and equipment that are in short supply at home, and imports and exports to support the coordination and upgrading of the domestic industrial structure. This plan focuses on the adjustment of the relationship between the key industries in the national economy, not only expounds the specific plan for the selection of leading industries, but also puts forward the countermeasures for the adjustment of China's industrial structure. This plan captures the essence of the problem of industrial structure in our country and makes full use of the thought of development economics to seek growth through structural adjustment.Solutions put forward the leading industry selection, and expounds the interaction between various industries, reflects the industrial structure in our country dual task about "fixes" and "upgrade", the current has not fundamentally finished the task and a new era economic structure adjustment problem on transformation of economic development patterns. But in formulating policies and guidance for the practice there is still of high reference value.

2. Understanding on regional industrial structure and leading industries in China

The scheme also summarizes and summarizes the regional industrial structure in China. The current industrial situation of the three major regions in China is characterized by: (1) dual reverse gradient distribution of resources, technology and capital; (2) structural differences and industrial linkage pattern of "resource complementarity" or "product complementarity" between the East and the west, which forms a pattern of resource exploitation and raw material industry in the West and manufacturing industry in the east. Vertical regional division of labor system with industrial products as the main part. The plan holds that the dual objectives of balance and efficiency should be taken into account, regional horizontal economic integration should be vigorously developed, the spatial flow of industrial factors should be promoted, accelerating the formation of a unified national market. The eastern part of China has strong capital strength and high technology level, while the central and western regions are rich in resources and have great market potential. It is the key to deal with the development relationship between the eastern, central and western regions by complementing and opening up resources, developing cross-regional investment and cooperation, developing regional division of labor and forming reasonable spatial industry and regional structure. We should cultivate regional leading industries, establish self-adjustment mechanism of industrial structures, promote rationalization of regional industries, properly tilt, rationalize division of labor, coordinate development and overall arrangement of regional industrial layout.

The plan first classified the regions according to the development status of each province: (1) there was a large gap in the economic development level of each province and region. The indicator of Per capital GDP between 700 yuan and 900 yuan in Heilongjiang, Guangdong, Jilin, Hubei and Shandong; Between 550 yuan and 700 yuan are Xinjiang, Shanxi, Tibet, Hebei, Fujian, Qinghai and Inner Mongolia. Between 450~550 yuan are Ningxia, Hunan, Anhui, Jiangxi, Gansu, Shaanxi, Sichuan, Henan; Less than 450 yuan are Yunnan, Guangxi, Guizhou. (2) according to the industrialization rate, regions can be classified into agricultural provinces (the industrialization rate is less than 55%), agricultural and industrial provinces (the industrialization rate is between 55% and 65%), and industrial provinces (the industrialization rate is greater than 65%); according to the heavy industrialization rate, it can be divided into three categories: heavy (heavy industrialization rate is more than 60%), light (heavy industrialization rate is between 50% and 60%) and light (heavy industrialization rate is less than 50%).

The problems existing in the change of industrial structure in China's provinces and regions are as follows: (1) The development of basic industries lags behind. The production growth of energy and raw materials lags behind that of processing industry, especially in the sectors of light, textile and food. (2) High-grade consumer durables and office supplies such as televisions, refrigerators, washing machines and photocopiers are developing simultaneously in all provinces, and the phenomenon of repeated industrial layout is very serious.

This plan makes a comprehensive and profound analysis of China's regional industrial structure. It clearly proposes that cultivating regional leading industries is an effective measure to promote the rationalization of regional industrial structure and solve the convergence of regional industrial structure.

3. Selection of leading industries of some representative developed provinces, medium developed provinces and underdeveloped provinces

The principles of formulating and applying regional industrial policies proposed in this plan are: (1) The principle of comparative advantage. According to the endowment difference of regional factors of production, regional leading industrial policy should make full use of the advantages and avoid the disadvantages, give full play to the comparative advantages, adjust the spatial allocation of resources, and accelerate the overall development speed of regional economy and national economy. (2) Principle of scale economy. According to the theory of division of labor, an agreed division of labor for the purpose of obtaining economies of scale is inevitable between regions with similar income levels and endowment levels of factors of production. The ratio of income level and factor endowment level is similar in the underdeveloped and developed areas of China, so the division of labor oriented by scale economy should be encouraged among homogeneous areas. This is conducive to the optimization of resource allocation and industrial restructuring within the scope of expanding market space, so as to improve the economic efficiency of the whole region and accelerate the development of national economy. (3) Regional multiplier principle. Regional specialization is the basic power to promote the development of regional economy. Therefore, in order to promote the development of regional economy to the greatest extent, regional industrial policy must give full play to the role of regional specialization and follow the principle of regional multiplier maximization.

In order to obtain the maximum regional multiplier effect under the condition of open economy, it is required to reasonably determine the leading industry sectors when formulating regional industrial policies. On the other hand, it also requires the comprehensive development of other related industries in the region on the basis of specialization. Regional multiplier effect is directly proportional to industry "influence coefficient" and "induction coefficient". Therefore, these two coefficients can be used to evaluate the regional multiplier effect.

The principle of scale economy is a characteristic principle in the selection of regional leading industries. This principle maintains that economies of scale can be achieved in homogeneous regions through agreement division of labor,which is very beneficial to upgrading China's economic scale structure, improving economic benefits and avoiding regional industrial structure convergence. The following table is the selection plan of key industries in the whole country and some representative developed provinces, medium developed provinces and underdeveloped provinces. The program is based on the analysis of the leading industries from the bottom up, and several representative provinces and regions are selected according to different levels of development. As the representative provinces and regions make choices according to their own selection index system, the selected region's leading industry can better reflect the direction of regional economic development and the comparative advantage of the region. However, because the index system of leading industry selection of each representative province is not uniformed, it is difficult to choose among provinces and regions, and it is difficult to carry out regional horizontal coordination. For example,in the scheme,food and textile industries was considered as leading indusry in many provinces, which is overcrowded and unreseasonable, so regional comparative analysis should be made.

Table 4-2 Representative Regions in China

Region	Leading Industry
The nation as a whole	Transportation, energy industry, iron and steel industry, chemical industry, machinery industry, textile and garment industry, the technology industry
Beijing	—
Tianjin	—
Hebei	—
Liaoning	High quality steel products, general machinery, transportation machinery and complete sets of equipment, daily machinery, light industry professional equipment, spare parts processing,home appliances, daily chemical industry, fine chemical industry,plastics industry,chemical fiber and textile,oil refining, electronics industry, fast food,paper and culture and education, sewing leather,feed industry, specialty industry, construction industry, etc
Shanghai	Sewing, printing, stationery, daily chemical industry, medical chemical industry, plastics industry, precision machinery manufacturing, automobile industry, shipbuilding industry, power plant equipment manufacturing, electrical and instrumentation manufacturing
Jiangsu	Microelectronics industry, machinery industry, textile industry, petrochemical industry, construction industry, food industry
Zhejiang	Electronic and communication equipment manufacturing, instrumentation manufacturing, chemical industry, textile industry, food industry, building materials industry
Fujian	Food industry, metallurgy industry, building materials industry, forest industry
Shandong	—
Guangdong	Mechanical industry, food industry, chemical industry
Guangxi	The food industry
Hainan	—
Shanxi	—
Inner Mongolia	Coal industry, power industry, metallurgy industry, building materials industry, chemical industry (including forest products chemical), textile industry, food industry
Jilin	—
Heilongjiang	—
Anhui	—
Jiangxi	—

continued

Region	Leading Industry
Henan	Food industry, textile industry, mechatronics industry, chemical industry, building materials industry and construction industry
Hubei	Machinery industry, textile industry and metallurgy industry
Hunan	Food industry, chemical industry, metallurgy industry, building materials industry
Sichuan	Machinery industry, construction and building materials industry, food industry (including beverage industry), cotton and linen textile industry
Guizhou	Machinery industry, food industry, metallurgy industry, power industry, coal industry
Yunnan	Food industry, metallurgy industry, phosphorus chemical industry, rubber industry, forest products processing industry
Tibet	—
Shaanxi	Electronic industry, civil machinery industry,national defense industry, textile industry, coal industry, nonferrous metal industry
Gansu	Light textile industry, petrochemical industry, power industry, mechanical and electronic industry, building materials industry
Qinghai	—
Ningxia	—
Xinjiang	—

Source:Shulian Zhou. Research on China's Industrial Policy[M].China fiscal and economic press, 1990, 1991.

4.3.2 Former national planning commission program

The former national planning commission, Gao Chunde, put forward the selection scheme of China's leading industry in the book "China regional industrial structure". The plan considers that China's industrial layout has the following problems:unbalanced regional economic development still exists,unreasonable industrial structure and regional economic layout between regions, further widening economic gap, and incomplete economic rationalization of the three major regions in the east, west and central China. The eastern region has plenty of physical and human capital, technical conditions are better with resources shortage, under these circumstances, China should focus on the development of high-tech industry, capital and technology intensive products, committed to the development of export industries and products, high consumption, resource intensive, and the stress of transportation industry gradually transferred to the abundant natural resources of the Midwest. However, in actual economic development process, the eastern region has far from finished. Regional comparative advantages have not been taken full use of, and the central and western regions have not started from their own endowments to cultivate and develop leading industries and key industries that can give full play to their advantages. In addition, the eastern region has not achieved the goal of improving the level and grade of processing industry and expanding the share of foreign market. The regional industrial division of labor and resource allocation in the eastern, central and western regions have not reached the pareto effective state.

In view of the above problems, the basic countermeasures proposed in this plan are as follow: (1) In a certain period of time, the overall economic layout will not take new large-scale expansion. (2) In terms of regional development strategy, specific development priorities of each region shall be determined on the basis of the overall goal of national economic construction. The eastern region will focus on the development of technology-intensive, knowledge-intensive and export-oriented industries, vigorously develop sophisticated new products, and gradually improve its industrial structure and product structure in order to improve its competitiveness in exports. In the central and western regions, we should give full play to the advantages of abundant resources and speed up the construction and development of basic industries such as energy, raw materials processing, especially coal and petroleum processing, non-ferrous metals smelting and production, electric power, iron and steel, and building materials. At the same time, speed up the construction of infrastructure such as transportation trunk roads, make full use of the role of the golden waterway, consolidate the foundation of agriculture, strengthen the survey and exploration of resources, pay attention to cultural and educational undertakings. (3) Develop key industrial belts across the country to enrich and strengthen the skeleton system for China's economic layout. (4) Actively promote the process of urbanization and develop economic zones with their own characteristics.

The plan proposes to further divide the western part of China into the near and far west. At the same time, the economic area is unbalanced, and a division scheme based on "typology area" is proposed. This is planned on the basis of the "four zones" in China, taking the provinces as the basic unit, according to the industrial processing level and structural characteristics of the provinces and regions, the provinces and regions in China are further divided into five economic zones, and put forward the key industries for the development of each region.

(1) Processing type area. Including Shanghai, Beijing and Tianjin. In the choice of leading industries, the plan propose to develop high-tech products, including consumer electronics durable goods, fine chemicals, precision machinery manufacturing, automobile industry, high-grade light textile industry and so on.

(2) Processing leading type area. Including Heilongjiang, Liaoning, Shandong, Hubei, Sichuan, Zhejiang, Jiangsu, Fujian and Guangdong provinces. Heavy processing provinces should focus on the development of chemical industry, iron and steel industry, machinery manufacturing and other industries, as well as the production and development of transportation equipment manufacturing, large mechanical and electrical equipment manufacturing and import substitution of significant heavy machine tools and mechanical as well as electrical equipment manufacturing. The light-processing leading provincial areas focus on the development of food industry, textile industry, electronic industry manufacturing and other industries.

(3) Resource-dominated typology area. Including Guizhou, Yunnan,

Inner Mongolia, Xinjiang, Gansu, Ningxia, Qinghai, Guangxi and other provinces and regions. With the development of water power industry, coal extractor processing industry, petrochemical industry, non-ferrous metal smelting industry, ferroalloy manufacturing, carbon products, chemical fertilizer manufacturing and other industries are considered as the focus of the economic.

(4) Resource processing mixed type area. Including Anhui, Jiangxi, Henan, Hebei, Hunan, Jilin, Shaanxi, Shanxi and other provinces. It focuses on coal mining and processing industry, electric power industry, non-ferrous metal smelting and processing industry, building materials industry, light textile industry and heavy machinery manufacturing.

(5) Other typological areas. Including Hainan and Tibet provinces. Hainan is an agricultural region with tropical characteristic cash crops, such as rubber and tropical fruits, and it will continue to be a key industry in the future. Tibet is a cold region with poor natural conditions and a small population.The characteristic agriculture that should suit local natural condition.

On the whole,the selection of leading industries in some provinces and regions is subdivided into different types by its main products. The plan is specific and detailed, with strong operability. The leading industries selected by each province and region can better reflect the development status and comparative advantages of the region, and the region is scientifically divided according to the scientific basis. However, it is difficult to reach a consensus in the coordination and integration between provinces and regions due to the inconsistency of specific indicators and the difference of development goals and specific conditions.

4.3.3 Development research center program of the State Council

The topic of "regional industrial policy research" hosted by the development research center of the State Council puts forward a choice of leading industries in China. The research involves a wide range of contents, including the historical process and current situation of industrial development in various regions, the process of industrial structure evolution, the content and effect of industrial policies, and the selection of leading industries is one of its main contents.

According to this study, there are many problems in the development of regional industrial structure in China: (1) The "dual structure" between industry and agriculture has not been eliminated. (2) Insufficient momentum for agricultural development. (3) Weak basic industries constitute the bottleneck of economic development. The first is the lack of energy, the energy industry has not developed as fast as the growth momentum of the strong processing industry. Secondly, the transportation capacity is seriously insufficient. In quite a number of provinces and regions, the growth rate of freight transport turnover is far lower than the growth rate of total social output value,which affects the smooth progress of industrialization. (4) Industrial imbalance. Some industries are excessively dependent on natural resources. The processing industry overexpands, the raw material production capacity and the processing capacity present "the inverted pyramid type"; Single pillar industry, lack of industry. (5) Low degree of cooperation and division of labor among enterprises, resulting in weak inter-industry correlation. (6) The production capacity of the product chain is not symmetrical, some industries are under construction, the production capacity is idle, and the products are overstocked; another part of the production capacity is insufficient, product demand exceeds supply. (7) Aging in product structures.

(8) Backward services industry.

From a strategic point of view, this plan points out that China's industrial restructuring and the selection of leading industries should follow three principles: (1) Coordination. Put the coordination of industrial structure in the first place, make the supply and demand between each industry chain roughly balance, and make up for the technical fault between each industry. (2) Evolution. We should improve the level of industrial structure and shorten the time span of industrial structure evolution. (3) Differentiation. According to their own characteristics of resource endowment and the stage of industrial structure evolution, they can put forward their different industrial structure evolution goals.

The results of the selection of leading industries in this program have the following characteristics: the key industries of the country and region are relatively consistent; In the sense of coordination, there are agriculture,raw materials industry, electric power industry, transportation, post and telecommunications (including communications) industry; In the sense of evolution, there are mechanical industry, petrochemical industry and electronic industry. In addition, the export of foreign exchange to promote large industries, such as the textile industry and household appliances industry.

The national industrial policy should not only give full play to the comparative advantages of different regions and form a pattern of complementary advantages, but also be conducive to the evolution and transformation of the industrial structure in the three zones of east, west and central China, so as to prevent the current single vertical division of labor system from deteriorating. In the 1960s, the key industries in the west could be divided into three categories: Firstly, basic industries such as energy and raw materials, which served the processing industry in the east and the central and western regions and promoted the regional economic development; Secondly, mechanical and electrical industries and high and new technology industries that provide major equipment for various industrial departments throughout the country; Thirdly, agriculture and consumer goods industry with local characteristics. The development of these three industries is not only conducive to the development of advantages, but also to change the situation of the initial level of industrial structure. The east should develop processing industry and continuously spread the traditional processing industry to the west. The central region should give full play to industries with regional comparative advantages and potential, constantly improve the technical level of products, reduce consumption and improve quality, so as to enable products to enter the broad international market. Due to the different selection standards and methods of different provinces and regions, this plan lacks the basic comparison among regions, has a high overlap in regional leading industries, and has no inter-regional coordination and screening, so it is not operable.

Table 4–3 Development Research Center of the State Council on the selection for China's Leading Industries

Region	Leading Industry
The national	Agriculture, raw material industry, electric power industry, transportation industry, post and telecommunications (including communication), receiving and unloading industry, petrochemical industry, electronic industry, textile industry (key industries)
In the east	Export-oriented, high-precision processing industry
In the middle	—
In the west	Energy, raw materials industry, electromechanical industry and high and new technology industry, agriculture and consumer goods industry with local characteristics
Beijing	The first industry, modern non-staple food base (including modern vegetables and meat eggs and milk base); In the second industry, machinery industry, chemical industry, household goods industry, textile industry, food industry; In the third industry, modern service industry, including information service industry, cultural tourism, financial industry, consulting industry, exhibition industry and so on
Tianjin	Microelectronics industry (including electronic machinery industry), light, micro car manufacturing, petrochemical industry
Hebei	Textile industry, metallurgy industry, construction (including building materials industry), chemical industry, mechanical and electrical and light industry in some industries
Liaoning	—

continued

Region	Leading Industry
Shanghai	—
Jiangsu	Science and technology industry, mechatronics industry, chemical industry dominated by petrochemical industry
Zhejiang	Machinery industry, electronics industry, petrochemical industry, fluorine chemical industry, etc
Fujian	Paper industry, building materials industry, electronic industry
Shandong	Power industry, textile industry, food and beverage industry, petrochemical industry as the main body of the chemical industry, machinery industry, building materials industry
Guangdong	Light textile industry, petrochemical industry, machinery industry, building materials industry
Guangxi	Food industry, machinery industry, non-ferrous metal industry, building materials industry
Hainan	Natural gas, petroleum, chemical industry, Marine industry
Shanxi	—
Inner Mongolia	—
Jilin	Petrochemical industry, automobile industry
Heilongjiang	Machinery industry, petrochemical industry; industries of coordinating significance; agriculture,raw materials industry, electric power industry and industries with apparent functions; Textile industry, food industry, building materials industry
Anhui	Mechanical industry (including electronics industry)
Jiangxi	Mechanical and electronic industry, food industry, textile industry, metallurgy industry, chemical industry, building materials industry
Henan	Chemical industry, non-ferrous metal industry, textile industry, food industry, machinery industry, electronic industry
Hubei	Machinery industry, textile industry, food industry, metallurgy industry, chemical industry, power industry
Hunan	Mechanical and electronic industry, petrochemical industry
Sichuan	Machinery industry, construction and building materials industry, food industry, textile industry featuring silk and hemp
Guizhou	Energy industry, non-ferrous metal industry and chemical industry, mechanical processing and light industry
Yunnan	Food industry, rubber, spice based tropical crop cultivation and processing industry, phosphorus chemical industry, nonferrous metal metallurgy industry, new product processing industry
Tibet	Agriculture,livestock and forest products processing industry, mining,internal and external trade, tourism
Shaanxi	Food and beverage industry, textile and clothing industry, household appliances industry, machinery and electronics industry, coal power industry
Gansu	Energy industry, metallurgy industry, flower market industry, food industry
Qinghai	Energy industry, chemical industry
Ningxia	Power industry, light textile industry, machinery industry
Xinjiang	Textile industry, food industry, petroleum industry, chemical industry

Source: Ministry of Industry and Information Technology of China.

Combining the above three schemes, it can be seen that this bottom-up scheme well reflects the development conditions of various regions, as well as the comparative advantages and disadvantages of regional development. But the disadvantages with this method are that it is not easy to reach a consistent conclusion in the bottom-up process, because the benchmark and index system selected by the provinces and regions are not consistent,and the goals and levels of development are not the same. On the one hand, it is difficult to choose the leading industry in a higher level region because it is difficult to select and compare the leading industry among regions. Reluctantly, on the other hand,even if in the provinces choose the leading industries, as well as the scheme on the basis of a higher level to choose the leading industry of the regional level, a bottom-up system of regional leading industry in China will be messy, as mentioned before, the number of the leading industry is not the key element for the dominant industry. Numbers are not playing an important role of leading industry in the national economy, sometimes the leading industry of the potential function could even hinder the economic development and the transformation of the pattern of economic development.

4.4 Selection of Leading Industries and Review of Industrial Policies

4.4.1 Relevant policies to support key industries during the ninth five–year plan

Period of the ninth five-year plan (1996–2000), China's economic "supply" era has ended, during this period, the government put forward two economic development strategic: one is the economic system, from the traditional planned economic system to socialist market system, the second is the development modes, from extensive to intensive changes.

The requirements of the ninth five-year plan for transforming the economic development mode from the industrial structure are to strengthen the development of primary industry and improve the supporting role of agriculture in the development of national economy. Adjust and improve the secondary industry, develop basic industry, revitalize pillar industries, take industry as the main force of economic growth and export expansion; We will give full play to the role of the tertiary industry as the main channel for employment.

1. Determination of national leading industries and key supporting industries during the ninth five-year plan period

During the ninth five-year plan period, in order to strengthen the basic position of agriculture, relieve the restriction of basic industries on the national economy, alleviate the contradiction of insufficient infrastructure development, and realize the upgrading of industrial structure in telecommunications, electronics, machinery, automobile and construction industries, so as to promote economic growth, the state has made efforts to promote agriculture, infrastructure and basic industries, pillar industries and light textile industries, as well as the key development targets in the tertiary industry and other fields have put forward comprehensive requirements.

2. Development of industrial leading industries

Pillar industries should be further oriented to the market and give full play to the role of the market in allocating resources. The focus of pillar industries is to raise the starting point of technology, fully introduce and absorb foreign advanced technology and foreign capital, so as to strengthen the domestic independent development and innovation capacity. Under the condition of insufficient technological innovation ability, the state should combine technology introduction, digestion and absorption to cultivate our competitive advantages.

At the industrial level, the focus of the mechanical industry is to improve the development and manufacturing of complete sets of large equipment in the electrical and chemical industries, and to improve the quality and performance of important basic machinery represented by machine tools and instruments. The machinery industry should develop new products, improve the manufacturing capacity of complete sets of equipment, and ensure the domestic demand for processing equipment needed for the manufacture of major technical equipment, upgrade and improve the production capacity of complete sets of large thermal power and hydropower equipment, focusing on the design of high-capacity, high-efficiency power generation equipment.

The electronic industry needs to focus on the development of integrated circuits, computer software development, communication equipment manufacturing, and new types of components, so as to improve the level of information systems and equipment in the national economy. The state will develop micron technology in integrated circuits, chip components in electronic devices, optoelectronic devices and new display devices. Development and production of computer hardware equipment and other accessories, digital program-controlled switches, mobile and optical fiber equipment, push basic software and application software in accordance with international standards.

Petrochemical industry focuses on deep processing and comprehensive utilization, research and development of synthetic fibers, synthetic rubber and synthetic resin. Oil refining industry should focus on improving product quality and grade, expand the scale of enterprise production. In terms of oil supply distribution, the state should improve the transportation efficiency of existing refined oil storage and transportation facilities, and gradually build and improve refined oil pipeline transportation. In the aspect of ethylene production, the state mainly transform and expand the original ethylene equipment, develop large-scale ethylene equipment and improve the quality of ethylene products.

The auto industry focuses on the production and supply of auto parts, mainly on the manufacture of economical cars and heavy vehicles, and strengthens the research and development system of auto technology.Accelerate the restructuring and transformation of the automobile industry, implement scale operation, set up large automobile and motorcycle production enterprises, support the rise of a number of key parts and components backbone enterprises, as well as establish a general domestic and foreign standard auto parts production system.

The state should increase the added value of the construction industry, gradually establish a construction market system, regulate the price of construction products, and improve the comprehensive utilization efficiency of land and buildings. The construction of building materials industry is to adjust the structure, save resources and energy, reduce the focus of pollution emissions, develop and promote the use of environment-friendly new building materials, vigorously develop commercial concrete, limit the use of cement accumulation and solid clay bricks, thereby improve the utilization efficiency of construction waste residue.

3. About agricultural development

The ninth five-year plan calls for strengthening agriculture and ensuring the steady growth of grain, cotton, oil and other basic agricultural products. Accelerate the development of chemical fertilizer as the focus of agricultural industry, chemical fertilizer industry to make full use of natural gas and raw materials, focus on the construction of large nitrogen fertilizer base, and actively develop phosphorus compound fertilizer and potash fertilizer. Pesticide production mainly increases the development of new varieties to reduce the pollution and harm of pesticides to human and environment. The state should increase the production and supply of agricultural film, adjust the structure of materials used for agricultural film, accelerate the development of small and medium-sized agricultural machinery and machinery for processing agricultural products, and improve large agricultural machinery.

4. Developing the tertiary industry

On the basis of the development of agriculture and industry, the state will develop production-oriented services.It advocate to develop emerging service industries such as information and technology consulting, legal consulting and accounting auditing services, and improve intermediary services such as asset appraisal, business agency and coordination. At the same time, we will standardize the development of the financial and insurance industries so as to guide the healthy development of the real estate industry. The state would improve the wholesale markets and logistics services for agricultural and sideline products, industrial consumer goods, and means of production, introduce and develop new marketing methods such as agency system and chain operation.

4.4.2 The focus industries and related policies during the tenth five-year plan

The tenth five-year plan has carried out the guiding ideology of development as the theme and structural adjustment as the key line. In the new era of China's accession to WTO, a new strategic has been put forward in view of three prominent contradictions existing in the economic structure: unreasonable industrial structure, unbalanced regional development and uncoordinated urban-rural development. Special industrial structure adjustment has put forward clear requirements and comprehensive deployment: to consolidate the basic position of agriculture in the national economy, speed up industrial restructuring and optimization of structure, develop the service industry, speed up the informationalization of the national economy, and further strengthen the construction of water conservancy, transportation, energy and other basic industries, etc., in accordance with the above ideas, the tenth five-year plan put forward the following industry development thoughts.

About the primary industry. Focus on optimizing varieties, improving quality and increasing benefits, so we will adjust the crop structure, variety structure and quality structure of planting industry, and develop high-quality, high-yield and high-efficiency planting industry. Continue to build high-quality cotton bases in xinjiang, double-bottom rape bases in the Yangtze river basin and green food bases. We will expand the acreage of feed crops, improve livestock and poultry breeds, and accelerate the development of animal husbandry, strengthen the degree of sustainable utilization of fishery resources, and develop aquaculture and pelagic fishery. We should adjust the pattern of agricultural production, develop characteristic agriculture, and form a pattern of large-scale and specialized production. We should push coordination between service and policy support for the export of agricultural products, and develop agriculture exports to earn foreign exchange.

About industry. In terms of raw material industry, we will actively develop the production industries of three major synthetic materials and fine chemical products, stainless steel and cold-rolled plates, alumina, rare earth deep-processing products, new dry-process cement, high-efficient fertilizers, pharmaceuticals and key intermediates that are in high demand.We should develop light industries such as wood pulp, high-grade paper and paperboard, new household appliances, differentiated fibers, industrial textiles, high-grade fabrics, brand-name clothing and deep processing of agricultural products.

Relying on major projects, we should revitalize the equipment manufacturing industry and improve the design, manufacturing and complete set of technical equipment. The development of CNC machine tools, instruments and basic components should put to an important position, so as to improve the quality and technical power. We will support the development of new types of high-efficiency power equipment such as large gas turbines, large pumped storage units and nuclear power units, ultra-high voltage power transmission and transformation equipment, complete sets of large metallurgical, chemical and petrochemical equipment, urban rail transit equipment, and new types of papermaking and prevention machinery. Development of agricultural machinery, civilian ships and economic cars. We will improve the manufacturing of automobiles and key components, develop efficient, energy efficient and low-emission automobile engines and hybrid power systems. Last but not least,we should develop the construction industry.

About the tertiary industry, this book develop a service sector oriented toward living consumption and promote tourism as a new economic growth point. We will strengthen the community service sector and further develop the commercial retail and catering industries. We will actively develop financial and insurance services for living expenses, popular entertainment industry, culture and sports industry. We will focus on production-oriented services, carry out chain operations, logistics and multimodal transport, transform and upgrade the traditional logistics, transportation and postal industries. Standardize accounting services, legal services, management consulting,engineering consulting and other intermediary services. We should also develop the information services industry, especially the Internet and information technology application consulting and database services.

About high and new technology industry, the tenth five-year plan build a number of major high-tech projects, including high-speed broadband information networks, deep submicron integrated circuits, biotechnology projects, and new launch vehicles. It propose to promote the industrialization of new and high technologies such as digital electronic products, new display devices, optoelectronic materials and devices, modern traditional Chinese medicine, and satellite applications, and support all industries in developing technology oriented products.

4.4.3　Key industries during the eleventh five-year plan

According to the requirements of the new industrialization road, the eleventh five-year plan take the cultivation of independent innovation ability as the key to enhance the competitive strength of the industry, it propose to develop the industry with comparative advantages, and focus on improving the technical level and competitive strength of the industry. The service sector should focus on supporting key areas and weak links in the service sector related to manufacturing, and supporting the growth and development of emerging service industries as well as new forms of business. It suggests to promote standardization of the service sector, provides standards for the service sector, and gradually improve industrial structure with priority given to the service economy.

1. Developing high-tech industries

With the goal of industrial agglomeration and large-scale development, the industrial chain of high-tech industry should be promoted from processing and assembly to independent research and production, the value chain of high-tech should be advocated, and the industrialization of independent innovation results of high-tech industry should be strengthened. Support and guide the formation of a number of independent intellectual property rights and core competitiveness of leading industries and outstanding performance of transnational high-tech research and production enterprises.

The electronic information industry was encouraged, with the focus on the production of integrated circuits, new components and other electronic information core products, give priority to supporting the research and development and production bases of wireless communication and network equipment and other information products, build application software and micro-electronic industry bases, cultivate optoelectronics industrial groups, and extend the electronic industrial chain. We will vigorously develop basic software and key application software, build nationwide digital television networks, mobile communications and new-generation information network infrastructure.

Developing new materials industry, new materials around information, aerospace, machinery and equipment, new energy, such as the needs of the development of the industry in the new period the development of special function. High performance structure materials, and new composite materials are encouraged and supported for the development of environmental protection and energy saving materials, as well as new materials research and development, and gradually establish the innovation system. The plan promotes the industrialization of high-performance new materials that are urgently needed in the aerospace,information and biotechnology industries.

2. Revitalize the equipment manufacturing industry

The emphasis on equipment manufacturing industry is to improve the research and development design ability of major technical equipment, push the manufacturing and system integration of core components. In the field of high-efficiency and clean power transmission and transformation and high-grade CNC machine tools and basic manufacturing equipment, the research and development of a number of important equipment has a significant impact on technological innovation and comprehensive strength improvement which plays a driving role. So we should develop and build a batch of large coal chemical complete set equipment, large ethylene complete set equipment, large metallurgical equipment, large coal mine comprehensive mining equipment lamp. Develop a number of large environmental protection equipment such as air pollution and urban industrial waste treatment, as well as large environmental protection and resource comprehensive utilization equipment.

Strengthen independent research and development and design capabilities for ships,promote the development of supporting marine equipment and large shipbuilding facilities, and focus on developing new types of ships and marine engineering equipment with high added value and high technology. We should build large shipbuilding bases, merge and reorganize small shipbuilding enterprises, eliminate backward ones, and rationally guide shipping enterprises to develop in a rational way, construct more than 10000 teu container ships, large energy and raw material transport ships and offshore petroleum engineering equipment and supporting equipment.

3. Promote the process of social and economic informatization

Drive industrialization with informatization, promote informatization with industrialization. The key point of informationization transformation of manufacturing industry is to promote intelligent production process and equipment and informationization of enterprise management. We should improve information technology in electromechanical and manufacturing industries, promote intelligent control and agile manufacturing technologies in mechanical manufacturing, and strengthen on-site monitoring and control of production processes. Accelerate the construction and popularization of the national basic information database, optimize the information resource structure, so as to realize the basic information sharing. We should strengthen the information technology in production, exchange, and circulation, and make further use of information resources as well as dissemination and utilization of information. Build and gradually improve broadband communications networks and steadily advance the development of communications and the internet. We should improve the safe transmission and use of information, promote the industrialization of information security products, strengthen the construction of information security infrastructure and the security protection of information network and national important information system. We should build and develop specialized information security services, such as assessment, consulting, and disaster preparedness, and improve the system for grading security protection and assessing information security risks.

4. Accelerate the development of consumer services and producer services

Raise the proportion of the service sector in the national economy, vigorously develop services for consumption and production, and develop new forms of business in the service sector.

Actively promote the practice of modern logistics management technology,guide enterprises to participate in the differentiation of internal logistics socialization, improve the degree of social division of labor. Cultivate and support specialized logistics enterprises, push the development of third-party logistics, establish and promote the construction of logistics standardization system. We should promote the informationization of the logistics industry and strengthen the development and utilization of innovative forms of logistics. Extend the enterprise's logistics industry chain, to achieve the enterprise procurement, production organization and product sales of a set of long industrial chain operation. Integrate logistics infrastructure and build large logistics hubs. We should develop and apply new information technologies, strengthen connectivity and supporting services of logistics hubs, promote efficient logistics services, develop intelligent transportation systems.

Develop the financial and insurance services in a well organized manner, actively guide and support private finance in various forms of ownership, small and medium-sized Banks, fund management companies, securities companies, financial leasing companies and other non-bank financial institutions, and faciliate finance channels for small and medium-sized enterprises and non-governmental organizations that provide microfinance. We should encourage financial innovation and support further improve the online financial service system, develop a variety of financial and foreign exchange hedging tools,and vigorously support overseas financial services and foreign exchange risk management. We should expand insurance services to all aspects of people's lives, develop old-age and medical insurance, agricultural and agricultural disaster insurance, and expand the channels for investment and application of insurance funds.

Keep up with the trend of upgrading in consumer consumption structure, enrich the content of consumer service industry, and constantly adapt to and meet the diversified service needs of consumers. We should raise the proportion of the commercial service sector, and encourage the development of consumer services that involve a variety of forms of ownership and different types of business.We should develop modern logistics and organizational forms such as franchise and chain operations. We will appropriately adjust policies concerning the real estate industry, improve the housing supply structure, focus on the construction of commercial housing and affordable housing, appropriately regulate the primary and secondary real estate markets and the rental market, expand financing channels for real estate development, supervise and standardize housing consumption credit. On the premise of maintaining the sustainable development of original tourism resources, we should innovate the forms and types of tourism development, develop sustainable and environment-friendly tourism forms and encourage scientific popularization, aerospace, marine and other special tourism and featured tourism commodities.

4.4.4 Changes in industrial policies from the ninth five–year plan to the eleventh five-year plan

From the ninth five-year plan to the eleventh five-year plan, the change of leading industries has always been accompanied by the main line of industrial restructuring and the theme of the transformation of economic development mode. The most important characteristic of the adjustment and change of the leading industry is to keep the balanced development of the industry. During the ninth five-year plan period, the leading industries of the national economy are mainly machinery, petrochemical, electronics, automobile and construction. Machinery industry, represented by the development and manufacture of complete sets of large equipment such as electric power, chemical fertilizer and ethylene, is the basis and bottleneck for the survival and development of other industries in the national economy. The petrochemical industry focuses on the deep processing and comprehensive utilization of petroleum, and develops the production of synthetic fibers, synthetic resins, synthetic rubber and ethylene. On the one hand, machinery and petrochemical industries are both capital-intensive heavy industries; on the other hand, these industries are basic industries, most of which depend on their production. The electronics industry focuses on integrated circuits, emerging components, computers and software, and mobile communications. What's more, the construction industry and automobile industry with strong industrial correlation function have also become the leading industries of the national economy. The leading industries during the tenth five-year plan period include foreign exchange earning agriculture, raw material industry and equipment manufacturing, high and new technology industry, etc. The new and high technology industry is quite different from the industrial development plan during the ninth five-year plan period. It is mainly represented by information technology, integrated circuits, biological engineering and new launch vehicles, etc. Emerging industries have become the leading industries of the national economy, indicating that China's industrialization has reached a new stage. The industrial sector is still dominated by basic industries such as equipment manufacturing and raw material processing. Different from the ninth five-year plan, the equipment manufacturing industry focuses on CNC machine tools, instruments and basic parts, ship equipment and devices. During the ninth five-year plan period, basic industries such as electric power and petrochemical industry are the focus, while the basic industries during the tenth five-year plan period included heavy industries such as machine tools and generator transmission and transformation devices, as well as intermediate products in light industries such as synthetic materials, fibers and paperboard. In accordance with the requirements of the new industrialization road, the eleventh five-year plan takes the enhancement of independent innovation ability as the central link, gives full play to the comparative advantage and competitive advantage of its own resources, and improves the technical level and competitiveness of the industry. The leading industries in this period are high-tech industry, equipment manufacturing, basic industries such as energy and raw materials, as well as production-oriented service industry. The content of high-tech industry is basically the same as that of the tenth five-year plan. The difference lies in that the eleventh five-year plan puts the high performance computer and network equipment of wireless communication and the electronic information industry represented by photoelectric communication into a prominent position. The biological industry focuses on biomedicine and genetic engineering, while increasing the production of new materials. At the same time, the equipment manufacturing industry, in addition to the content of the tenth five-year plan period, also increased the shipbuilding manufacturing industry during the eleventh five-year plan period. In terms of basic energy industry, the focus during the eleventh five-year plan period is on renewable energy and sustainable construction of energy production and supply. The emphasis on raw material industry development lies in structural reorganization and layout adjustment, which is the biggest difference in the tenth five-year plan. Besides, the eleventh five-year plan also put transportation, modern logistics, financial services, information services and other production-oriented services in the focus of industrial planning, in order to make them better serve industrialization. Under the requirements of expanding domestic demand and changing the mode of economic development, the content of consumer services was enriched during the eleventh five-year plan.

4.5 Experiences on Leading Industries and Economic Development Mode

To study the choice of China's leading industries and the transformation of the economic development mode, it is necessary to compare and study the successful experiences and lessons from other countries to avoid repeating the detours. Countries with different stages of economic development have different economic development strategies. But what's the same in the process of economic development? Economic development mode depend on the expansion of the total economic scale is not enough to achieve the optimal scale and economic benefit, we also should adjust industrial structure to achieve industrial upgrading. Leading industry replacement is the catalyst to achieve this goal. This chapter compares four typical countries that have experienced the change of leading industry and successfully realized economic take-off, summarizes the general change trend and policy direction, and provides reference for the choice of leading industry and the transformation of economic development mode in China.

4.5.1 Cases from the USA

1. The history of the change of leading industries in the United States

For a long time before the 1880s, the United States was in the stage of agricultural economy, and agriculture was the dominant part of the national economy. From 1607 to 1776, 90% of the colonies were engaged in agriculture, fishing, and natural resources extraction. After the civil war, the United States gradually established a political system combining federal centralization and state and local decentralization, and capitalism developed rapidly. By the end of the 1870s, the first industrial revolution was completed. Since then, the United States has transitioned from an agricultural country to an industrial country. Since 1776 the change of the leading industry in America has gone through four stages:

(1) Before the late 19th century, dominated by agriculture and textiles. The specific resource conditions and capitalist system conditions in the United States, the increasing international market demand for American agricultural products in the last 50 years of the 19th century created superior conditions for the development of American agriculture. Before the first industrial revolution, industrial development was mostly limited by power energy, which was decentralized, concentrated and difficult to alter. With the emergence and promotion of steam engine, agricultural productivity was greatly improved, and industrial development gradually got rid of the limitation of location and could be successfully carried out in places far away from natural resources. Driven by the first industrial revolution, agricultural productivity in the United States increased by 44.19% between 1840 and 1900. From 1865 to 1914, the productivity of the entire American economy, including industry, increased by about 20%. Agricultural productivity was much higher than the average level of the

entire American economy during the same period. After the 1860s, the United States successfully realized the mechanization of agricultural production by virtue of advanced agricultural production technology. At the same time, agriculture, as a leading industry, led to the emergence and development of a series of manufacturing sectors. In 1880, the manufacturing industry of the United States accounted for 26%, 30.6% for textiles, leather and shoes, 19.3% for forestry products, and 75.9% for the national economy. [①] Among the industrial composition,textile industry occupies the dominant position. In 1860, the output value of cotton textile industry in the United States was second only to the agricultural processing industry, accounting for 15.8% of the output value of the entire industrial sector. The development of the textile industry led to an increase in the demand for textile machinery and stimulated the development of the machinery manufacturing industry, as well as the development of cast iron, machine tools and metal processing and sewing machinery manufacturing related to the machinery manufacturing. With the development of textile industry and food manufacturing industry, the United States gradually formed an industrial structure dominated by labor-intensive light industry and successfully realized the primitive accumulation of capital in the early stage of industrialization.

(2) From the 1880s to the early 20th century, the second industrial revolution, basic industrial construction is the abbreviation of the comprehensive industrialization of the United States. In 1890, the total industrial output value of the United States surpassed that of Britain,France and Germany, ranking first in the world. In 1920, exports increased about 23 times as much as in 1860, and imports increased more than 13 times, much faster than industrial growth. Because of the need for economic exchanges between different regions

---

① Fett, Culbert. A history of the American economy[M]. Liaoning People's Publishing House, 1981.

and the strong support of the government, the construction of railway transportation again set off a peak, which laid the foundation for the United States to become the main artery of the industrial empire. Railway construction has given full play to its leading role of industrial association. Under the driving force of railway industry, other basic industries, such as steel, oil and coal, have also developed vigorously, and the basic industry itself has led to the rise and development of other industrial sectors. Agricultural products manufacturing, textile industry, wood processing, tobacco, papermaking and other light industrial manufacturing sectors have become the main industrial sector. Due to the development of basic industry and its driving role, the United States became a country with complete industrial sectors and a modern industrial system at the end of the 19th century.

In the early 20th century, the second scientific and technological revolution marked by the development of electric power and internal combustion engine provided strong material and technological support for the rise and development of the steel and automobile industries in the United States. During this period, the iron and steel industry and automobile industry were the leading industries of the national economy. The development of the American steel industry began with the improvement and gradual establishment of the large-scale coking process. With the invention and use of electric power, the steel industry made great progress in the smelting furnace. Metallurgical technology has not only increased steel output, but also improved quality and reduced costs. At the same time, metallurgical technology also stimulated the development of iron and steel processing industry and other machine tool industry. American iron and steel industry in the United States to realize industrialization has the decisive significance, in the iron and steel industry, the United States not only become the world's largest producer of manufactured goods, and the agricultural machinery, machine tools, electrical equipment and other industrial products are widely sold in the world market, more than 100 years, iron and steel industry has always been a symbol of American economic power.

(3) In the 1920s, the American automobile industry promoted the use of manufacturing process mechanization, assembly line technology, parts generalization and production standardization, and the automobile industry developed rapidly and became the leading industry of the American national economy. Since 1905, the United States automobile production jumped to the first place in the world, the United States automobile production accounted for 73.33 percent of the world in 1910. The rapid development of automobile industry has led to the rapid development of machinery manufacturing, rubber tires and other industries in the same period. The automobile industry has not only driven the development of other industries with extensive industrial correlation effect, but also changed the consumption pattern of Americans. The United States was the first country to enter the stage of mass consumption described by Rostow. Cars, buildings, electrical equipment etcs. played a huge role in promoting the development of the American economy and the change of consumption pattern during this period. Installment business and franchise system came into being, making the development and prosperity of insurance banking and industrial service industry in the United States, and stimulating manufacturers and technicians to promote their technology and services at an unprecedented speed and scale.

(4) Since the 1970s, when the automobile and steel industries in the United States were in decline, the rapid development of high-tech industries represented by information technology, microcomputer technology, new materials and new energy, space technology and marine technology led to profound changes in the American economy. In order to meet the needs of war, technology-intensive industries in the United States began to develop intensively during world war II, and

44technology-intensive industries such as semiconductors, communications and electronic computers had developed greatly at that time. Since the 1980s, the production of American microcomputers has been growing at an annual rate of 30%, the production of integrated circuits has been growing at a rate of more than 30%, and the international market share of optical fiber has been growing at a rate of 40%~50% every year. High-tech industry has become the industry with the fastest growth momentum. At the same time, the high-tech industry in the United States continues to penetrate into the traditional industry and modern service industry, changing the production mode of each industry. The third industrial revolution promoted automation and information technology in production, and also brought about a new business environment, which led to more people engaging in the management and coordination of non-directly productive services. Life service industry, business service industry and public service industry are growing. Thus, the United States entered a "post-industrial era" dominated by tertiary industry. Since the 1990s, the us government has put forward the idea of "information superhighway", taking the high-tech industry represented by the information industry as the leader of economic development, trying to get rid of the crisis and enhance international competitiveness. Information technology industry has played an irreplaceable role in the growth of the national economy of the United States. It has also changed the production and operation mode of American enterprises, the demand structure of American people and the economic development mode.

2. Policies and measures adopted by the us government to support pillar industries

Although the United States is a country of economic liberalism, the U.S government also attaches great importance to special period of supports for certain industries. After the civil war, the United States entered the period of high protective tariff system, and the trade protection legislation emerged one after another. Tariff legislation mainly targeted at some agricultural products and advanced woolen, cotton, linen, cloth, steel and other industries. By imposing high protective tariff system on these industries, it not only inhibited imports, but also appropriately protected and stimulated the development of domestic agriculture, textile industry and manufacturing industry. From the second world war to the 1980s, the US government greatly promoted the development of capital-intensive industries represented by the two leading industries, steel and automobile, through policies such as depreciation preferential treatment, accelerated equipment renewal and tax deduction for enterprise investment. In addition, in order to maintain the autonomy of its pillar industries, the us government has strengthened its legislation on foreign investment intervention and trade protection.

The American government also attaches great importance to the support of the high-tech industry. Promoting the development of high-tech industry is one of the themes that the government pays most attention to and gives priority to. First, the US government has made science and technology a top priority. The federal government has increased spending on research and development, while improving the research system, especially by giving strong support to cooperative research between enterprises and research institutes, and promoting the research and development and industrialization of new and high technologies. Second, the government encourages enterprises to research and innovate and promotes the development of high-tech industries. On the one hand, anti-trust laws have been liberalised to allow companies to jointly develop new products. The other is tax support for new industries. Third, the US government supports the development of venture capital and USES the market to guarantee the capital needed to develop high-tech industries. Fourth, the government provides a huge market for high-tech industries through military orders.

In the face of the competitive pressure in the high-tech field from Japan and other countries in the new era, the United States focuses on the high-tech industry represented by the information industry and provides various guarantees in terms of organization, legislation and implementation. The US government has identified information, automation, environment, defense technology and other key areas to tackle, among which the high-tech industry is the most attractive.

3. Experience and lessons from the change of American leading industries

For a long time, the American-style industrial policy was only an auxiliary measure for market failure, and did not directly interfere with the market and specific resource allocation. It was mainly manifested in industrial policies like legal protection and infrastructure construction. On the one hand, it creates a good market competition mechanism and an open enterprise development environment. On the other hand, it also provides a perfect infrastructure and a world-renowned technology and education platform. But American-style industrial policy has its drawbacks:

First, the important features of the industrial policy is a programmatic, did not make specific to the development of pillar industry and leading industry of the long-term planning, more is not clearly the best standard of industrial structure and leading industry, but through a way to create the economic environment for the industry adjust, or are the problems in the process of natural development of the economy to take remedial measures. Although subjective policy mistakes can be avoided, the self-adjustment effect of market mechanism in the process of structural adjustment is generally lagging behind, which cannot quickly make up for the damage of industrial structure caused by market failure, which inevitably brings adverse effects to economic development.

Second, American industrial policy lacks some necessary

regulatory authority and means, and regulatory agencies are also subject to the executive, legislative and judicial branches, which are independent and mutually restrictive. The inconsistencies among the three can often reduce the power of regulatory agencies. Moreover, regulatory agencies themselves are industrial in nature, driven by different purposes, lack of coordination with each other,even contradictory. The lack of close coordination and cooperation between industrial policies and trade policies is also a defect of American industrial policies, especially in the automobile, steel and electronics industries of the United States after the cold war.

Because of this, since the middle and late 1980s, the United States has begun to attach importance to the guiding role of the government in the adjustment of industrial structure. The American government has to actively participate in the formulation and implementation of domestic industrial planning and international trade policies, and consciously use the macro-planning means of the government to cooperate with market forces to optimize the industrial structure.

4.5.2 Cases of Japan

1. The evolution of the internal structure of Japan's industry and the changes of its leading industries after World War II

After World War II, Japan's economy was in ruins. The Japanese government in order to quickly recover from the post-war difficulties, positive intervention in the economy, the coal, electric power, steel and other basic industries as the leading industry of the recovery period, formulated a series of such as raw materials distribution, financial loans tilt, price subsidies development measures, such as the basic industry in 1950, quickly return to the highest level before the war, the other light industry manufacturing in basic industries also leads to the rapid recovery. In 1955, the whole industrial system of Japan was restored to the highest level before the war, which laid a solid foundation for the further development of Japanese economy.

From the 1950s to the 1970s, Japan moved from the initial introduction and imitation of technology to the improvement of technology and import and export products, entering the era of technological innovation. Japan's leading industries began with automobile, machinery, petrochemical, non-ferrous metals, electrical, electronic and other industries. During that time, the auto industry was particularly notable. In 1970, Japan became the second one in the world compared to the United States as a major producer of automobiles, and in 1980 it surpassed the United States. Under the industrial policies, the automobile industry, steel, aluminum, rubber, paint, glass and other industries have developed rapidly.

After the 1973 oil crisis, the Japanese government adopted a series of policies to support high-tech industries in order to adjust the domestic industrial structure and maintain its international competitiveness. Japan introduced "special electron industry and special machinery industry are temporary measure law", made "electronic computer changes plan in an advanced degree". However, this industrial restructuring did not bring a significant boost to economic growth. After completing the task of catching up with technology, Japan itself has not quickly established an effective and unique scientific research mechanism. In fact, Japan has not been able to identify new leading industries since the 1980s, thus unable to identify new economic growth points with the development of new technologies.

2. Main policies and measures of the Japanese government to revitalize leading industries

The Japanese government's active strengthening and guidance of industrial policy contributed a lot to the rapid development of Japan after the second world war. The highly protected road, which aims to cultivate the leading industry with strong international competitiveness, is a great creation in theory and practice of Japan's economic catch-up and industrial upgrading.

The Japanese government chooses and determines the leading industry as the main direction of economic development through the formulation of medium and long-term plans, and plans the industrial structure in the implementation process, so as to make it gradually develop to a higher level. From the mid-1950s to the early 1970s, Japan's industrial structure was characterized by the rapid transformation of its leading industry from textile industry to heavy chemical industry, driven by large-scale equipment renewal. During this period, shipbuilding, steel, electric power and other basic industries developed rapidly. In order to catch up with the European and American countries, the leading industries such as petrochemicals, automobiles and household appliances rose rapidly under the strong support of the government. In 1963, the ministry of foreign trade formulated the "vision of trade and industry policy in the 1960s", which clearly regarded the development of heavy industry as a long-term vision. In 1980, MIT put forward the slogan "build a nation with technology" in the "conception of trade industry in the 1980s", and concentrated on developing a series of emerging industries such as new energy, new materials, aerospace technology, information and biological engineering. In addition to medium-and long-term planning, the Japanese government has kept the tax burden at around 20%, far lower than other developed countries, in order to accelerate capital accumulation and stimulate economic growth. At the same time in the tax special policy, the government also implemented some key industries to accelerate the depreciation of equipment policy. Japan has successively revised a series of financial regulations such as banking law, import and export banking law and development banking law, which provide legal basis for the state to directly intervene in financial activities. The government also set up the development bank of Japan, the export-import bank of Japan and 10 public treasuries, which are highly targeted and have a profound impact on the development of leading industries. In order to support promising leading industries and promote industrial rationalization, the government decided to transform "excessive competition" into "effective competition", and to form scale economies by "rationalization cartels" for some key supported industrial organizations. Since the mid-1960s, government intervention has led to a wave of big mergers in the car industry, the steel industry and emerging technologies.

Japan is a good country to combine industrial policy and trade policy. After the world war, the Japanese government advocated "export first doctrine" and implemented the policy of revitalizing export. Government has promulgated the "important machinery import tax system", "important machinery special depreciation system", etc., the integrated use of a variety of preferential and industrial policy, not only for the export of Japanese manufacturing opened up a broader space, also make the domestic development of much-needed foreign exchange income, to accumulate capital, to form the virtuous circle of import and export trade and the domestic industry.

The Japanese government also attaches great importance to the guidance of industrial policy on technological progress. First of all, the government implements the policy of "absorptive" technology development, vigorously introduces European and American technologies, insists on the method of gradual progress and gradual upgrading in the process of introduction,and strictly checks and approves each technology. Second, the government has set the main goal of cutting-edge technology. In the 1980s, the strategic decision of "building a nation by science and technology" was established, and high technology was actively applied to specific industries. Third, the government has increased investment in scientific research through various means. Japan attaches great importance to independent research and development in key industries. On the one hand, it provides various preferential treatment to non-governmental research institutions, and on the other hand, it actively promotes technology transfer from government and university research units to enterprises.

3. Japan's experience and lessons in developing leading industries

The development of Japan's leading industries can proceed smoothly under the careful guidance of the government is a prerequisite. First, Japan's policy measures to support pillar industries are in line with its national conditions. The Japanese people's continuous support for domestic products is an important prerequisite for Japan to successfully protect its domestic market. The traditional characteristics of Japanese households make their propensity to save high,which provides an extremely favorable condition for domestic capital accumulation. Second, the formulation and implementation of industrial policy cannot be separated from the close cooperation among various departments. The formulation and implementation of Japan's industrial policy is the result of mutual coordination and cooperation among various government departments, specialized government departments, non-governmental industry organizations, various industrial review councils and financial capital groups. Third, government intervention does not completely replace the market mechanism. In the cultivation of leading industries, the Japanese government attaches great importance to the cultivation of enterprises' self-generating ability and does not allow enterprises to rely on the state for a long time. The government only provides support in the most critical development links, and sets the period of support, promotes the accelerated independence of the industry, emphasizes the orientation of the market, and puts enterprises under competitive pressure. Finally, the key to its success is to follow the general rules of industrial structure evolution and timely guide and support the upgrading of industrial structure. In the process of Japan's economic catch-up, the general rules of structural evolution were not violated. Although the Japanese government has played a non-negligible role in the growth of the leading industry, the role of the Japanese leading industry in economic development and the transformation of the economic development mode cannot be completely attributed to the government's preferential policies and support, and the natural coordination and mutual competition of the entire industrial system cannot be ignored.

In the process of Japan's economic take-off, the experience of the revitalization of its leading industries is undoubtedly the most successful model, which has a unique analytical value and reference significance for the later countries. However, all policies that actively guide economic development will make mistakes. Sometimes, the government determines the leading industry in a certain period and accelerates its development by various means, but it fails to grow into the leading industry due to the wrong choice. Japan's aircraft industry is the most typical example. Sometimes, even though the government chooses the leading industry correctly, it designs a failed development strategy. Whether the government-chosen leading industry can withstand the test of competition remains to be tested by the market. It is not the government that can create and change subjectively. This is the lesson that Japan's industrial policy brings to us.

4.5.3 Cases from Germany

1. The evolution of German industrial structure and the development and transformation of leading industries after World War II Germany is a later-developed country in Europe. Before the first world war, Germany took coal mining, steel, electric power and other basic industries as its leading industries, led the development of machinery manufacturing and chemical industry, and established a

relatively complete industrial system dominated by heavy industry. World War II brought a devastating blow to the German economy. From the end of the war to the mid-1970s, the economy of the federal republic of Germany recovered rapidly and developed rapidly. During this period, heavy industry was further given priority, machinery manufacturing became the largest industrial sector, and the electrical and electronic industry,automobile and aviation industry and chemical industry also developed rapidly. Germany's machinery manufacturing industry was quite developed as early as the end of the 19th century. After the second world war, the machinery manufacturing industry provided the urgently needed machinery and equipment for the recovery and development of Germany's national economy. The recovery of Germany's national economy also provided a huge demand market for the machinery manufacturing industry. As an important pillar industry of Germany, German machinery manufacturing is not only the largest job market, but also has a broad domestic and foreign market. With the development of social economy, German machinery manufacturing industry has also improved the technical requirements and quality requirements step by step. Germany has a wide variety of machinery products with good quality, among which printing and papermaking machinery, textile machinery, wood processing machinery, metallurgy and steel rolling machinery and machine tools are the very famous. One of the characteristics of German machinery manufacturing industry is that small and medium-sized enterprises are the main, not like the United States and Japan which are mass production with low cost to obtain a competitive advantage, machinery manufacturers generally tailor, to variety small batch, which meet the market requirements. Due to the advantages of technology and quality, German machinery manufacturing in the world could maintain competitive advantages.

After the second world war, under the high attention of the German government, the German automobile industry recovered rapidly and developed at a high speed. In the mid-1950s, it became the world's second largest producer of automobiles following the United States. After the 1990s, the German automobile industry faced great difficulties due to the fierce competition in the international market. After World War II, Germany's chemical industry recovered and developed rapidly. After 1950s, Germany's chemical industry turned to petroleum as the main raw material and set up a number of petrochemical enterprises. Before the oil crisis in 1973, Germany's chemical industry was growing at an average annual rate higher than the industrial average, and its output was growing substantially. To 1990 Germany caustic soda output occupies the 4th place in the world, polyethylene production occupies the 3rd place in the world, plastic production occupies the 2nd place in the world, the production such as fertilizer, synthetic fiber, paint fuel, synthetic detergent occupies the front row in the world.

German electronic industry started late, the government realized the importance of the electronic industry, the development of the electronic industry to give all kinds of preferential treatment and support. In the 1980s, Germany's electronics industry had a considerable scale and competitiveness,and became the second largest industrial sector after the machinery manufacturing industry. Germany's medical electronics, control equipment, electronic instruments and meters had great competitive advantages. The electronic information of Germany not only enters the service industry, but also transforms and improves the traditional industry. The technical level and technological content of the traditional industry are improved. The output of steel and coal continues to decline, and it is replaced by the high-quality special steel and coal mining technology equipment which are in the leading position in the world. Up to now, Germany's automobile, machinery manufacturing, chemical, electrical and electronic industries and other leading industries have grown and become the backbone of German industry.

2. Main policy measures and characteristics of the German government supporting leading industries

After the war, federal Germany chose to implement the capitalist market economic system, market forces regulate economic activities on their own,government intervention only in some necessary occasions. For the leading industries with good development prospects and strong market competitiveness, the government allows market competition to determine their formation and development. The role of the government is to create conditions for competition, so as to better protect and promote competition. In addition to maintaining a free and competitive market, the German government provided the basic conditions for ensuring economic development, such as vigorously developing transportation, energy, urban public facilities and posts and telecommunications. In addition, Germany has established a complete social security system, which reasonably corrects the unfairness and imbalance brought about by the market distribution principle, which is conducive to the market competition environment and the improvement of workers' initiative in production.

While emphasizing market forces, Germany did not ignore the significance of industrial policy. Through "orderly adaptation", "purposeful preservation" and "far-sighted shaping", industrial policy can be applied to remedy different types of industrial problems, including market organization and fiscal policy. Market organization tools are designed to regulate market fundamentals and market elements. Fiscal policy has two forms: monetary intervention and physical intervention. The former is tariff policy, financial assistance and various tax incentives, while the latter is to exert influence on demand and production through national finance.

Like many developed countries, Germany attaches great

importance to scientific research and technological development. Germany pursues the strategy of "building a nation by science and technology". The development of science and technology starts from the enterprise first, causes the enterprise to take the initiative to carry on the technical transformation, and gives the encouragement and the support. The government actively assists enterprises in technological progress, especially in basic scientific research and high-tech development, and provides legal, financial, tax and subsidy policy support for technological transformation of enterprises.

The difference between Germany and other countries also lies in taking measures to actively support the development of small and medium-sized enterprises from various aspects. In the 1960s and 1970s, the federal government issued the "law on maintaining stability and economic growth" and later passed the "industrial sector and regional economic policy principles" to regulate the government's behavior towards small and medium-sized enterprises. The federal republic of Germany is known for its decentralized policy of market power. German SMES have an extremely important economic position,which is also an important reason for the efficiency and vitality of the German economy and the effective and flexible industrial policies.

3. Comparison and enlightenment of the road of revitalizing the leading industries of Germany and Japan after the war

After the war, Germany and Japan both achieved rapid economic development and had many similarities in revitalizing leading industries, such as attaching importance to the development and application of new technologies. However, the two have fundamental differences in the guiding ideology and policy of economic development strategy.

(1) They have different forms of policy intervention. Japan's national guidance planning intervention, its industrial policy is general by firstly department of industrial policy after listen to the opinions of

the private sector organizations and certifying, comprehensive development and then formulate industrial policy planning, coordination and takes corresponding department after the review, through before you can perform, the whole industry policy formulation and implementation process and each link of the Japanese government has strong initiative and a larger degree of participation. Germany, on the other hand,takes the form of cooperative consultation and intervention with social organizations and individuals. The role of the government is mainly to provide a corresponding policy and institutional framework for industrial development and inter-industrial cooperation and competition, so as to make the market mechanism more flexible and allocate various resources more effectively. The German government pursues economic liberalism and does not advocate subjective selection of leading industries or special policy support for certain industries. Subjective intervention makes them the focus of industrial development.

(2) Different emphases of the policy system. Japan pays more attention to the industrial structure adjustment policy, the policy focus is always on the "industrial structure upgrade". Although Japan has an anti-monopoly law, it puts more emphasis on "concentration of production and priority to economies of scale". However, Germany attaches great importance to the maintenance of market competition order. In order to protect free competition, German social market system gives priority to anti-monopoly.

(3) Different attitudes towards trade and capital liberalization. Japan's industrial policy aims to pursue the rapid development of the overall economy, actively encourages and supports the development of certain domestic industries through industrial support and cultivation, and strictly restricts the foreign direct investment in certain industries and other trade protection measures to protect the development of certain domestic industries, so as to enhance its international

competitiveness. Under the guidance of the Japanese government, the industrial structure is dominated by export,and most of its leading industries are also export industries. Germany actively advocates free trade, encourages exports, but does not restrict imports, opens its market to foreign countries, and always adopts a laissez-faire domestic and foreign investment policy. Japan's policies have been criticized and resisted in the international trade market.

4.5.4 Cases of South Korea

1. South Korea realized the evolution of industrial structure and the change of leading industries during the economic take-off period

From the early 1960s, South Korea began to enter a planned period of economic development. The South Korean government chose the development path of import substitution and the light industry represented by the fiber manufacturing industry got the first rapid development under the support of the government. Between 1960 and 1970, the average annual growth rate of the fiber industry was 30%. After the development of light industry had a certain strength, the Korean government shifted the focus of development to heavy industry in the 1970s. In the late 1960s, the government dominated the national economy with industries such as steel and oil refining. After 20 years of large-scale development, these industries became the pillar industries of South Korea in the early 1980s.

Shipbuilding and automobile industry are the leading industries developed in the 1970s and 1980s. In 1970, the Korean government formulated the basic plan for the revitalization of the shipbuilding industry, from which the shipbuilding industry was included as one of the leading industries. In 1993, South Korea received shipbuilding orders worth 7.35 billion US dollars, with a total tonnage of 9.52 million tons, surpassing Japan and ranking first in the world. Similar to the shipping industry, the automobile industry in South Korea also rose rapidly and achieved greater success. South Korea's machinery industry started late and did not develop until the 1970s. After the 1990s, South Korea's industrial dominance shifted to the electronics industry with a faster development speed. In 1991, South Korea became one of the world's top five electronic products producing countries. The development direction of South Korea's electronics industry gradually shifted from the production of household appliances to the production of industrial electronic products. In addition, South Korea's entertainment, film and television services have also developed rapidly, quickly occupying the southeast Asian market.

2. Main policies and measures to develop leading industries in the process of economic take-off of the Korean government

South Korea can successfully build a number of leading industries, the government implemented a series of support and coordination policies. First, the government clearly defines the industrial development goals and priorities, and implements a strong policy orientation. After the war, South Korea's industrial structure upgrading and the development of leading industries mainly rely on the power of the government. Since the 1960s, a series of development plans and policies for leading industries have been introduced and put into practice in the form of industrial revitalization law and cultivation law. Second, give priority to merit-based support to promote enterprises to form economies of scale and international competitiveness. The South Korean government on the development of large enterprise groups always throughout the history of the rise of South Korea 30 years, government industrial policy as far as possible let enterprises have money, technology and market development ability into the leading industry domain, at the same time do not have the potential of development and hopelessly out of enterprise, prevent excessive seek and waste of resources. In the early 1980s, major sectors of South

Korea were monopolized by large enterprise groups or chaebol. The strong strength of large enterprise groups is a strong guarantee to promote the optimization of industrial structure and the substantial support of leading industries. Finally, protect domestic leading industries in opening up.South Korea's export-oriented economic development path is bound to rely on opening to the outside world. However, in order to prevent the domestic industry from being strangled by multinational companies in the growth period, the South Korean government has implemented a foreign economic policy to protect the national industry. South Korea strictly restricts foreign direct investment, focusing on foreign government loans and commercial loans. On the import policy, South Korea has also adopted a set of strict and effective self-protection measures. These policies not only focus on restraining external shocks, but also focus on cultivating the competitiveness of domestic key industries.

3. Problems in South Korea's leading industries and countermeasures

Although South Korea's industrial policy has brought 30 years of prosperity and development to South Korea, from the perspective of the development of leading industries and industrial restructuring, the South Korean industry guided by the government and encouraged by exports also has serious problems.

Firstly, the imbalance of industrial structure is aggravated. South Korea's conglomerates are producers of unbalanced industrial structures. On the one hand, the chaebol's blind investment in the heavy chemical sector in the 1970s squeezed the development of light industry and agriculture. On the other hand, the South Korean government gives priority to the policy support for large enterprises, and small and medium-sized enterprises are excluded by large enterprises and neglected by the government. Their status is deteriorating and their development is sluggish. South Korea's economy is highly centralized and monopolized, affecting the operation of the market mechanism, a large number of small and medium-sized enterprises are pushed into difficulties, seriously restricting the competitiveness of South Korea's economy.

Secondly, the development of South Korea's leading industries realized by the government's special policies still lacks sufficient capability of technology development. The foundation for the development of enterprises' own technologies is weak. Under the distortion of policies, enterprises lack the enthusiasm to develop new technologies, and the oligarchic economy even hindering the formation of a free competition system to pursue technological advantages.

Finally, trade frictions between South Korea and other developed countries are increasingly intensified by highly protective and export-oriented policies in leading industries. In response to the above problems, since the 1980s, the Korean government has changed the policy of government-led industrial development in the past. According to the principle of market economy, the Korean government promotes internal and external competition and gradually reduces government protection, support and restriction measures for industries. Industrial policy changed from direct government intervention to indirect and neutral government support. Since the 1980s, the government has issued measures to strengthen the quality of enterprises, the law on restricting monopoly and fair trading, the long-term plan for revitalizing small and medium-sized enterprises and other regulations to prevent the monopoly of big chaebol and support small and medium-sized enterprises. In 1993, the South Korean government began to implement the policy of specialization of the chaebol enterprises, requiring each chaebol to engage in no more than two or three specialized operations in order to concentrate on improving international competitiveness.Since the 1980s, the Korean government has also gradually increased investment in technology development and research, then promoted industrial technology promotion measures. They has also shifted from giving priority to specific industries to focusing on technology development, increasing labour productivity, and giving priority to policies that promote support for technology development.

4.6 Summary of This Chapter

1. The choice of leading industries and the transformation of economic development mode should not only follow the law of economic development, but also be combined with the reality of China's economic development. Under the macro-control of the government, the leading industry and the adjustment of industrial structure should be taken as the starting point to actively seek for the transformation of economic development mode. However, active regulation by the government does not mean abandoning the basic principles of the market economy and changing the mechanism of free operation of the economy. On the contrary, only by making the market economy free and smooth can the economy maintain dynamic development. This is the premise that China should first abide by when formulating industrial planning and policies.

2. With the construction and real estate industries and manufacturing industries as the leading industries in this round of economic growth, we should focus on supporting communications equipment, computer and other electronic equipment manufacturing, electrical, machinery and equipment manufacturing, wood processing and furniture manufacturing, garment, leather, down and its products industries. They are not only an important support for the current national economy, but also an industry conducive to achieve the goal of comprehensive development and maintaining an effective mode of economic development. So we should strengthen policy information

service and make it in a healthy and free development environment. At the same time, these industries should be encouraged to develop to industrial clusters, speed up resource integration and improve the competitiveness of the industry. We will vigorously support technology development and research activities in leading industries and related key industries, advocate independent innovation and effectively improve the self-upgrading capabilities of these industries themselves. At the same time, the manufacturing industry should be encouraged to take an active part in international competition and achieve the elimination of the fittest in the international market.

3. The supporting and supplementary role of consumer service industry and production service industry to the leading industry cannot be ignored. The development of the service industry is not only resource-saving, environmentally friendly and sustainable, but also people-oriented. Developing the service sector will not only facilitate the transformation of economic development from external demand to domestic demand, but also facilitate the expansion of employment and the upgrading of the industrial structure. Economic development is dominated by the tertiary industry and supplemented by other industries. Combined with the previous research results, this book argues that we should develop consumer services, which mainly include wholesale and retail trade, residential and other social services, accommodation and catering, and education. At the same time, production-oriented service industry, such as financial insurance and real estate service industry, is the leading industry and the support industry of other important industries, and is also the object that industrial development planning and industrial policies should focus on.

Chapter 5　Current Situation and Future Prospects of China's Economic Development Mode

5.1　Analysis of the Contents of China's Economic Development Mode

5.1.1　Elements and structures of China's economic development

This chapter uses Solow growth model to estimate the contribution of growth factors to economic growth, and to analyze the quantitative relationship of economic growth factors, so as to reflect China's current development mode. When a country's economic development mainly depends on the increase of large input of factors, then the economic development is characterized by the extensive mode of quantity expansion. If the economic growth is brought about by technological progress or the increase of total factor productivity, the mode of economic development tends to be intensive type.

This part uses the model of the previous chapter fomula (39) to complete the estimation. The estimated results of OLS and MLE are as follows:

OLS:

$$\ln(Y) = 0.002768 + (-0.0195\ln L) + 0.2147\ln K + 214.299\ln R + (-0.1832\ln E) + (-0.1055\ln I)$$
$${\scriptstyle(0.5571,-3.4962)}{\scriptstyle(0.1608,0.0134)}{\scriptstyle(5.8247,36.79)}{\scriptstyle(0.2304,-0.7950)}{\scriptstyle(7.7001,-0.01370)}$$

$$(1)$$

sigma-squared 0.6471 gamma 0.75 log likelihood function=−0.00011

    MLE:

$$\ln(Y)=0.00149+8.5573\ln L+0.4093\ln K+(-2.4342\ln R)+(-2.4386\ln E)+(-1.027\ln I)$$
$$\small (0.4337.0.1973)\quad\quad (0.1014,4.0353)\quad\quad\quad (5.0370,-0.4832)\quad\quad\quad (0.1736,-0.1405)\quad\quad\quad (4.733,-0.217)$$

(2)

sigma-squared 0.8093 gamma 0.9079 log likelihood function=−0.00738

The results of OLS and MLE estimation show that MLE has a good reliability. MLE estimates show that during 2002–2007, China's economic development mode tends to be capital-based and labor-intensive. The efficiency coefficient of labor force and capital is positive. Capital and labor still play an important role in the process of economic development in China. The coefficient value of labor force to output is larger than that of capital to output, which indicates that the contribution of labor force to economic development is still considerable, and the demographic dividend of our country has not disappeared at this stage; the R&D coefficient is negative, which indicates that the R&D input of our country has not exerted the scale effect, and the R&D input-output efficiency is not high; the environmental input efficiency of China is negative, under this economic development mode. The environmental emission pressure of the exhibition has been obvious. Energy input efficiency coefficient is negative, indicating that the overall energy use in China is inefficient, energy use technology is low, resulting in serious waste of energy, which shows that China's economic development at this stage is energy inefficient and environment unfriendly.

5.1.2 Analysis of the industrial structure of China's economic development

This book take advantage of the relevant data of input-output tables in 1997, 2002, 2005 and 2007 to analyze the industrial structure of China. The data of output value of each industry accounted for the total output value of that year are shown in Table 5-1. According to the data, in 1997–2007, the construction industry, agriculture, forestry, animal husbandry, fishery, heavy industry in manufacturing industry such as chemical industry, metal smelting and calendering industry, general and special equipment manufacturing industry, transportation equipment manufacturing industry, light industry manufacturing industry such as food and tobacco processing industry, communication and computer electronic equipment manufacturing industry, non-metallic industry, etc. contributed most to the total economic output. Mineral products, clothing, shoes and hats, and textile industries contribute a lot to the national economic output. Transportation, warehousing, wholesale and retail industries in the service industry also play an important role in the national economy.

Construction and real estate related industries accounted for 9.6% of the total output of the national economy in 1997, 11.5% in 2002, 9.3% in 2005, and 9.5% in 2007 respectively. The proportion was relatively stable. The proportion of manufacturing industry in the total output of the national economy was 55.2% in 1997, 45.44% in 2002, 50.95% in 2005 and 54.65% in 2007. The proportion of manufacturing industry in the national economy has always been a large part. The proportion of light industry manufacturing represented by textile industry in manufacturing industry has been stable at about 8% from 1997 to 2007, which indicates that the proportion of heavy industry manufacturing industry in the national economy is dominant. The contribution of service industry to output was 17.3% in 1997 and maintained at about 30% in other years. Based on the above analysis, it can be seen that the contribution of agriculture, forestry, animal husbandry and by-fishery to total output declined from 1997 to 2007. The contribution of manufacturing industry was too large to be ignored, and the ratio increased slightly. The contribution of service industry to output did not increase significantly. Therefore, the mode of economic development of China in this period was biased towards heavy industry manufacturing industry.

Table 5–1 Proportion of Output to Total Output Value (2002–2007)

1997		2005		2007		2012	
Agriculture	0.123	Chemical industry	0.074	Construction business	0.077	Agriculture, forestry, animal husbandry and fishery	0.091
Construction business	0.087	Construction business	0.074	Chemical industry	0.076	Construction business	0.090
Chemical industry	0.076	Agriculture, forestry, animal husbandry and fishery	0.073	Metal smelting and calendering	0.075	Chemical industry	0.069
Food manufacturing and tobacco processing	0.069	Metal smelting and calendering	0.058	Agriculture, forestry, animal husbandry and fishery	0.060	Wholesale and retail business	0.055
Business	0.055	Manufacturing of communication and electronic equipment	0.052	Food and tobacco processing	0.051	Metal smelting and calendering	0.049
Textile industry	0.046	Food manufacturing and tobacco processing	0.048	Manufacturing of communication and electronic equipment	0.050	Food and tobacco processing	0.046
Non-metallic mineral products industry	0.044	Manufacturing of general and special equipment	0.046	Manufacturing of general and special equipment	0.048	Transportation and warehousing	0.045
Machinery industry	0.041	Transportation and warehousing	0.045	Transportation equipment manufacturing industry	0.040	Manufacturing of general and special equipment	0.041
Metal smelting and calendering	0.039	Production and supply of electricity and heat	0.037	Transportation and warehousing	0.039	Communication and electronic equipment	0.041
Clothing and leather manufacturing	0.030	Wholesale and retail business	0.036	Production and supply of electricity and heat	0.038	Transportation equipment manufacturing	0.031
Garment and leather manufacturing industry	0.028	Transportation equipment manufacturing	0.033	Wholesale and retail business	0.035	Public administration and social organizations	0.031

continued

1997		2005		2007		2012	
Social service industry	0.028	Electrical machinery and equipment manufacturing	0.030	Electrical machinery and equipment manufacturing	0.033	Textile industry	0.029
Electrical machinery and equipment manufacturing	0.027	Non-metallic mineral products industry	0.029	Textile industry	0.031	Production and supply of electricity and heat	0.025
Transportation equipment manufacturing industry	0.025	Textile industry	0.029	Non-metallic mineral products industry	0.028	Estate	0.023
Metal products industry	0.025	Public administration and social organizations	0.024	Petroleum and nuclear fuel processing industry	0.026	Finance	0.023
Manufacturing of electronic and communication equipment	0.022	Petroleum and nuclear fuel processing industry	0.023	Finance	0.024	Accommodation and catering	0.023
Administrative organs and other industries	0.022	Textile and apparel industry and its products	0.023	Textile and garment industry	0.022	Electrical and equipment manufacturing	0.023
Manufacture of paper and cultural and educational supplies	0.020	Accommodation and catering	0.021	Metal products industry	0.022	Papermaking and cultural and educational supplies system	0.022
Electricity and steam production and supply	0.019	Manufacture of paper and cultural and educational supplies	0.020	Public administration and social organizations	0.019	Textile and garment manufacturing industry	0.021
Freight transport and warehousing industry	0.018	Metal products industry	0.019	Manufacture of paper and cultural and educational supplies	0.018	Education	0.020
Financial and insurance industry	0.016	Leasing and business services	0.019	Accommodation and catering	0.018	Petroleum and nuclear fuel processing	0.019
Agriculture	0.015	Chemical industry	0.019	Construction business	0.018	Agriculture, forestry, animal husbandry and fishery	0.019
Construction business	0.012	Construction business	0.019	Chemical industry	0.016	Construction business	0.019

continued

1997		2005		2007		2012	
Chemical industry	0.011	Agriculture, forestry, animal husbandry and fishery	0.018	Metal smelting and calendering	0.014	Chemical industry	0.018
Food manufacturing and tobacco processing	0.011	Metal smelting and calendering	0.017	Agriculture, forestry, animal husbandry and fishery	0.014	Wholesale and retail business	0.017
Business	0.011	Manufacturing of communication and electronic equipment	0.017	Food and tobacco processing	0.013	Metal smelting and calendering	0.014
Textile industry	0.010	Food manufacturing and tobacco processing	0.013	Manufacturing of communication and electronic equipment	0.012	Food and tobacco processing	0.013
Non-metallic mineral products industry	0.009	Manufacturing of general and special equipment	0.012	Manufacturing of general and special equipment	0.012	Transportation and warehousing	0.013
Machinery industry	0.009	Transportation and warehousing	0.011	Transportation equipment manufacturing industry	0.012	Manufacturing of general and special equipment	0.013
Metal smelting and calendering	0.009	Production and supply of electricity and heat	0.011	Transportation and warehousing	0.011	Communication and electronic equipment	0.010
Garment and leather manufacturing industry	0.008	Wholesale and retail business	0.009	Production and supply of electricity and heat	0.008	Transportation equipment manufacturing	0.007
Social service industry	0.007	Transportation equipment manufacturing	0.007	Wholesale and retail business	0.008	Public administration and social organizations	0.007
Electrical machinery and equipment manufacturing	0.007	Electrical machinery and equipment manufacturing	0.007	Electrical machinery and equipment manufacturing	0.006	Textile industry	0.006
Transportation equipment manufacturing industry	0.006	Non-metallic mineral products industry	0.006	Textile industry	0.005	Production and supply of electricity and heat	0.005
Metal products industry	0.004	Textile industry	0.005	Non-metallic mineral products industry	0.005	Estate	0.005

continued

1997		2005		2007		2012	
Manufacturing of electronic and communication equipment	0.004	Public administration and social organizations	0.004	Petroleum and nuclear fuel processing industry	0.005	Finance	0.005
Administrative organs and other industries	0.003	Petroleum and nuclear fuel processing industry	0.004	Finance	0.004	Accommodation and catering	0.003
Manufacture of paper and cultural and educational supplies	0.002	Textile and apparel industry and its products	0.002	Textile and garment industry	0.003	Electrical and equipment manufacturing	0.002
Electricity and steam production and supply	0.001	Accommodation and catering	0.002	Metal products industry	0.002	Papermaking and cultural and educational supplies system	0.002
Garment and leather manufacturing industry	0.001	Manufacture of paper and cultural and educational supplies	0.002	Public administration and social organizations	0.001	Textile and garment manufacturing industry	0.002
		Metal products industry	0.001	Manufacture of paper and cultural and educational supplies	0.001	Education	0.002
		Leasing and business services	0.001	Accommodation and catering	0.001	Petroleum and nuclear fuel processing	0.001

Data source: China Statistical Bureau.

5.1.3   Analysis of demand structure of China's economic development

Economic development includes three major needs: consumption, capital formation and net exports. This section analyses the characteristics of China's economic development mode from the demand structure [1] . From 1991 to 2010, the contribution of

---

[1]   All data in this section are from the Zhongjing Network and the Annual Statistical Yearbook.

consumption to the economy was gradually reduced except in the year of 2005 and 2007. In 1991, 65.1% of the contribution of China's economic development came from final consumption, which reached 76.8% in 1999. By 2010, the contribution of consumption to economic growth had dropped to 36.8%. In the final consumption, the proportion of consumption distribution between residents and government is relatively stable. In 1991, the proportion of residents and government in total consumption expenditure was 76.15% and 23.85%, respectively. In 2010, the proportion of residents and government in total consumption expenditure was 71.31% and 28.69%, with little change for 20 years. The contribution rate of capital to economic growth increased from 24.3% in 1991 to 91.3% in 2009. In 2010, the contribution value fell back to 54%. The overall contributions of total capital formation to economic growth has increased steadily. Among the total capital formation, the proportion of total fixed capital formation and inventory to total capital formation in 1991 was 77.15% and 22.85%, respectively. The proportion of fixed assets investment to total capital formation has exceeded 90% since 1998. The ratio of fixed capital formation and increase in inventory to total capital formation in 2010 was 95.12% and 4.88%, respectively. It can be seen that fixed capital is the main source of capital formation in China. Investment driven by production. The contribution of net exports to economic growth fluctuated greatly from 1991 to 2010, but the proportion of total imports and exports in GDP rose steadily from 1991 to 2010. In 1991, China's imports and exports contributed 33.11% of GDP, of which import accounted for 47.04% of total imports and exports, while export accounted for 52.96% of total import and export. In 2010, the contribution of total imports and exports to GDP was 50.02%, of which 53.05% was contributed by exports. From 2003 to 2008, the contribution of China's total imports and exports volume to economic growth was more than 50%, which reached 65.3% in 2006. In summary, from the early 1990s to the early 21st century, China's economic growth mode has changed from consumption-oriented to investment-oriented and export-oriented.

Table 5–2 Demand Structure of China's Economy

Indicator Name	Annual Contribution Rate of GDP: Final Consumption Expenditure	Annual Contribution Rate of GDP: Total Capital Formation	Annual Contribution Rate of GDP: Net Exports of Goods and Services	The Year-on-Year Stimulation of GDP: Final Consumption Expenditure	Pulling GDP Year-on-Year: Total Capital Formation	A Year-on-Year Boost to GDP : Net Exports of Goods and Services
2019-06	55.30	25.90	18.80	3.40	1.60	1.20
2019-03	65.10	12.10	22.80	4.20	0.80	1.40
2018-12	71.60	20.40	8.00	4.60	1.30	0.50
2018-09	74.00	35.90	−9.90	4.80	2.20	−0.60
2018-06	79.60	33.00	−12.60	5.30	2.00	−0.80
2018-03	79.20	40.40	−19.60	5.40	2.50	−1.20
2017-12	46.20	29.10	24.70	3.10	1.80	1.50
2017-09	64.00	31.00	5.00	4.30	1.90	0.30
2017-06	49.40	47.50	3.10	3.40	2.90	0.20
2017-03	74.50	26.30	−0.80	5.10	1.60	0.05
2016-12	75.10	40.20	−15.30	5.10	2.50	−0.90
2016-09	58.80	45.00	−3.80	3.90	2.80	−0.20
2016-06	56.00	49.40	−5.40	3.80	3.10	−0.30
2016-03	77.40	36.90	−14.30	5.20	2.30	−0.90
2015-12	63.50	39.00	−2.50	4.30	2.40	−0.20
2015-09	51.30	59.10	−10.40	3.50	3.70	−0.60
2015-06	60.60	47.00	−7.60	4.20	2.90	−0.50
2015-03	64.10	16.70	19.20	4.50	1.00	1.20

Source: China Statistical Bureau.

5.2 An Analysis of China's Leading Industries — Based on China' s Real Estate Industry

5.2.1 The background of the prosperity of China's real estate industry

Since the housing system reform in 1998, China began to

implement the commercialization of housing, the welfare housing system comes to an end, losing constraints of the real estate market and the release the potential in housing market. After that, China's real estate industry has entered a period of sustained and rapid development. Because of its strong industrial linkage, real estate promotes the development of steel, cement, chemical raw materials and other forward related industries in the national economy, as well as financial services, information consulting and other backward related industries. China's construction and real estate related industries absorb a large number of rural surplus labor force, and promote the employment of labor force. Real estate related industries have become the leading industries of the national economy, supporting the rapid development of China's economy. However, at the same time, China's real estate market is also facing the problem of overheating and housing bubbles: the investment rate in real estate is still high, and new real estate is in short supply with more and more demand, the housing price rises too fast, especially in the housing market. Developers and government hype, together with the domestic speculative groups and foreign hot money join in, the real estate market speculation is becoming more and more frequently. In recent years, housing prices in most parts of China have been rising continuously, and there has been an irreversible trend. The real estate market has become an important area for developers and investors to accumulate wealth. A large number of people who hold large amounts of real estate resources make a forturn from Chinese real estate for ten years, but some residents can not afford to buy houses. They face enormous repayment pressure. The real estate market has greatly changed the income distribution pattern of people's wealth. On the one hand, more and more funds are invested in the real estate market. On the other hand, people's housing needs are not only expanding in quantity, but also the housing quality requirements. However, the growth of real estate commodity supply seems to be more and more unable to catch up with the growth of demand, and the voice of the real estate bubble is getting bigger. The original policy which strongly supported real estate as the leading industry of the national economy has contracted in an all-round way. Instead, the government has issued a series of macro-policies to regulate and control the overheating in the real estate market. The overprosperity of the real estate market and the real estate bubble have aroused widespread concern. Could the real estate related industries continue to prosper and guide the sustainable development of economy?

5.2.2 The current status of China's real estate market

This section analyzes the development status of China's real estate industry in the past 1997–2010 years from three aspects: real estate prices and sales volume, real estate investment and the financing sources for the real estate industry.

1. China's real estate prices and sales volume analysis

According to the data, the real estate sales area of our country in 2010 was 1047.645 million square meters, an increase of 9.55% over the previous year in 2009, the sales area increased by 43.63%, 11.63 times as much as in 1997, and the average growth rate of real estate sales area in 13 years was 19.84%. The real estate market in China has shown a small cycle (peak to trough) from 2004 to 2009. In 2004, the area of housing sales increased by 13.39% compared with 2003. Affected by the global financial crisis, housing sales showed a negative growth rate of –14.72% in 2008. In 2009, China's economic recovery, real estate sales rebounded to a growth rate of 43.63%. The growth rate of real estate prices was relatively that year stable in 1998–2003, except for a slight decrease in 1999. In addition, it is noted that the growth rate of commodity house prices in 1999 and 2008 was negative, mainly due to the impact of the Asian financial crisis in 1998 and the global financial crisis in 2008. It can be seen that the impact of the Asian financial crisis on China's real estate market price lagged behind about a year, while the impact of the 2008 global financial crisis on the real estate market emerge immediately that year. The growth rate of China's commercial housing prices began to be very unstable in 2003. There were two cycles in the growth rate of 2003–2009 years, of which the growth rate of commercial housing prices was very low in 2006 and 2008. Price growth rate declined sharply in 2006 and 2009. The growth rate in 2006 was 10 percentage points lower than that of 2005, while the price growth rate in 2009 was 16.43% lower than that of the previous year. At present, China's real estate was in a period of rapid recovery and prosperity, which reflected in the rebound in transaction volume, rising house prices and sustained growth. Apart from the reverse trend in 2003–2005, the real estate prices in other years are stable, which implied that speculation in China's real estate market was very active in 2003–2005. Before 2003, the growth rate of commercial housing sales was much larger than that of housing price, but after that, the growth rate of housing price gradually approached the growth rate of commercial housing sales, and the gap convergent.

2. China's real estate investment analysis

In 1997, the national investment in fixed assets of real estate was 317.84 billion yuan, reaching 4825.94 billion yuan in 2010, an increase of 33.16% over the previous year, and the investment in 2009 was 1.52 times that of 1997. In 1997, real estate investment in fixed assets accounted for 12.74% of the total social investment in fixed assets, which reached 23.65% in 2003, and then declined slightly. In 2010, real estate investment in fixed assets accounted for 17.35% of the total social fixed assets investment. From the experience of real estate bubble bursting countries, real estate investment generally accounts for 20%~25% of the fixed assets investment in the whole society, and if the percentage is more than 30%, it might implies bubbles. During the past 13 years, the proportion of real estate development in fixed assets investment in the whole society is 10%~25%, which shows that the scale of real estate investment in China is reasonable and safe. In the past 1997–2009 years, the amount of investment in commercial real estate was the largest, followed by the investment in office buildings, then the investment in real estate of affordable housing, followed by the development of high-grade apartments and real estate in villas, and finally the investment in residential real estates development. Driven by large-scale investment in real estate, the number and growth of newly-built and completed real estates in China have continued to grow. In 2010, the construction area of commercial housing in China reached 4.05 billion square meters, an increase of 26.53% compared with that of 2009. The completed housing was 787 million square meters, an increase of 8.347% over the previous year. At the same time, the vacant area of newly added commercial housing in China is becoming smaller and smaller. In 1997, the vacant area of new commercial housing was 31.399 million square meters, reaching 41.31 million square meters in 1999, while the vacant area of completed housing in the same period was 55.97 million square meters, which is equivalent to that of housing completed housing in that year. Since 2000, the vacant area of new houses has decreased year by year, and it was negative in 2007. It is noted that the vacancy area of housing in 2007 and 2009 are negative, indicating that the demand for commercial housing in these years exceeded the supply. It shows that after 2000, both the rigid demand for housing and speculative demand are increasing. The continuous and rapid growth of investment in real estate coexists with the continuous decrease of vacancy area of newly added commercial housing. The market demand of commercial housing in China is very strong.

3. Analysis of the sources of funds of Chinese real estate enterprises

In 2009, the total investment funds for real estate development in China amounted to 5779.9 billion yuan. The first source of investment funds for real estate development is deposit and advance receipt, up to 280.6 billion yuan, an increase of 75.3% compared with the previous year, accounting for 48.45% of the total investment in real estate development in that year; the second largest source of funds is self-financing of real estate development enterprises. In 2009, the number of self-financing funds for real estate investment in China was 179.91 billion yuan, an increase of 17.22% compared with 2008, accounting for real estate development. 31.05% of the total investment, followed by domestic bank loans, totaling 113.64 billion yuan, an increase of 49.42% over the previous year, accounting for 19.66% of the total investment in real estate. It is noted that most of China's real estate development funds come from the sales of commercial housing. During 1997–2009 years, the proportion of domestic bank loans in Chinese real estate enterprises has been maintained at around 20% of the total investment funds of real estate and 2005 at a minimum of 18.31%. Self-financing accounted for 25.48% of the total investment funds in real estate in 1997, and has been growing steadily since then, reaching 38.64% in 2008. Except for the slight decrease to 26.91% in 2000. According to the data of Table 5-3, the ratio of bank loans to Chinese real estate enterprises is not high. However, the proportion of bank loans in China's real estate funds is greatly underestimated. In fact, driven by the huge profits of the real estate industry, a considerable part of self-financing comes from bank loans. It is assumed that 70% of the self-financing of real estate comes from domestic loans, so the proportion of bank loans of real estate enterprises is more in line with the actual situation. If domestic bank loans plus 70% of self-financing funds are taken as real domestic real estate loan funds, the proportion of

domestic loans in the total real estate financing sources is around 40%.
That is 41.71% in 1997, 39.63% in 2004 and 46.25% in 2008
respectively. In the mature real estate market of developed countries,
bank loans could not exceed 40%. In that case, the dependence of real
estate enterprises on banks increases the bubble of the real estate
market, and also greatly increases the risk of banks and other financial
institutions.

Table 5–3 Data on Indicators of Real Estate in China (1997–2009)

Year	Sales Area of Commercial Housing (10000 m²)	Residential Area of Completed Housing (10000m²)	New Vacant Area of Houses (10000 m²)	Value Added of Real Estate (RMB 100 million)	Investment in Fixed Assets in Real Estate (100 million)	Total Domestic Loan of Real Estate Enterprises (100 million)	Total Self-financing of Real Estate Enterprises (100 million)	Average Price of Commercial Housing (RMB/m²)	Cost of Building and Security Materials for Residential Buildings (100 million)	Land Acquisition Cost (RMB 100 million)
1997	9010.2	40550.2	31539.9	2921.1	3440.7	911.2	972.9	1997.2	16259.6	247.6
1998	12185.3	47616.9	35431.6	3434.5	3896.9	1053.2	1166.9	2062.6	18879.5	375.4
1999	14556.5	55868.9	41312.4	3681.8	4342.1	1111.6	1344.6	2052.6	20367.0	500.0
2000	18637.1	54859.9	36222.7	4149.1	5194.4	1385.1	1614.2	2111.6	22192.7	733.9
2001	22411.9	57476.5	35064.6	4715.1	6644.6	1692.2	2183.9	2169.7	25248.5	1038.8
2002	26808.3	59793.6	32985.4	5346.4	8154.4	2220.3	2738.4	2250.2	29231.3	1445.8
2003	33717.6	54971.5	21253.9	6172.7	13143.4	3138.3	3770.7	2359.5	37391.9	2055.2
2004	38231.6	56897.3	18665.7	7174.1	16678.9	3158.4	5207.6	2713.9	48974.8	2574.5
2005	55486.2	66141.9	10655.7	8516.4	19505.3	3918.1	7000.4	3167.7	62593.4	2904.4
2006	61857.1	63046.9	1189.8	10370.5	24524.4	5356.9	8597.1	3366.8	77496.9	3814.5
2007	77354.7	68820.8	−8533.9	13809.8	32438.9	7015.6	11772.5	3863.9	97290.1	4873.3
2008	65969.8	75969.1	9999.2	14738.7	40441.8	7605.7	15312.1	3799.9	123934.2	5995.6
2009	94755.0	82101.5	−12653.5	18654.7	49358.5	11364.5	17949.1	4681.1	162114.2	6023.7

Source: China Statistical Bureau.

Notes: The commodity house prices here do not use statistical data. They are obtained by dividing annual sales by sales area. Residential construction and security costs include: real estate construction and installation projects and equipment and tools acquisition costs.

Data source: 1997–2009 years of raw data came from "China real estate statistical yearbook 2010", "China real estate and construction enterprises Yearbook 2010", China economic network database db.cei.gov.cn. Data for 2010 are from annual statistical reports.

5.2.3 Causes for the prosperity of China's real estate industry as a pillar industry

1. Strong demand in real estate market

The scarcity of land strengthens both the speculative demand and rigid demand for real estate. Land is the foundation of real estate development. As a scarce factor of production, land supply is short of elasticity. Generally speaking, with the growth of the total social demand, the smaller the supply elasticity, the faster the relative growth of factor prices. China has a large population and the land area suitable for population is very limited. China's land is owned by the state, the rights to use and ownership are separated, and the government's control over the use of land is very strict. Therefore, the contradiction between the scarcity and monopoly of land resources, the quantity of land supply, the factors of land location, the heterogeneity of land and the increasing demand for land, as well as the diversity and speculation of demand, leads to the increasing in land demand. The restriction of land supply is far from adapting to the growth of land demand. Land price is the standard of real estate. The scarcity of land strengthens the rigid demand of real estate commodities. Although land is a real asset, it is a virtual capital because it is not a labor product and has no value. The scarcity of land strengthens the speculation expectation of investors, coupled with the high profits of the real estate industry, which makes a large number of speculating funds pour in. The irreversibility of the rise of land price and real estate price leads to the abnormal prosperity of the real estate market in China.

2. Real estate promotes the development of the whole society

Land is the basic condition of real estate construction, and land is an important source of local financial revenue in China. In 1997, the cost of real estate land acquisition in China was 24.76 billion yuan, which reached 6.02 billion yuan in 2009, and increased by 2.43 times in the last 13 years. In 1998, the cost of land acquisition increased by 51.61% over the previous year, with an average increase of 27.83% between 1997 and 2009. Land acquisition cost is not only an important part of fiscal revenue, but also the main force to stimulate the GDP. Therefore, the development of real estate has received strong support from the government. What's more, the real estate industry has a wide range of industrial linkages, and its prosperity and development drive the development of related industries forward and backward. In recent years, the price of raw materials based on steel has risen substantially, and the prosperity of the real estate market has led to a chain reaction of the upstream and downstream industries such as steel, cement, glass and so on, and the service industry for real estate has also sprung up in large numbers. In addition, the development of the real estate market has shifted a large number of rural surplus labor force and increased employment.

5.3   Prospect of China's Real Estate Market and Outlook of Future Leading Industries

5.3.1 The measurement of the bubble in China's real estate market

Many developed countries and regions in the world have experienced the real estate bubble. The bursting of the real estate bubble has brought great harm to society and economy. Japan, the United States, Ireland and other developed countries have been affected by the real estate bubble for a long time. Until now, some countries still shrouded in the shadow of the real estate bubble bursting. In view of this, this part first investigates whether bubbles exist in the booming real estate industry when it is a leading industry, so as to analyze prospects of China's leading industries.

1. Is China's real estate markets overheated?

The development of real estate involves the supply, demand, transaction and financial market of real estate. The following data is the CPI-reduced rate of house price, the growth rate of real estate sales, and the growth rate of real estate domestic loans to examine the evolution of China's real estate market. In order to estimate the real estate market bubble, this part classify and examine the indicators in Table 5-4. The criteria are: the distribution of the indicators deviates from the range of standard deviation which has not exceeded one time of the expected value, that is $EX-\sigma<X\leqslant EX+\sigma$, which is defined as the normal area; the range of standard deviation exceeding one time and less than two times belongs to the alert area. Specifically, it can be divided into the following two cases: if on the left side, namely $EX-2\sigma<X\leqslant EX-\sigma$, it is defined as a subcooled zone; if on the right side of the central value, it is defined as a subcooled zone; if on the right side of the central value, it is $EX+\sigma<X<EX+2\sigma$, it is defined as a subcooled zone; if on the left side of the central value deviates more than twice the standard deviation, i.e. $X\leqslant EX-2\sigma$, it is considered as a subcooled zone; and on the right side of the central value, that is $X\geqslant EX+2\sigma$. From the Table 5-4, it is known that the real estate market in China showed a small cycle (peak to trough) from 1992 to 2010. In 1993, the sales of commercial housing increased by 35.87% compared with that of the previous year. Affected by the global financial crisis, the sales of housing showed a negative growth rate of −17.26% in 2008. In 2009, China's economic recovery, the growth rate of commercial housing sales rebounded to 30.38%. In 1992, 2005 and 2009, the growth rate was in the alert zone of single bubble index. During 1992–2010, the growth rate of commodity house prices was extremely unstable, and the range of rise and fall was quite different, especially in 1993–1995; between 1997–

2005 and 2007–2010, the growth rate of commodity house prices experienced a period of subcooling and serious bubble. The trend of the growth rate of commercial housing sales is basically consistent with the growth rate of sales area. In 1992, 1993, 2005 and 2009, the individual indicators are in the bubble warning zone. During 1992–1994 and 2000–2007, the growth rate of sales area of commercial housing was far greater than that of house price, which indicated that the demand of real estate market was very strong. During 1992–2010, the average growth rate of domestic bank loans of real estate enterprises in China was 23.17%. The growth rate of domestic bank loans of real estate enterprises increased sharply in 2002–2003 and 2008–2009, among which the individual indicators in 2003 and 2009 were in the bubble warning zone.

This book select five indicators to analyze the growth of individual indicators in the real estate market, such as the first five indicators in Table 5-4. From 1992 to 2010, China's real estate investment in fixed assets accounted for about 15% of the total social investment in fixed assets, slightly increased to 18.28% over the few years. This index indicates that the scale of real estate investment in China is reasonable and safe. The ratio of house price to urban real income shows that the house price after CPI reduction is 5~8 times than that of urban real income, and the index values in 2009 and 2010 are in the overheated zone. At the same time, the real estate price rise rate is 0.715 times than the real income growth rate of cities and towns on average. In the investigation, the variance of this index is small, indicating that the price rate has little change. Although the growth rate of domestic bank loans of real estate enterprises has changed greatly during 1992–2010, the variance of the ratio between the growth rate of real estate loans and the growth rate of bank loans is small, and the fluctuation range is relatively stable. Only the index value of 2000 falls out from the bubble zone. From 1992 to 2010, the ratio of ready-to-sell commercial housing to completed commercial housing in China showed a decreasing trend, from nearly 50% in 1995 to −33.045% in 2010. This change shows that the market demand of commercial housing in China is much higher than that of supply.

The above indicators show that China's real estate market has shown some characteristics of bubbles, but it is not enough to judge whether there is evidence of bubbles in China's real estate only from these indicators. The ratio of the difference between each index value and the expected value and the tolerance value of the interval in which the index value is located, that is, the difference between the upper and lower limits, is used to express the foam degree of the five index values. The foam value of each year is taken as the average value of the five index values. The absolute value of the ratio is greater than 1 if the deviation of each index value from the expectation in specific year exceeds the tolerance of the interval, which indicates that there is real estate bubble, otherwise there is no bubble. According to the results of Table 5-5, it can be concluded that there are obvious bubbles in the real estate market in 1998, 2003 and 2010, which can also be regarded as the turning point of China's real estate development. Due to the data, we can not deny that there is no bubble in other years. In order to further test the bubble of China's real estate market and examine the intrinsic causes and impact of the real estate boom, we will use relevant models and dynamic panel data to prove our conclusions further.

Table 5–4 Development of China's Real Estate Industry (1992–2010)

	Ratio of Investment in Real Estate Development to Investment in Fixed Assets	The Ratio of Housing Price Growth Rate to Urban Real Income Growth Rate	Ratio of Real Estate Loan Growth Rate to Bank Loan Growth Rate	The Ratio of House Price to Urban Residents' Income	Ratio of the Area of Commercial Housing for Sale to the Area Completed	Growth Rate of Real Estate Investment	CPI Reduced Growth Rate of Housing Price	Growth Rate of Sale Area of Commercial Housing	Sales Growth Rate Reduced by CPI	Real Estate Domestic Loan Growth Rate
1992	9.049	1.505	—	7.274	—	54.021	22.947	29.458	42.624	—
1993	14.821	1.139	—	7.124	—	62.261	20.444	35.871	46.757	—
1994	14.987	0.032	—	5.362	37.868	24.142	0.813	7.502	8.248	—
1995	15.730	0.668	—	5.743	46.847	18.892	19.687	8.545	23.588	—
1996	14.037	1.016	—	5.639	48.554	2.096	22.775	-0.070	18.493	—
1997	12.744	1.285	—	6.174	43.045	-1.196	16.476	12.317	24.720	—
1998	12.723	0.794	1.005	6.391	30.634	12.059	7.023	26.057	30.909	15.582
1999	13.744	0.015	0.665	6.154	32.013	11.917	0.122	16.290	16.392	5.545
2000	15.141	0.190	4.092	6.297	25.763	17.673	1.031	21.895	22.692	24.606
2001	17.048	0.279	1.696	6.116	24.962	21.438	2.446	16.843	18.828	22.173
2002	17.910	0.253	1.852	6.192	23.352	18.570	5.276	16.399	20.589	31.210
2003	18.273	0.323	1.959	6.146	18.682	23.271	2.786	20.492	22.647	41.342
2004	18.670	1.356	0.053	6.920	9.969	22.833	12.032	11.807	21.278	0.642
2005	17.921	1.359	2.599	7.305	-3.874	17.292	19.127	31.097	42.160	24.052
2006	17.657	0.520	2.332	7.188	-10.794	18.090	6.601	10.299	15.853	36.725
2007	18.415	0.825	1.920	—	-27.634	23.196	11.152	20.035	28.057	30.963
2008	18.054	-0.201	0.527	—	0.864	18.954	-2.677	-17.258	-20.483	8.410
2009	16.136	1.759	1.559	8.126	-30.378	13.903	31.375	30.379	47.005	49.421
2010	17.352	0.463	0.530	7.813	-33.045	24.902	3.342	9.554	12.480	10.552
Ex	15.811	0.715	1.599	6.586	13.931	21.280	10.672	16.185	23.307	23.171
σ	2.476	0.557	1.036	0.759	26.228	14.401	9.548	12.097	15.119	14.101
Over cold	X≤10.86	X≤-0.4	X≤-0.5	X≤5.07	X≤-38.5	X≤-7.52	X≤-8.42	X≤-8.01	X≤-6.93	X≤-5.03
Cold	10.86<X≤13.33	-0.4<X≤0.158	-0.47<X≤0.563	5.07<X≤5.827	-38.5<X≤-12.30	-7.52<X≤6.878	-8.42<X≤1.125	-8.01<X≤4.087	-6.93<X≤8.188	-5.032<X≤9.07
Normal	13.33<X≤18.29	0.158<X≤1.271	0.563<X≤2.636	5.827<X≤7.345	-12.30<X≤40.159	6.878<X≤35.681	1.125<X≤20.22	4.087<X≤28.282	8.188<X≤38.426	9.07<X≤37.27
Heat	18.29<X≤20.764	1.271<X≤1.828	2.636<X≤3.672	7.345<X≤8.104	40.159<X≤66.386	35.681<X≤50.08	20.22<X≤29.768	28.282<X≤40.38	38.426<X≤53.545	37.27<X≤51.37
Over heat	X>20.764	X>1.828	X>3.672	X>8.104	X>66.386	X>50.08	X>29.768	X>40.38	X>53.545	X>51.37

Source: China Statistical Bureau.

Note: (1) *The commodity house prices here do not use statistical data. The annual sales volume divided by sales is deducted by the consumer price index.*

(2) *According to the World Bank's algorithm, the ratio of house price to income is derived from the average single price of commercial housing/average household income = average selling price of commercial housing * average household population * per capita urban residential area / per capita real income of urban residents * average household population.*

(3) *The vacancy rate of commercial housing is the most popular indicator in the world. The formula is: vacancy area over half a year or more is uninhabitable/completed area of the whole society. Since 1994, China has been counting the number of vacant commercial houses, including those completed but not sold or rented. In 1998, the National Bureau of Statistics divided the vacant area into more than one year and less than one year. Since 1999, it has been clear that the vacant area should be deducted from non-saleable and rentable areas such as demolition and reconstruction, unified construction, public supporting, enterprise self-use and swing houses. But the vacancy released by the National Bureau of Statistics is only an increment, not an indicator of stock. Limited to the nonuniformity of index value change and the availability of data, we use the ratio of commercial housing for sale and completed commercial housing to reflect the vacancy of commercial housing in China from the perspective of market supply and demand of commercial housing, and divide the difference between the area of completed housing in the current year and the area of actual housing sales in the current year by the area of completed housing in the current year.*

Data sources: 1991–2010 year data from China Economic and trade database db.cei.gov.cn, "China real estate statistical yearbook 2010", "China real estate and construction enterprises Yearbook 2010".

Table 5–5 Foam values of five indicators[①]

	1998	1999	2000	2001	2002	2003	2004	2005	2006	2007	2008	2009	2010
1	4.149	−0.42	2.553	0.749	−0.076	−0.502	1.157	0.425	3.061	1.054	0.452	0.132	6.022
2	1.424	0.026	0.340	0.499	0.454	0.579	2.43	2.435	0.933	1.478	−0.361	3.153	0.830
3	−0.29	−0.18	0.679	0.047	0.393	0.674	−1.497	0.482	0.625	0.655	−1.038	−0.02	−1.035
4	3.710	0.215	−0.69	−1.309	−0.340	4.652	0.944	−0.03	−0.79	—	—	0.419	1.621
5	0.318	0.110	0.726	−0.290	−0.820	1.090	0.190	−0.07	−0.21	−1.59	−0.249	−1.69	−2.260
Sum	9.314	−0.24	3.608	−0.304	−0.390	6.493	3.224	3.235	3.622	1.602	−1.196	1.995	5.179
Foam	1.863	−0.05	0.722	−0.061	−0.078	1.299	0.645	0.647	0.724	0.401	−0.299	0.399	1.0356

Source: China Statistical Bureau.

2. Measurement and evaluation of China's real estate bubble
(1) Establishment of econometric estimation model

---

① Indicator value: the ratio of real estate development investment to fixed assets investment, the ratio of house price growth rate to real income growth rate of cities and towns, the ratio of real estate loan growth rate to bank loan growth rate, the ratio of house price to income of urban residents, and the vacancy rate of commercial housing are expressed by 1, 2, 3, 4, 5, respectively. The last one is the average bubble value of each index.

Based on the basic principles of the theoretical model of real estate bubble, this part designs the econometric model of real estate bubble test. The theoretical model assumes that real estate price changes are determined by both economic fundamentals and speculation in the real estate market. From the perspective of real estate commodity demand, the economic fundamentals affecting the real estate market mainly include the level of economic development, urbanization, financial development and so on. From the perspective of the supply of commercial housing, the main factors affecting the real estate price changes are the cost of housing construction, such as the cost of land acquisition, installation of residential building materials and so on. In addition, real estate commodities are also an important investment, so there will be a lot of speculation in the real estate market. Real estate speculation ichange their behavior through speculators' anticipation of real estate price changes, and this speculation acts on real estate prices again. Based on this assumption, we use Levin and Wright (1997) model to divide real estate prices into two parts, one is the basic price determined by economic fundamentals, the other is the price determined by non-economic factors. The formula is expressed as:

$$P_t = P_t^m + G_t, G_t = E_t G_{t+1} / 1 + r_t \tag{3}$$

P_t^m: implies the basic price of the economy; r_t: real interest rate; G_t: discount of expected capital gains for speculation; $E_t G_{t+1}$ represents the expected return of the commodity housing owner for the next period. According to the assumption of adaptive expectation, we can take it as a function about the rate of change （π） of real estate prices in the past:

$$E_t G_{t+1} = f(\pi_{t-1}, \pi_{t-2}, \cdots, \pi_{t-n}), \pi_{t-1} = (P_{t-1} - P_{t-i-1}) / P_{t-i-1}, i = 1, 2, \cdots, n \tag{4}$$

(2) Variable setting and data source

①Interpreted variables RP_{it}. RP_i is the real average house price of 31 regions in the whole country in t period. This variable is the real average house price obtained by dividing the sales volume of commercial housing in 31 provinces (cities) to the actual sales of that year, and then adjusting the consumer price index of the residents in this region. ①

②Explanatory variables of basic house price. Dependent variable RR_{it}, represents real estate mortgage rates, we choose the interest rate of bank loans for more than five years and get the real interest rate level after CPI reduction in different regions. The real per capita GDP adjusted by CPI in 31 provinces (cities) of China in different years is selected by using $RGDP_{it}$ as an index to measure the real income and development level of residents in different regions. Thus, the real basic house price is expressed as:

$$RP_{it}^r = \delta_0 + \delta_1 RR_{it} + \delta_2 RGDP_{it}, \text{ in which } \partial RP_{it}^r / \partial RP_{it} < 0 \ \partial RP_{it}^r / \partial GDP_{it} > 0 \quad (5)$$

③The explanatory variables of non-basic house prices. We assume that the real estate market meets the rational expectations hypothesis, that is, the non essential part of the current housing price is caused by the changes in the previous prices. That is $P_{it}^e = E_{it-1}G_{it} = f(\pi_{it-1})$, in which π_{it-1} indicates price changes of early stages, $\partial f / \partial \pi > 0$, in this model, we use the lagged item of house price.

④Other variables. In order to reflect the regional differences in the real estate market more accurately, we introduce the regional dummy variables v_{it} ②, we introducing the interactive terms of

---

① Loan interest rate more than 5 years' is calculated by the relevant data of the national research network database and the official website of the people's Bank of China.

② In this book, we divided 31 provinces into four regions: 1, representing the developed areas, mainly including the provinces, the cities, the 2 and the more developed regions, including 3, sub developed regions, including 6 central provinces and municipalities. The area 4 represents, Hong Kong and Macao only. This book mainly refers to the per capita GDP ranking of the corresponding provinces according to geographical location factors. Liang Yunfang (2007) used the eastern, central and western regions sorted by per capita GDP. This paper argues that the sorting by per capita GDP is unreasonable, because the eastern, central and western regions sorted by per capita GDP can reasonably reflect the location factors of housing prices to a certain extent, but the per capita GDP in our model is also an explanatory variable. Considering that the variables may produce collinearity problems when regression occurs, we do not think it is in favor of dividing the region according to the per capita GDP ranking.

regional virtual variables and the first period of house price delay $\pi_{it-1}v_{it}$, and interaction term between regional dummy variables and per capita GDP $RGDP_{it}v_{it}$, in which μ_{it} represents a random error term. The regression model of empirical analysis describes   as follows:

$$RP_{it} = \delta_0 + \delta_1 RR_{it} + \delta_2 RGDP_{it} + \delta_3 \pi_{it-1} + \delta_4 \pi_{it-2} + \delta_5 v_{it} + \delta_6 \pi_{it-1} v_{it} + \delta_7 RGDP_{it} v_{it} + \mu_{it}$$

(6)

（3）Regression results and analysis[①]

This part uses panel data of 31 provinces (cities) from 1997 to 2009 to make GLS regression for the above models. The estimated values of each parameter are shown in Table 5-6, and the coefficients of the two models are compared in Table 5-7. Both models have high significance and strong explanatory power. The regression results show that:

The coefficients of the random effect model and the fixed effect model are basically the same. Hausman test can not reject the original hypothesis. The two models have high explanatory power for real estate average price (R-sq value is larger). Obviously, the results of the random effect model in this paper are better than those of the fixed effect model. The test of significance between groups (0.9487) and the overall statistical significance (0.9603) of the random effect model are stronger than those of the fixed effect model (0.8177, 0.9050). In the stochastic effect model, the coefficient of real interest rate is negative at the significant level of 5%, but not significant. Every 1% increase in lending rates, house prices will fall by 1.466%. This is basically consistent with Liang Yunfang's (2007) panel data based on error correction model and Zhang Yali's (2011) dynamic panel data based on expected income model. The medium and long-term loan interest rate has no significant impact on housing prices, which is also the reason

---

①   The Stata10 software is used to estimate and test the model in this book.

why the current government's control policy of continuously raising the interest rate of personal housing loans and raising interest rates to deal with the overheating in real estate has little effect.

Table 5–6 Random Effect Model GLS Regression Parameters[①]

Explanatory variables	Coefficient value	Standard error	Z-value	$P>|z|$	95% confidence interval (upper and lower limits)	
interest	−0.0146559	0.0115224	−1.27	0.203	−0.0372394	0.0079277
lpgdp	0.200756	0.041619	4.82	0.000	0.1191842	0.2823278
lphprice_1	0.8466455	0.0631218	13.41	0.000	0.7229291	0.9703619
lphprice_2	0.0164411	0.0389528	0.42	0.673	−0.0599051	0.0927872
region_2	−0.1011221	0.3920977	−0.26	0.796	−0.8696194	0.6673753
region_3	0.7187923	0.3355405	2.14	0.032	0.061145	1.37644
region_4	1.315092	0.3625758	3.63	0.000	0.6044561	2.025727
reg*lpgdp_2	−0.1592196	0.0568153	−2.80	0.005	−0.2705755	−0.0478636
reg*lpgdp_3	0.0095782	0.0642506	0.15	0.881	−0.1163508	0.1355071
Ireg*lpgdp_4	−0.0757512	0.0484013	−1.57	0.118	−0.170616	0.0191136
Ireg*lphpr_2	0.218132	0.0768822	2.84	0.005	0.0674457	0.3688182
Ireg*lphpr_3	−0.0967491	0.0884786	−1.09	0.274	−0.270164	0.0766657
Ireg*lphpr_4	−0.0704985	0.0710822	−0.99	0.321	−0.2098171	0.06882
cons	−0.7340642	0.2256428	−3.25	0.001	−1.176316	−0.2918124

---

① In the regression results, in addition to the medium and long term interest rate term, other explanatory variables take paired values. Interest denotes interest rate, lpgdp denotes GDP per capita, lphprice 1; 2 denotes house prices with lag of one and two periods, region denotes region, cons denotes control variable, the same as the following table.

Table 5–7 Comparison between Fixed-effect and Random-effect Models

Variable	Fixed effect	Random effect	Difference
interest	0.2099192	−0.0146559	0.2245751
lpgdp	0.0906949	0.200756	−0.1100611
lphprice_01	0.8575004	0.8466455	0.0108549
lphprice_02	0.0068991	0.0164411	−0.0095419
region_2	0.3211736	−0.1011221	0.4222957
region_3	0.8901368	0.7187923	0.1713445
reg*lpgd_2	−0.1531528	−0.1592196	0.0060667
reg*lpgd_3	−0.0266634	0.0095782	−0.0362416
reg*lpgd_4	−0.037306	−0.0757512	0.0384452
region_4	1.642185	1.315092	0.3270931
reg*lphp_2	0.145159	0.218132	−0.072973
reg*lphp_3	−0.090608	−0.0967491	0.0061411
reg*lphp_4	−0.1780108	−0.0704985	−0.1075122

Unlike Liang Yunfang et al. (2006), the price fluctuation in the previous period has a lagging effect on the current housing price. The difference is that the coefficient of the first order lag and the two order lag factor is more significant. The first order lag term 0.8466 shows that when the expected housing price rises by 1%, the real house price will be pushed up by 0.8587%, nearly doubled, indicating the real estate market bubble, and the real estate market bubble is expected to be promoted. The first-order lag coefficient of house price is greater than the second-order lag coefficient, and the effect of the next-order expectation is greater than that of the next-order expectation on the current house price. This shows that the current real estate market in China is effective, which is in line with the assumptions in our theoretical model. This also reflects the obvious positive feedback effect of speculation in China's real estate market. When the expectation of house price rising is realized and people made forturn from market speculation, the expectation of price rise will be further strengthened.

Real per capita GDP has a positive impact on housing prices. For every 1% increase in real per capita GDP, house prices will rise by 0.2%. The price of real estate rises with the improvement of economic development, but the effect of rising income level with the rise of house price is not significant. In addition, the real per capita GDP coefficient is far less than the first-order lag coefficient, which shows that the role of promoting the real estate market bubble expectation is significantly greater than the impact of per capita GDP. This further proves that the reason for the sustained rise of real estate prices in China lies in anticipation and speculation rather than economic fundamentals. Many scholars put forward that the rise of house price in China is caused by the increase of land purchase cost, housing construction cost, installation cost of building materials, and wage rise of construction workers.

The coefficients of fictitious variables confirm the regional characteristics of China's real estate bubble. Real estate speculation and location factors are closely related, which is in line with the reality. We believe that housing prices are related not only to the actual level of development, but also to geographical location. The regional 1 and regional 2 we set are concentrated on coastal areas, with advantageous geographical location, convenient transportation, prosperous commercial trade and better quality of life. The degree of opening to the outside world is relatively high, as well as the level of financial development. The floating population is large, the rigid demand for real estate and speculative demand are large, and the aggregated liquidity capital is rich. The estimated coefficients of virtual variables show that the coefficients of developed regions 1 and 2 are contrary to those of sub-developed regions 3 and 4. When we set the dummy variable, we set the area 1 as the reference variable, assuming that the housing price of the area 1 is reasonable, then it must be sub-developed area 3 and developing area 4 that promote the formation of housing price bubbles, which is obviously not in line with the reality. Because the prosperity of the real estate market is largely restricted by the purchasing power of the region, only the formation of effective demand can have a substantial impact on housing prices. From this perspective we concluded that the developed coastal areas are the main force to promote the real estate bubble in China.

From the coefficient value of the interaction term between the regional fictitious variable and the first-order lag term of house price, the interaction term of the fictitious variable and the first-order lag term of house price has negative coefficients for regional 3 and regional 4, but the value of regional 2 coefficients is positive, which indicates that speculation in developed areas strengthens the role of promoting house price, but speculation in sub-developed areas weakens house price. In China, real estate developers and real estate speculators generally enter the first tier cities, because speculators in large cities are more speculators, and speculators tend to imitate each other, leading to irrational rise in house prices. In areas where speculators are less, the extent of the expected impact of housing prices may not be obvious or unanticipated, even contrary to expectations, thereby speculation is not profitable. That is why the real estate bubble generally first appears in large cities with relatively high economic development level.

The coefficients of the interaction between regional fictitious variables and real per capita GDP are only positive but not significant. However, the individual coefficient of per capita GDP and regional fictitious variables has positive effects on housing prices, that is, real per capita GDP and geographical location have positive effects on housing prices respectively.

In summary, the empirical analysis in this section shows that the real estate market bubble exists in China, and expectation and speculation are the important reasons to promote the real estate bubble. The positive feedback effect of speculation in China's real estate market is obvious. Demand increases with the rise of housing prices. When the expectation of rising housing prices is realized and profits from speculation in the market, the expectation of rising prices will be further strengthened. The effect of bank's medium and long-term loan interest rate on house price is not significant. Real estate price increases with the improvement of economic development level, but the effect of real income level on house price is not so obvious. The reason for the sustained rise of real estate price in China lies in anticipation and speculation rather than economic fundamentals. Housing price is positively related to GDP per capita, but it is also related to regional development. The developed coastal areas are the main drivers to promote the real estate bubble in China.

5.3.2 The prospect of China's real estate industry and the outlook of the leading industry in the future

The research in the last section shows that there is bubble in the real estate industry of China from 1998 to 2010. The experiences of the real estate market development in developed countries shows that the bursting of the real estate bubble is extremely harmful. It will distort asset prices, imbalance the allocation of market resources, and pose a great threat to the stable and healthy development of the overall economy. The prosperity of the real estate industry is closely related to the banking and financial industry. Once the real estate bubble bursts, the scale of bank assets will shrink, the value of real estate loans as collateral will decline, the default rate of bank loans will rise, and the shrinkage of bank capital will reduce the supply of credit, lead to the breakdown of the supply chain of bank funds, and bring about the financial crisis. If the regulator's policies are inappropriate and measures are taken to keep downward pressure on house prices, the bubble will collapse. The bursting of the real estate bubble has a rapid and strong impact on the financial system. China's financial system is relatively fragile. Once the real estate bubble bursts, it will lead to more misconduct loans. A series of bad debts will lead to financial system and even the overall economic crisis.

There is no doubt that the real estate industry, as the dominant part of the national economy until it becomes the pillar of the national economy, plays a very important role in the process of economic development. However, the long-term excessive prosperity and expansion of the real estate industry squeezed out the resources needed for the development of other industries, and inhibited the development of other industries. The prosperity of the real estate market means that the real estate investment has a high rate of return, which makes many investors gain surplus profits and absorb more funds in the virtual economy on a large scale. Many non-real estate enterprises even turn their main business to the real estate industry. A large number of enterprises in the real estate industry under the lure of huge profits, the original funds used to expand reproduction are invested in the real estate industry, resulting in production-oriented enterprises lack of funds. In this way, a large amount of funds and resources accumulated in the whole economy and society to the real estate industry, occupying the resources of other industries, especially the manufacturing industry, resulting in serious deformity of the national economic industrial structure. This development mode, which relies on large-scale investment and ignores technological innovation, is unhealthy and unsustainable.

Therefore, in order to achieve a healthy and sustainable development mode, it is necessary to make preparatory choices for the new leading industries in the future when the life cycle of the old leading industries gradually declines. From the analysis of Chapter IV, we can see that the communication and electronic information industry can be the leading industry in China in the future. The innovation plasticity of the telecommunication electronic information industry is very great. At the same time, its huge domestic market can stimulate domestic demand and employment. It is also resource-saving and environment-friendly. The telecommunication electronic information industry also has a strong industry-related role and can be widely penetrated into all sectors of the national economy. The new competition pattern of the electronic information industry in the international market has brought great opportunities and challenges to China's communication and electronic information industry. Innovation and technology R&D are the key to the sustainable development of telecommunications and electronic information industry. Although China and most countries are at the starting line in the new round of competition, China's innovation and R&D are still weak. Innovation is not only important for emerging industries and high-tech industries, but also indispensable for the transformation of traditional industries and the development of service industries. In the final analysis, the direction of the transformation of the mode of economic development is to achieve an innovative way of development, which is the foundation of sustainable economic development.

The characteristics of resource and capital saving, environment friendliness, domestic demand orientation and employment expansion in service industry should also be regarded as the key industries of national economy. Productive service industry serves the development of real economy and is an auxiliary industry of national economy. Consumer services, such as animation and other creative industries, entertainment industry is conducive to expanding domestic demand, but also resource conservation and environmental friendliness, of course, their development also needs continuous innovation to develop. Social welfare and social security service industry is the industry that should be vigorously developed in the face of aging population. It will be China's new economic growth point in the future. To develop social welfare and security services, not only we should strengthen the investment and construction of the public service system of social security, we should also encourage and advocate private capital to join the social welfare industry and promote the development of social security and welfare industry through various means and wide channels.

Chapter 6　Policy Suggestions on the Development of Leading Industries and the Change of Economic Development Mode in China

6.1　Principles for Developing Leading Industries and Changing the Mode of Economic Development

6.1.1　Grasp the opportunities for leading industries replacement

Accelerating the adjustment and upgrading of the economic structure can smoothly realize the transformation of the mode of economic development. The process of industrial structure change and adjustment is also the process of leading industry selection and replacement. Generally speaking, the main industries with competitive advantages are those producing upstream products or industrial clusters, which play a leading and commanding role in the industrial chain. The formation of this leading industry and its leading role need the support of other industries and the drive of related industries. The process of the leading industry and other related industries, coordinating role is the process of dynamic adjustment of industrial structure and constantly moving towards rationality and perfection. Therefore, in order to realize the smooth transformation of the mode of economic development and solve the transformation problems faced in the current development process, it is necessary to concentrate on cultivating and developing leading industries. Choosing domestic demand-driven industry with moderate investment leverage, strong employment-driven effect, outstanding technology spillover effect, resource-saving and environment-friendly industry as the leading industry, and forming leading industry clusters, promoting the improvement of the overall industrial quality, and driving the economic development mode to multi-objective direction.

When the original leading industry which is suitable for the economic conditions and development requirements is no longer suitable for the new development requirements, or when the original leading industry is unsustainable under the requirements of the new development mode, or when the life cycle of the original leading industry is approaching the end, that is, it's time for the replacement of the leading industry, the transition of the new and old leading industries will bring new development opportunity to all industries of the national economy. In the process of economic development, the backward industrial structure will transform and adjust independently and dynamically when the competitive advantage of the leading industry is formed. The industrial structure is to rationalize in the process of forming the competitive advantage and eliminating the inferior industry. As a result, some industries can not develop and grow because they are suppressed and hindered by the original industrial structure and industrial policy; while some industries have gone to the declining stage of life cycle, they still enjoy the benefits of industrial policy tilt, in this way the transition process of leading industries is the process of re-integration of resources, re-adjustment of industrial pattern and strength, and a great opportunity for industrial development.

6.1.2 Coordinating leading industries and supporting industries

The adjustment of industrial structure accompanied by the transformation of economic development mode needs to accurately select and properly cultivate, while the selection and cultivation of leading industries need to coordinate closely with other related industries. If there is only the prosperity of the leading industry in the national economy, without the assistance of the related supporting industry, or the underdevelopment of the supporting industry for the leading industry, or the coordinated development of the supporting industry for the leading industry, it may weaken the strength of the leading industry and hinder the development and growth of the leading industry. At the same time, the development of the leading industry and the development mode are unsustainable.

With leading industry or leading industry cluster as the core, the industries derived from the development of leading industry have forward, backward and side links with the surrounding industries. They are the supporting industries in which leading industry plays a role in the national economy and provide reliable guarantee for the development of leading industry. We should take the leading industry as the core and the central link of the industrial chain, extend the industrial chain as far as possible, and increase the circuitous degree of the labor division in the industrial chain. Not only can we expand the scope of industrial clusters centered on leading industries and enhance their competitive advantages, we should also facilitate the division of labor and cooperation among industries within leading industrial clusters, internalize the external effects among industries and realize the optimal allocation of resources. Whether it is a leading industry or a coordinated supporting industry, its role can be maximized only when it has scale effect. When the leading industry achieves the best scale and the scale effect is released, the guiding role of the leading industry can be brought into play. At the same time, the supporting industry also needs to have the corresponding scale to cope with the leading industry, so coordinating the supporting industry also needs appropriate guidance, so as to develop in a moderate scale.

The coordination between related industries and leading industries is also reflected in the spatial distribution of related industries and leading industries. Reasonable distribution of related industries can ensure the agglomeration effect of leading industries and supporting industries in space. At the same time, it can also prevent the unreasonable distribution of leading industries and related industries from restricting each other, excessive concentration of industrial layout and disorder distribution. The common development of leading industries and related industries can constitute the driving force of economic development or transformation of economic development mode. Any isolation that only pays attention to the leading industry but ignores the related industry, or ignores the key point of the leading industry, is not conducive to a healthy and smooth development of the economy.

6.1.3   Strengthen government guidance on the basis of market regulation

To give full play to the role of leading industries in the transformation of economic development mode, we must begin with the basic role of market regulation. According to the spontaneous function of the market, we should cultivate the leading industries, and make the industries survive independently and become stronger gradually through market competition, the disadvantaged industries gradually withdraw from the market. Market competition can survive the fittest, give full play to the market function of optimizing the allocation of resources, each industry in the process of self-evolution through competition and complementarity could achieve symbiosis and elimination, in this way the leading industry come into being because of its strong self-supporting ability, as well as its increased development potential. In addition, according to the industrial development sequence formed by market self-regulation, it follows the law of regional development and also suitable for the whole development.

However, while the market plays a fundamental role, the imperfection of the market economic system and the difference of regional development factors and development degree may hinder the exertion of the basic role of the market, or even make the regulatory role of the market basis ineffective. Therefore, in order to make up for the shortage of the market, shorten the slow process of adjusting the industrial structure and transforming the mode of economic development relying solely on the market mechanism, it is necessary to strengthen the government's guidance to the development of the leading industries, and give play to the government's support and guidance role in the process of transforming the economic development. The government's macro-control role in the process of leading industry development and the transformation of economic development mode mainly includes direct financial, fiscal and tax policies and subsidies, and also indirectly creates a good environment for the development of leading industry and the transformation of economic development mode from system to policy. Obviously, strengthening the government's role of guidance and regulation is not all about the government. The guiding and supporting role of the government in the development of leading industries and the transformation of the mode of economic development is mainly reflected in the adoption of some reasonable and effective measures to strengthen industrial development and enhance industrial competitiveness. The supporting and guiding policies should first follow the principle of fairness.

6.2 Suggestions on Transforming the Mode of Economic Development

6.2.1 Electronic information industry

With the emergence of new devices and products such as internet TV, tablet PC and smart phone, the technology integration of electronic information industry extends to terminal services and computer networks. At the same time, the competition pattern of the electronic information industry has changed greatly. The pattern of global electronic information industry dominated by the company and the Intel has been challenged by apple. The change of the competition pattern of electronic information industry brings a new round of opportunities to China's electronic information industry. Electronic information industry has recovered from the internet bubbles since 2001, and new applications and services of electronic information have grown rapidly. China has proposed the development of "new generation of information technology" as a strategic emerging industry for the development of the national economy. The development of a new generation of IT industry focuses on mobile communications, triple play, internet, integrated circuits, cloud computing, high-end software, high-end servers and information services. This kind of strategic emerging information technology industry is driven by innovative technology. It is not only a new growth point of consumption, but also has strong industrial radiation capacity. On the one hand, it can improve the technology and competitiveness of the entire electronic information industry, and on the other hand it could it could change the mode of economic development. In particular, the Internet of Things (IOT) technology is another innovation of the information industry revolution. It aggregates and integrates modern network technology, artificial intelligence and other technologies and applies them. The internet of Things has a long industrial chain, which helps to drive the synchronous development of a series of industries, such as microelectronics, sensors and radio frequency identification systems. At the same time, it has a wide range of applications, covering almost all industries. In the era of the internet, all countries stand on the same starting line. Therefore, for China, it is key for industrial transformation and upgrading, and also a major opportunity for the transformation of economic development mode.

Electronic information technology plays a booster role in the upgrading of industrial structure and the transformation of development mode. Using information technology to transform traditional industries will improve the management and manufacturing enterprises, optimize the industrial structure and facilitate the transformation of the mode of economic development. Information technology can not only improve the level of enterprise informatization and product grading, but also expand the market space of information industry, so that information industry can give full play to the leading and commanding role in the market. To give full play to the leading and promoting role of electronic information industry in the transformation of economic development mode, we also need to better promote the integration of information technology and other industries, and give full play to the application level of information technology in key sectors of various industries. Encourage and strengthen support for the pilot area of information technology integration with other industries, and focus on the application of the Internet of Things as a breakthrough window. In addition, while strengthening the information construction and developing the information industry, the state should pay attention to the pollution and resource waste caused by the production process of the electronic information industry. Encourage enterprises to improve environmental protection standards of electronic products, develop energy-saving and environmental protection electronic information technology and products, and guide enterprises to conduct ecological design and green manufacturing. Referring to foreign industry standards, we should apply green materials and technologies that meet the standards to promote the sustainable development of information industry.

6.2.2 Strategic emerging industries

To cultivate and develop strategic emerging industries, we must first strengthen the power on independent innovation capability. The construction of independent innovation capability is key to the cultivation and development of new industries, and key to the transformation of economic development mode in the future. The construction of independent innovation capability of strategic emerging industries mainly focus on basic and leading industries. It is the birthplace and production place of frontier technology and core technology as well as technology transformation capability. The development of strategic emerging industries must take enterprises as the main body, combine production, education and research, and give full play to the role of enterprises as the main body of technological innovation. Establishing large-scale enterprises with backbone, focusing on the research and development of key common technologies and cutting-edge technologies, building a number of high-level research incubation platforms, and ultimately realizing the industrialization of scientific research achievements. To speed up the cultivation of strategic emerging industry market, there is still a considerable distance between the success of technology research and industrialization in the initial stage of strategic emerging industry development. Market demand creates opportunities for technological development. Technology is constantly improved in the process of market application. Meanwhile, technological improvement further promotes market maturity. In the early stage of the development of emerging industries, market and business model can be realized by improving the supporting infrastructure. Establishing a system of industry standards and technical standards for important products are conducive to the development of strategic emerging industries, so does optimize market access and administrative procedures, and standardize market-oriented operation.

The government should devote itself to creating a good environment for the development of strategic emerging industries, guide them, and provide necessary support for the development of strategic emerging industries through the formulation and implementation of relevant supporting policies such as finance, taxation and subsidies and so on. By integrating existing policy resources, on the one hand, the government sets up special funds for the development of strategic emerging industries to provide tax incentives and subsidies for the construction and development of the whole innovation industry chain, such as key R&D technologies, industrialization of major innovation achievements, and basic innovative projects. At the same time, the government should strengthen its guidance to speed up the promotion and application of resource-saving and efficient energy-saving products. In terms of financial support, the government should increase the credit support of financial institutions for venture capital in high-tech industries, encourage private investment, give full play to the financing capacity of multi-level capital markets, improve the GEM market system, develop bond market and venture capital funds, and establish relevant supporting policy and improve regulatory systems.

6.2.3 Promoting the integration of services and other industries

Productive service industry plays an important role in the process of industrialization. The transformation of economic development mode is to promote the integration of service industry and other industries. As an intermediate input, producer-oriented service industry directly enters the production process, which has significant externality and industrial agglomeration effect. Therefore, we should give full consideration to urbanization and industrialization, as well as economic, social and environmental factors, and scientifically plan and promote the agglomeration and integration of producer services as a whole. With the construction of functional areas and agglomeration areas as the carrier, the mechanism of market-oriented and specialized services can be realized with institutional innovation. The government offers planning layout and necessary policy support, aims at eliminating the differences between the producer service industry and the manufacturing industry in terms of resource utilization price and tax revenue, and focus on giving policy support and preference to the producer service industry cluster.

In order to adjust and upgrade the industrial structure and realize the transformation of economic development mode, it is necessary to strengthen the interrelationship between industries and build an interactive mechanism conducive to the integration and development of service industry and manufacturing industry. To strengthen the integration of producer services with other industries, we must further deepen the specialized division of labor within the industry and focus on technology research and development and market expansion. We will separate some non-core service links, set up specialized supporting service departments, form an industry system with significant core competition and close supporting services to realize the continuous development of industry chain in technology and scale. For some industrial agglomeration areas, it actively promotes the opening up of industries, targeted to attract the entry of relevant service industries, and transforms the pure manufacturing agglomeration area into the agglomeration area with both production and service, which not only extends the industrial chain but also enlarges the scale of agglomeration area. To achieve the integration of production and service among industries, it is necessary to establish information sharing platform, promote cooperation and interaction between manufacturing and service industry, and realize seamless connection between service and manufacturing links.

Conclusions

Based on the input and output table of the economic development mode, the book calculates the relevant input and output coefficients of the 42 industries in China for 2002–2007 years, and investigates the domestic demand inducing effect, import and exports inducing effect, investment multiplier, labor employment driving function, energy consumption coefficient, environmental emission coefficient and technology spillover effect. The industries that are conducive to the transformation of the current economic development mode are analyzed. Next this book synthesizes the goal of the transformation of the mode of economic development and the importance of balancing various factors of development, uses the generalized stochastic frontier production function model to make an empirical analysis, and draws a consensus on the choice of industries that are conducive to the transformation of the economic development mode. The conclusions of this study are as follows:

(1) Considering the empirical results of intermediate input-output efficiency, domestic demand-induced, labor-driven, import-export-driven effect, investment multiplier-driven effect, energy-saving and environmental protection effect, R&D spillover effect and input-output efficiency, this book holds that the construction industry and real estate related industries are the leading industries of our national economy in the investigation period. Communication equipment and computer and other electronic equipment manufacturing industry, wood processing and furniture manufacturing industry, garment, leather, down and its products industry are also candidates for leading industry in this period.

The comprehensive input-output efficiency of wholesale and retail industry, residential service industry and education industry is relatively high. This kind of consumer service industry also could be the candidate industry of leading industry. Consumer service industry can not be neglected in the process of economic development mode transformation, no matter what the domestic demand pulling role is, or what the labor employment driving role are energy conservation and environmental protection. What's more, the comprehensive input-output efficiency of the financial insurance industry with the productive services is relatively high. At the same time, the development of the industry has a strong industrial correlation with the construction, real estate and manufacturing industries. It should be regarded as the auxiliary industry of the leading industry of the national economy.

(2) During the survey period, the input structure of China's economic development is mainly labor and capital investment type; the industrial structure is biased towards the second industry; the industrial structure is dominated by heavy industry; the demand structure is capital intensive and imports and exports dominant type, the proportion of consumption to total demand is very limited. Therefore, the mode of economic development in this stage is extensive. During the period of investigation, the mode of economic development in China is effective in terms of labor force and capital intensive. Labor and capital inputs are still the main contributing forces to the development of national economy, thereby labor and capital are still in the stage of increasing marginal return of factor input on the whole.

China's energy input is generally negative efficiency, energy utilization is inefficiency, transportation process loss is serious, coupled with the low level of technology in some industries, energy use is generally at a negative efficiency, and China's energy input and output are inefficient. The effect of R&D input on total economic output is not insufficient, because the total R&D input does not reach the minimum threshold of the scale effect of R&D input. In addition, the distribution of R&D investment among industries is uneven, some industries have excessive R&D investment, and other industries have insufficient R&D investment, which leads to the overall low efficiency in R&D. At present, the scale effect of R&D investment in China has not taken excellent advantage.

(3) The construction industry and real estate related industries are the leading industries in China at this stage. The estimation results of stochastic frontier production function show that the comprehensive input-output efficiency of construction industry and real estate related industries is obvious. Combining with the calculation of the correlation coefficients of input-output model based on economic development mode, it can be seen that the consumption-pull coefficient of real estate industry is higher in 2002–2007 than other industry, and the employment-pull coefficient of labor force in construction industry is large and obvious. The environmental emission coefficient of construction industry is also investigated. It shows that the construction industry is environmentally friendly, and the construction industry also has a large R&D spillover effect. During the period of investigation, the stochastic frontier production efficiency of China's manufacturing industry was relatively high, among which light industry was dominated by communication equipment, computer and other electronic equipment manufacturing, wood processing and furniture manufacturing, garment and leather down and its products, and heavy industry was dominated by electrical, machinery and equipment manufacturing, transportation equipment manufacturing, general and special equipment manufacturing. Consumption pull coefficient, import and export inducement effect and labor employment driving coefficients of telecommunication equipment, computer and other electronic equipment manufacturing industry are somewhat larger than others. What's more, telecommunication equipment and computer and

other electronic equipment manufacturing industry are energy-saving and environment-friendly. The stochastic frontier production efficiency of wood processing and furniture manufacturing industry, garment, leather, down and its products industry is high, the imports and exports inducement effect is obvious, and the investment multiplier and labor employment driving factor are higher than other industries. However, the unsustainability of China's real estate prosperity and accumulated risks within indicating that China's leading industry should focus on the telecommunications and electronic information industry. Facing an increasingly grim situation of aging, China should develop social security and welfare services, entertainment and animation and other cultural industries,only in this way can China accomplish innovative transformation of economic development mode and achieve high-quality development.

References

Relevant Chinese Government Reports and Documents

1. Current economic situation and future economic construction guidelines [N]. People's Daily, 1981-12-15(3).
2. Government Report in 1983 [N]. People's Daily, 1983-06-24(1).
3. Proceed along the road of socialism with Chinese characteristics-Report on the Thirteenth National Congress of the Communist Party of China[R]. 1987-10-25.
4. Jiang Zemin. Speed up the pace of reform and opening up and modernization,win a greater victory in the cause of socialism with Chinese characteristics-Report of 1992 at the Fourteenth National Congress of the Communist Party of China[R]. 1992-10-12.
5. Li Peng. The proposal of the CPC Central Committee on formulating the "95" plan for national economic and social development and the vision for 2010[N/OL]. People's network, 1995-09-25.
6. Li Peng. Report on the "Ninth Five-Year" plan for national economic and social development and the 2010 objective outline[N/OL]. People's network, 1996-03-18.
7. Jiang Zemin. The proposal of the CPC Central Committee on formulating the "95" plan for national economic and social development and the vision for 2010[N/OL]. People's network, 1996-03-17.
8. Jiang Zemin. Hold high the great banner of Deng Xiaoping theory and push the cause of building socialism with Chinese characteristics to the full in twenty-first Century[N/OL]. People's

net, 1997-09-13.

9. Recommendations of the CPC Central Committee on the formulation of the Tenth Five-Year Plan for national economic and social development [N/OL]. People's network, 2000-10-11.

10. Outline of the Eleventh Five-Year Plan for national economic and social development[N/OL]. People's network, 2006-03-07.

11. Hu Jintao. Speech at the provincial Party level cadre training class of the Central Party school[R]. 2007-06-25.

12. Hu Jintao. Holding high the great banner of socialism with Chinese characteristics and striving for a new victory in building a moderately prosperous society in all respects[R]. 2007-10-15.

13. Hu Jintao. The important leading cadres at the provincial and ministerial levels should thoroughly implement the important speech on the seminar on accelerating the transformation of the mode of economic development[R].

14. Wen Jiabao. Government report in 2010[R/OL].People's network, 2010-03-05.

15. Hu Jintao. Join forces to meet challenges and promote sustainable development. Speech on APEC[R]. Xinhua news agency, 2009-11-15.

16. Hu Jintao. Deepen exchanges and cooperation and achieve inclusive growth. Speech at the Fifth APEC Human Resources Development Ministerial Conference[R]. Xinhua news agency, 2010-09-16.

Chinese and English monograph

1. Arnold J. P. Shortage Economics[M]. Economic Science Press, 1986.

2. Janos. Kornai. The Socialist System: The Political Economy of Communism[M]. Princeton University Press, 1992.

3. Kornai, Zhang An. Translation of socialist system-Communist political economy[M]. Central Compilation and Translation Press,

2007.

4. Edward F. Denison. The Sources of Economic Growth in the United States & the Alternatives Before us[M]. Committee for Economic Development, 1962.

5. Simon Kuznets. Quantitative aspects of economic growth in various countries[M]. Commercial Press, 1999.

6. Moses Abramowitz. Thinking about growth and other essays of economic growth and welfare[M]. Cambridge University Press, 1989:3-377.

7. Hennery B. Chenery. Structure Change and Development Policy[M]. Oxford University Press, 1984.

8. Hertz. Cao Zhenghai and Pan Zhaodong. Translation. Economic development strategy[M]. Economic Science Press, 1991.

9. Walt W. Rostow. Economics of Take-off into Sustained Growth[M]. Macmillan & Martin, Ltd., 1964.

10. D.H. Meadows. The Limits to Growth [M]. Universe Books, New York, 1972.

11. Walter W. Rostow, He Liping et al. From the take-off to the continued growth of economics [M]. People Press, 1988.

12. Walter W. Rostow, Guo Xibao and Wang Maosong. The stage of economic growth: A Non Communist Manifesto [M]. China Social Sciences Press, 2001.

13. Joseph Schumpeter. Translated by Yi Jiaxiang,Xiong Zhu, He Wei, et al. Economic development theory [M]. Commercial Press, 2009.

14. Karl Marx. Capital(Volume 3) [M]. People's Publishing House, 1975.

15. Ronald E, Miller and Peter D. Blair. Input-output Analysis: Foundation and Extension[M]. Englewood Cliffs, N J Prentice-Hal, 1985.

16. Hoffman. The growth of industrial economy[M]. Modern University Press, 1958.

17. Zhou Zhenhua. The structural effect of modern economic

growth[M]. Shanghai Sanlin Bookstore, 1995.

18. Zhou Zhenhua. Industrial structure optimization[M]. Shanghai: Shanghai People's Publishing House, 1992.

19. Zhou Zhenhua. A systematic analysis of the economic theory of industrial policy[M]. People's University Press, 1991.

20. Cai Fang. A turning point: new stage of China's economic development[M]. Social Science Literature Press, 2008.

21. Cai Fang. 30 years of economic transformation in China[M]. Social Science Press, 2009.

22. Wu Jinglian. The choice of China's growth mode [M]. Shanghai Far East Press, 2006.

23. Tan Chong Tai. Development economics [M]. Economic Publishing House, 2002.

24. Guo Xibao edited. Development economics [M]. Higher Education Press, 2011.

25. Guo Xibao edited. Selected works of development economics classics [M]. China Economic Publishing House, 1998.

26. Fang Jia. Research on industrial structure problems[M]. Renmin University Publishing House, 1996.

27. Liu Wei. Book on industrial structure in the process of industrialization[M]. Renmin University Publishing House, 1995.

28. The Research Group of the Development Research Center of the State Council. The strategic focus of changing the mode of economic development[M]. China Development Press, 2010.

29. Yang Gongpu, Xia Da Wei. Modern industrial economics[M]. Shanghai University of Finance and Economics Press, 1999.

30. Su Dong Shui Shui. Industrial economics[M]. Higher Education Press, 2000.

31. Jane Xinhua. Industrial economics[M].Wuhan University Press, 2002.

32. Li Yue, Li Ping, editor in chief. Industrial economics[M]. Dongbei

University of Finance and Economics Press, 2002.

33. Jane Xinhua. China's economic restructuring and transformation of development mode[M]. People's Publishing House, 2010.

34. Mao Lin an. Industrial economics[M]. Shanghai People's Publishing House,1996.

35. Long Maofa, Ma Mingzong. Introduction to industrial economics[M]. Southwest University of Finance and Economics Press, 1996.

36. Jiang Xiaojuan. Industrial Structure Upgrading at the Turn of the Century [M].Shanghai Far East Press, 1996.

37. Li Wuwei. Changes in the mode of economic growth[M]. Shanghai Xue Lin Publishing House.

38. Guo Wanda edited. Modern industrial economics dictionary[M]. CITIC Publishing House, 1991.

39. He Chengying. China's industrial structure theory and policy research[M]. China Financial and Economic Publishing House, 1997.

40. Lin Yin. Towards China's industrial structure in twenty-first Century[M]. Capital University of Economics and Trade Press, 1998.

41. Yu Rengang. The leading industry[M]. The People's Press, 2003.

42. Hu Zixiang. China's pillar industry development strategy[M]. Economic Management Press, 1996.

43. Liu Lisheng, Tan Xiangjun and Ji Wenting. The way to revitalize Chinese and foreign pillar industries[M]. China Economic Press, 1997.

44. Jiang Shi Yin. Regional industrial structure and selection of leading industries[M]. Shanghai Sanlian Press, 2004.

45. Zou Xiaojuan. Research on the evolution of China's leading industries (1949–2000)[M]. People's Press, 2011.

46. Li Dashan. The theoretical and empirical analysis of regional industrial structure[M]. Tianjin People's Publishing House, 1998.

47. Cui Gonghao, Wei Qingquan. Regional analysis and planning[M]. Higher Education Press, 1999.

English Papers

1. Moses Abramowitz. Resource and output trends in the United States since 1870[J]. American Economic Review, 1956(46):5-23.
2. Chenery H.. Patterns of Industrial Growth[J]. American Economic Review, 1960(50).
3. Robert Solow. Technical Change and the Aggregate Production Function[J]. The Review of Economics and Statistics, 1957, 39(3): 312-320.
4. Fang Fuqian. A study of inadequate consumer demand among Chinese residents based on data for urban and rural areas in different provinces[J]. Social Sciences in China, 2009(3):21-40.
5. Kuznets Simon. Economic Growth and Income Inequality[J]. The American Economic Review, 1955(45).
6. Lucas R. On the Mechanics of Economic Development[J]. Journal of Monetary Economics, 1988(22).
7. R. Solow. Technical Change and the Aggregate Production Function[J]. Review of Economics and Statistics, 1957.
8. Ranis G. and John C.H. Fei. A Theory of Economic Development[J]. American Economic Review, 1961.
9. Thakur,S.Y.. Industrialization and Economic Development: An Appropriate Strategy for the Underdeveloped Countries[J]. Popular Prakashan, Bombay, 1985.
10. Cella,Guido. The Input-output Measurement of Interindustry Linkages[J]. Oxford Bulletin of Economics and Statistics, 1984(46):73-84.
11. Creamer D.. Measuring CaPital InPut for Total Factor Productivity Analysis: Comments by sometime estimator[J]. Review of wealth and income, 1972(18):55-78.

12. Romer Paul M. Increasing Returns and Long-run Growth[J]. Journal of Political Economy, University of Chicago Press, 1986, 94(5).

13. Fukui Y.. A More Powerful Method for Triangulizing Input-output matrics and the Similarity of Prodution Structers[J]. Econometrica, 1986(54):1425-1433.

14. Geoffrey J.D. Hewings; Manuel Fonseca; Joaquim Guilhoto; Michael Sonis. Key sectors and structural change in the Brazilian economy: A comparison of alternative approaches and their policy implications[J]. Journal of Policy Modeling, 1989, 11(1):67-90.

15. Werner Baer, Manuel A.R. da Fonseca, Joaquim J.M. Guilhoto. Structural changes in Brazil's industrial economy, 1960–1980[J]. World Development, 1987, 15(2):275-286.

16. William G. Tyler. Brazilian industrialization and industrial policies:A survey[J]. World Development, 1976, 4(10-11):863-882.

17. Hi-Chun Park and Eunnyeong Heo. The Direct and Indirect Household Energy Requirements in the Republic of Korea from 1980 to 2000-An Input-output Analysis [J]. Energy Policy, 2007(35): 2839-2851.

18. Hong-Tao Liu, Ju-E Guo, Dong Qian, You-Min Xi. Comprehensive Evaluation of Household Indirect Energy Consumption and Impacts of Alternative Energy Policies in China by Input-output Analysis[J]. Energy Policy, 2009(37): 3194-3204.

19. Ghosh S. & Roy J. Qualitative input-output analysis of the Indian economic structure[J].Economic Systems Research, 1998(10): 263-273.

20. Schnabl H. The subsystem-MFA: a qualitative method for analysing national innovation systems: the case of Germany[J]. Economic Systems Research, 1995(7): 383-396.

21. Verspagen B. Measuring intersectoral technology spillovers: estimates from the European and US Patent OECD databases[J].

Economic Systems Research, 1997(9): 47-66.

22. Edward N. Wolff. Spillovers, linkages and technical change[J]. Economic Systems Research, 1997(9): 9-24.

23. Rogeio Montemayor Seguy and Jesus A. Ramirez. The Use of Input-output Analysis in an Econometric Model of the Mexican Economimy[J]. Annals of Economic and Social Measurement, 1975(4): 531-552.

24. Shelby D. Gerking, Input-output as a Simple Econometric Model[J]. The Review of Economics and Statistics, 1976, 58(3):274-282.

25. West G.R.. Approximating the moments and distribution of input-output multipliers[J]. Working Papers in Economics, 1982.

26. West G.R.. A stochastic analysis of an input-output model[J]. Econometrica, 1986,54(2): 363–374.

Chinese Papers

1. Cai Fang. The transition of China's economy and its challenges to development and reform[J]. Chinese Social Sciences, 2007 (3) :4-12.

2. Cai Guodong. The bottleneck of industrial structure upgrading in China and its breakthrough ideas[J]. Finance and Economy, 2009 (6) :10-13.

3. Chen Hongwei, Li guiqin and Chen hong. Measurement and comparative analysis of total factor productivity in China's three primary industries[J]. Research on Financial and Economic Issues, 2010 (2) :28-31.

4. Hu Chunli. Reasons and essence of China's upgrading of industrial structure[J]. China Investment, 2009 (11) :78-79.

5. Huang Taiyan. The connotation and Realization Mechanism of transforming the mode of economic development[J]. Qiushi, 2007 (18) :6-8.

6. Kim Pei. Changes in the mode of economic growth[J]. China's Industrial Economy, 2006 (5) :5-14.

7. Yifu Lin, Su Jian. On the transformation of China's mode of economic growth[J]. Management World, 2007 (11) :5-13.

8. Liu Shucheng. On Good and Rapid Development[J]. Economic Research, 2007 (6) :4-13.

9. Li Shaorong. Industrial structure and economic growth[J]. China's Industrial Economy, 2002 (5) :14-21.

10. Liu Wei. Historical changes in economic development and reform and fundamental changes in the way of growth[J]. Economic Research, 2006(1) :4-10.

11. Lv Zheng. Promoting the Fundamental Change of Development Mode through Structural Adjustment[J]. Qiushi Truth, 2009 (9) :40-42.

12. Meng Yao and Ma Yanjun. Strategic choice of China's industrial structure optimization and upgrading [J]. Economy and Management, 2005 (6) :12-14.

13. Ni Yan. Direction and Path of Industrial Structure Adjustment[J]. Contemporary Economy, 2010 (1) :66-67.

14. Shi Jinchuan. On the mode of economic development and Its Transformation- theory, history, reality[J].Social Sciences, 2010 (4) :12-18.

15. Tao Changqi and Qi Yawei. Spatial difference of total factor productivity in China and its causes analysis[J]. Quantitative Economic and Technical and Economic Research, 2010 (1).

16. Tao Xiao Ma, Xing Jianwu, Huang Xin, Zhou Wen. Research on energy price distortion and factor substitution in China's industrial sector[J]. Quantitative Economic and Technical and Economic Research, 2009 (11) :3-16.

17. Wan Jianxiang. Equilibrium Path between Industrial Structure and Equity under Economic Growth[J]. Economic Latitude, 2009

(5) :19-23.

18. Wang Jixia. Analysis of the relationship between the optimization and upgrading of industrial structure and the stage of economic development[J]. Longitudinal and Horizontal Economy, 2009 (11) :71-73.

19. Wang Xiaolu, Liu Peng. China's economic growth mode transformation and growth sustainability[J]. Economic Research, 2009(1) :4-16.

20. Wang Yueping and Ge Yuejing. An analysis of the characteristics of industrial linkages between input and output of China's industrial structure[J]. Management World, 2007 (2) :61-68.

21. Wang Yueping. Strategy and thinking of China's industrial structure adjustment in 12th Five-Year[J]. China Economic and Trade Guide, 2009 (21) :18-20.

22. Wei Jie and Ren Baoping. Theoretical and empirical analysis of factor productivity and economic growth quality[J]. Journal of Shanxi University of Finance and Economics, 2009 (11) :36-44.

23. Wu Shuqing. Changing the mode of economic development is the key to achieving sound and rapid development of the national economy[J]. Frontline, 2008(1) :17-19.

24. Xu Guibin. Economic Development, Industrial Upgrading and Market Form[J]. Finance and Trade Economy, 2007 (3) :18-23.

25. Xue Bai. Transformation of Economic Growth Mode Based on Industrial Structure Optimization[J]. Management Science, 2009 (10) :112-120.

26. Yun Weihong. Leading Factor of Production Replacement and Evolution of Economic Development Stage[J]. Economic Latitude, 2009 (1) :4-9.

27. Zhang Ping. China's policy orientation to accelerate the transformation of the mode of economic development[J]. China Development Observation, 2010 (4) :8-9.

28. Zhang Xiaoxue and Chen Wanming. Research on factor accumulation, structural change and China's economic growth[J]. Economic Longitude and Latitude, 2009 (6) :17-20.

29. Zhang Zhuoyuan. Changing the Mode of Economic Growth: Government Reform is the Key[J]. Macroeconomic Management, 2006 (10) :37-38.

30. Zhao Wei. The current stage of China's social and economic development: the judgement of three points of view[J]. Social Science Front, 2007 (5) :42-49.

31. The Research Group of The Ministry of Economics of the Chinese Academy of Social Sciences. China entered the second half of industrialization[J]. Chinese Academy of Social Sciences, 2007 (9).

32. Zheng Yuxin. Measurement of Total Factor Productivity and Stage Rule of Economic Growth Mode[J]. Economic Research, 1999 (5) :55-60.

33. Liu Lun Chang, Zhao Jingxing. On the main factors affecting the mode of economic growth and its transformation[J]. China's Industrial Economy, 1999 (10):30-35.

34. Liu Shaowu. Reflections on the role of institutional arrangements in the transformation of the mode of economic growth[J]. Managing the World, 2000 (6): 182-183.

35. Jin Pei. Changes in the mode of economic growth[J]. China's Industrial Economy, 2006 (5) :5-14.

36. Yang Wenjin, Yang Liuqing. Briefly on the conditions and social impact of the transformation of the mode of economic growth[J]. Economist, 2007 (1):32-37.

37. Justin Lin Yifu, Su Jian. On the transformation of China's economic growth mode[J]. Management World, 2007 (11) : 5-13.

38. Wang Xiaolu, Liu Peng. China's economic growth mode transformation and growth sustainability[J]. Economic Research, 2009 (1):4-16.

39. Yang Shuhua. Path Analysis of the Change of Economic Development Mode in China Based on the Perspective of Economic Driving Force[J]. Economic Dynamics, 2009 (3): 30-33.

40. Gu Haibing, Shen Jilou. Qualitative and Quantitative Study on the Change of Economic Growth Mode in China in Recent Ten Years[J]. Economic Dynamics, 2006 (12).

41. Gaofeng. Research on the Evolution of Economic Growth Patterns in Developed Countries and Its Practical Significance[J]. Foreign Theoretical Trends, 2006 (3).

42. Lv Zheng. Several Issues on Changing the Mode of Economic Growth[J]. Frontline, 2006 (4).

43. Yu Ting, Li yan. A breakthrough in transforming the mode of economic development-visiting chang xiuze [J]. Economic Daily, 2007.

44. Guan Aiping and Wang Yu. Selection Base of Regional Leading Industries[J]. Statistical Research, 2002 (11): 37-40.

45. Zhang Genming. Selection Analysis of Leading Industries in High-tech Zones Based on DEA Model[J]. Research on Technology, Economy and Management, 2008 (2).

46. Hu Jianji, Zhang Jin. Selection of leading industries based on Industrial Development Research[J]. Industrial Economic Research, 2009 (4):38-43.

47. Jia Xiaofeng. An Empirical Study on the strategic choice of China's leading industries[J]. Finance and Trade Economy, 2004 (6).

48. Zheng Jiangsui. Selection Principles of Regional Leading Industries[J]. Guangming Daily, 2008 (5).

49. Wang Jianming, Jiang Yuantao, Wang Zongjun. Selection model and empirical analysis of leading industries in small and medium-sized cities[J]. Science and Technology Progress and Countermeasures, 2004 (11): 34-36.

50. Wang Yaping, Zhou Dequn, Zhang Ling. Theoretical model and

empirical research on the choice of leading industries in energy based cities[J].System Engineering, 2007 (2): 81-86.

51. Zhao Chengbai. Selection of industrial leading industries under new industrialization[J]. Statistics and Decision Making, 2005 (22):40-43.

52. Liu Aiwen, Zheng Dengpan. Based on BP logic fuzzy neural network, the selection of leading industries in Resource-based Cities: a case study of[J]. Science and Technology Management Research, 2010 (6): 153-156.

53. Guan Aiping and Wang Yu. Benchmark Study on Selection of Regional Leading Industries[J]. Statistical Research, 2002 (12).

54. Qian Xueya and Yan Qinfang. Principles and Evaluation System of Leading Industries Selection[J]. Statistics and Exploration, 2002 (1).

55. Jiang Zhaoxia. Analysis of choice of leading industries[J]. Lanzhou University Journal, 2007 (4): 124-128.

56. Yan Kewu and Zhu Jinfu. Deficiencies and Improvements of Analytic Hierarchy Process in Multiobjective Decision Making[J]. New Exploration of Theory, 2007 (5):10-11.

57. Zhao Yulin, Zhang Qiannan. Selection of strategic leading industries in Shaanxi Province[J]. Journal of Zhongnan University of Economics and Law, 2007 (2):30-35.

58. Wang Zhongzhi and Lin Bingyao. A comparative study of cluster theory and leading industry theory[J]. Geographic Science, 2005 (1) :23-28.

59. Zhang Junyi and Su Weici. Research on leading industry selection based on shift-share analysis-a case study of chongqing municipality[J]. Journal of Chongqing Normal University (Natural Science Edition), 2010 (3).

60. Han Jiangbo. Based on the mutual promotion between the core technology chain and the core industry chain based on the

transformation of the mode of economic development[J]. Social Science, 2009 (3).

61. Wu Yanpeng. Selection of leading industries in Central China[J], 2009(5).

62. Chen Lilong, Hu Zhenhua. Selection and Empirical Study of Industrial Leading Industries in Central China: Based on New Industrialization[J]. Productivity Research, 2011 (3).

63. Yang Can. Research on the Measurement Method of Industrial Linkage and Its Application[J]. Statistical Research, 2005 (9).

64. Cai Rongxin. Inclusive Growth: Theory Development and Policy System[J]. Leadership Science, 2010 (12).

65. Li Gang. Source Basis, Theoretical Framework and Policy Direction of Inclusive Growth[J]. Economist, 2011 (7).

66. Huang Yiyou. On the Selection of Industrial Priorities in China in this Century[J]. Management World, 1988 (3).

67. Li Poxi, Xie Fuzhan and Li Nurturing. Analysis and Countermeasures for the Development of "Bottleneck" Industries[J]. Economic Research, 1988 (12).

68. Zhou Hanqi. Based on grey situation decision making model, Wuhan's leading industry selection[J]. Changjiang Forum, 2010 (5) :28-31.

69. Deng Julong. Course on Grey System[M]. Central China University of Technology Press, 1985.

70. Zhu Zhengming, Netizens, Shao Chong. Discussion on Leading Industries in China's Industrial Structure[J]. Managing The World, 1988 (1).

71. Institute of quantitative and economic research, Chinese Academy of Social Sciences. Research on technology progress and industrial structure[J]. Quantitative Economic and Technical Research, 1988 (1).

72. Xie Fuzhan and Li Nurturing. Strategic Choice of Industrial

Structure Adjustment[J]. Managing The World, 1990 (4).

73. Wang Jiaqiong and Li Weidong. Reanalysis of the benchmarks and methods for the selection of leading industries in cities[J]. Quantitative Economics and Technical and Economic Studies, 1999 (5).

74. Zhao Fuhou. Analysis of Leading Industries in FDI Based on Analytic Hierarchy Process[J]. Industrial Engineering, 2010 (8).

75. Cai Yi. Application of principal component analysis in comprehensive evaluation[J]. China Statistics, 2005 (2).

76. Huang Guitian, Qi Wei. Regional Leading Industry Choice from the Perspective of Industrial Relevance[J]. Learning and Exploration, 2010 (6).

77. Qi Fang. The choice method of city leading industry based on analytic hierarchy process (AHP) is divided into[J]. Economic Research Guide, 2008 (19).

78. Ru Shao Feng, Tian Zhen. Research on the selection of industrial leading industries based on DEA model[J], 2009 (3).

79. Linli. Application of DEA in China's Industrial Structure[J]. Statistics and Decision-making, 2006 (9).

80. Wu Haimin et al. DEA of industrial operation is effective: a new benchmark for selecting leading industries[J]. Shandong Economy, 2006 (6).

81. Zhang Genming and Liu Tao. Analysis of Leading Industries Selection in High-tech Zones Based on DEA Model[J]. Research on Technology, Economy and Management, 2008 (2).

82. Yang Xuechun, Su Yang, Wang Maojun. Selection of regional industrial leading industries based on input-output data: take[J]. Journal of Capital Normal University (Natural Science Edition), 2010 (6).

83. Zhao Bin. Selection of leading industries in Northwest China[D]. Doctoral Dissertation of Beijing Jiaotong University, 2011.

84. Ye Anning. Leading industry selection benchmark research[D]. Doctoral Dissertation of XiaMen University, 2007.

85. Zhang Youguo. The impact of the mode of economic development on China's carbon intensity[J]. Economic Research, 2010 (4).

86. Guo Zhaoxian. China's carbon dioxide emissions growth factor analysis based on SDA decomposition technology[J]. China's Industrial Economy, 2010 (12).

87. Guo Zhaoxian. China's carbon emissions factor decomposition: Based on LMDI decomposition technology[J]. China's Population, Resources and Environment, 2010 (12).

88. Liao Mingqiu. Based on the input-output model of energy conservation and emission reduction, studied[J]. China's Industrial Economy, 2011 (7).

89. Xu Yingzhi, Peng Huanhuan. Export-oriented Economy and Energy Conservation and Emission Reduction: An Empirical Study Based on Energy Input-output Table[J]. Soft Science, 2010 (4).

90. Zhang Qizai, Guo Zhaoxian, Bai Mei. Coordinate the industrial policy research on the relationship between maintaining growth and changing the mode of economic growth[J]. China's Industrial Economy, 2009 (3).

91. Li Na,Wang Fei.The evolution of China's leading industry and its citing research: Based on DPG method [J]. Quantitative Economics and Technology Economy Research, 2012 (1).

92. Jinduo Wu, Haiyu Yang. The Potential of Service Economics in China-On the Perspective of Efficiency[J]. 4th International Conference on Management and Service Science, 2010.

93. Jinduo Wu. The Study On Energy Efficiency In Africa, 2011 International Conference on Energy and Environment[R]. Volume I, working paper,IEEE Catalog Number :CFP 11131-PRT,ISBN:978-1-61284-113-7.

94. Guo Xibao, Wu Jinduo. Econometric Analysis of the Bubble Degree

in China's Real Estate Market[J]. Jianghan Forum, 2012(5).

95. Guo Xibao, Wu Jinduo.The Situation of Henan Industrial Structure and the Policy Thoughts of Its Adjustment and Upgrading during the Twelfth Five-Year Plan Period. Edited by Fan Hengshan, A Study on Some Issues of Promoting the Rise of Central China during the Twelfth Five-Year Plan Period[M]. Wuhan University Press, 2011.